ANGIE ZELTER is a well-known campaigner on and human rights issues. She works at the g abroad, encouraging and supporting global interest, and showing by her example, creative and nonviolent ways to resist the cruelty, waste and pollution of society's present-day structures. She is a founder member of the Institute for Law and Peace, Trident Ploughshares, the International Women's Peace Institute – Palestine, Faslane 365 and Action Atomic Weapons Eradication. She is a recipient of the 1997 Sean McBride Peace Prize (for the Seeds of Hope Ploughshares action), and the 2001 Right Livelihood Award (on behalf of Trident Ploughshares). She now lives in Wales working with others to manage woodlands for local use whilst preserving bio-diversity and on various local organic food growing projects.

As Action AWE founder, she was also one of the four activists who made history in 1996. The four women were on trial after causing an estimated £1.5 million worth of damage to a Hawk. The aircraft was to be exported to Indonesia where it would have been used to continue the genocidal attacks on East-Timorese villagers. She was acquitted by an English jury on the grounds that the use of the aircraft by the Suharto regime would have been a breach of international humanitarian laws. She is a well-travelled campaigner on human rights and environmental issues and has been active in nuclear disarmament since the early '80s. In 2012, Zelter was nominated for the Nobel Peace Prize.

Action AWE is a UK-based grassroots peace campaign dedicated to banning and eradicating nuclear weapons. Action AWE come together as groups and individuals to undertake nonviolent action against the Atomic Weapons Establishment (AWE). They use education and outreach to raise awareness of the humanitarian, health and security consequences of nuclear weapons. Their basic mission is to halt nuclear warhead production at the currently operating nuclear facilities, AWE Aldermaston and AWE Burghfield. Britain has over 180 nuclear warheads in its current nuclear weapons system, called Trident. Action AWE's campaign is focused on the UK government's pledge to improve and replace the nuclear submarines that carry Trident. If this pledge is fulfilled, by 2016 the UK government would have spent an estimated £76–100 billion to build a new generation of UK nuclear weapons. This is more than the current planned public spending cuts of £81 billion. Action AWE mobilises for concerted, persistent, politically effective actions to highlight and prevent the deployment and renewal of Trident, and to build public and parliamentary pressure for Britain to disarm and join other countries in nego-tiating a global treaty to ban nuclear weapons.

World in Chains

*Nuclear Weapons, Militarisation
and their Impact on Society*

Edited by
ANGIE ZELTER

Luath Press Limited
EDINBURGH
www.luath.co.uk

First published 2014

ISBN: 978-1-910021-03-3

The paper used in this book is recyclable. It is made from
low chlorine pulps produced in a low energy, low emissions manner
from renewable forests.

Printed and bound by
Bell & Bain Ltd., Glasgow

Typeset in 11 point Sabon
by 3btype.com

DEDICATION

These essays are dedicated to the next generations.

In the past I have often wondered why obviously unethical or inhumane horrors were able to take place, what people were doing at the time to prevent them or what kind of resistance was happening, how many people knew and tried to stop the genocide, slavery, poverty and pollution... I want those who come after my generation to know that yes we do know of the dangers of nuclear war, of climate chaos, of environmental destruction. This book will show you that there were many people working to try to change the structures that keep our world in chains. Working around the world, on many of the interconnected problems we face, there are many millions of us trying desperately hard to resist the abuses of power and to enable constructive, sustainable and humane transformation to a better world. I am not sure we will succeed but we are trying.

We are aware of our responsibility to you, the future.

Contents

Foreword

A. L. KENNEDY

A. L. Kennedy is a writer and broadcaster and proud to have occasionally demonstrated at Faslane amongst better and braver company.

THIS IS ONE of the most important books you may never read. You may even give it to someone else to not read after you. I don't mean that badly, or as any kind of criticism, it is simply very hard to read, or think, about oneself and all of ones loved ones – all of the people one knows – strangers, everyone… being evaporated, or burned alive, being poisoned, blinded, tormented, genetically altered, starved, deprived of all they own and so forth… Thinking about nuclear weapons is just hard. And you bought the book, you made an effort, maybe you don't have to think… After Richard Feynman helped develop the bomb, he would see ground zeros, possible targets on all sides, imagine expanding rings of damage – who wants to live like that?

That's even without recalling the way survivors of the Hiroshima and Nagasaki blasts wandered through the ruins with their arms outstretched – as if B movie horror flicks had been prescient about the way the undead would walk – slowly, stumbling, moaning and keeping their raw flesh from touching other areas of raw flesh. Who wants to think about that? When there's X-Factor and Strictly? Or when there's the Welfare State to bury? When you can't pay your bills? When the Red Cross feel they have to intervene to assist the poor in your country, a 'first world' country, who wants to think of something apparently much more distant and long ago like having to pay for weapons which threaten Armageddon all the time, every moment of every day, watching and wakeful when we are not? Who wants to consider how unclean and foolish one would feel when voting for and indulging regimes that find threatening hell on earth consistently acceptable, useful, statesmanlike?

I'm only thinking about all this, because I was asked to write a foreword here that is in some way cheering and light-hearted. Which is tricky – because human beings apparently love to make money out of misery and death and nuclear weapons are as far as we have managed to go in that line. We can subtly starve or diminish, threaten others, secretly massacre, openly massacre, abuse, but nuclear weapons – they're the ultimate, the daddy, the glitzy, showbiz, phallic death threat to everyone. They put you at the sexy, exclusive high table of wannabe mass murderers. Which isn't funny. It will only be funny when it has gone, when the madness has passed.

As I was growing up, my government used to run films on TV about how much they were doing to detect nuclear weapons when they were on their way, or had already exploded. Even though I had no idea about what death meant, their reassurances worried me. Telling me how to Protect and Survive using door frames and paper bags seemed inadequate. As a teenager, I hoped we would get the three minute warning so that everyone could have sex for three minutes – the impending extinction of all life everywhere seemed the only reason that would ever happen for me and three minutes didn't seem too long to put up with something if it turned out not to be nice. I still wasn't worried about death. I was approaching the perfect age for military recruitment – I had very little to lose, was strong, ingenious and – in my head – immortal. But I wasn't quite pliable enough mentally to think nuclear weapons weren't too complex and dreadful a toy for any of us to play with. As an adult, I was able to know that putting my head in a paper bag, or following the pointless last minute instructions of my government, listening to the specially selected soothing voices, would simply keep me occupied while those responsible for my impending death scrambled for safety. Which was, I suppose, why my government quietly discontinued the broadcasts, helped me not think.

In middle age, I was able to inspect a nuclear bunker in Berlin – a really classy one – the privacy-free toilets to discourage suicides, the outer door with a small thickened glass panel through which to scream goodbye, the generator with limited fuel, the kitchen with limited food, the bunks stacked deep and high and so horribly reminiscent of a concentration camp... it was very clear that survival would not be the best option. Which was unthinkable. And not funny. And we couldn't even use the bunker – it was a museum piece. Now there was no bunker – but still bombs. All over the world, a range of inadequate shelters, or defunct shelters, but still bombs. All over the world, the possibility of accidents, of 'defensive' escalations. All over the world, the need to keep arms manu-facturers busy, well-rewarded and secure. All over the world, people dying in the unpeaceful peace nuclear weapons have created, starving and living diminished lives, paying for the weapons which are killing them in so many ways. All over the world, politicians deciding they need the power of life and death and using it badly.

Not funny. But as my German editor and I stumbled away from the bunker we did laugh. We laughed uncontrollably. We laughed the way people do when they would rather not cry in public. We laughed the way that angry, outraged people do when they remember to think the unthinkable. Thinking the unthinkable is a very tiny step away from doing what you have been told is undoable – reforming what is deeply wrong in the world. To paraphrase Bevin – what we were able to do wrong, we will be able to put right.

And then we will be able to really laugh. Because it will be over. And while we laugh, we'll keep wakeful and watching so we don't go wrong again.

Acknowledgements

Thanks to all the contributors who have provided their essays freely. They point to the changes needed to re-structure society so that it is based on compassion, co-operation, love and respect for all. Their words inspire us to resist the growing militarisation and corporatisation of our world.

Thanks to Camilla, David, Mick, and other friends for their encouragement and help.

Special thanks to Gavin of Luath for once more generously publishing a book needed by a current campaign – Action AWE (Action Atomic Weapons Eradication) www.actionawe.org

CHAPTER ONE

Introduction

ANGIE ZELTER

A peace, justice and environmental campaigner

OUR WORLD IS IN CRISIS. We mostly live in dysfunctional, nationalistic states led by corrupt politicians and their corporate interests, who are more concerned with short term money-making and growth at any cost than in the fate of the vast majority of the population. A population that just wants to live in peace and security. Rather than dealing with the true underlying causes of insecurity (unequal distribution of resources, environmental degradation, human rights abuses, climate chaos... to name but a few), our states support the institutions and corporations that perpetuate and profit from injustice and inequality. We, the public, for many complex reasons allow them to get away with it. Governments manipulate fears that they then use to justify their erosion of domestic civil liberties, foreign military interventions and nuclear blackmail.

Despite the horrors of colonialism and the disastrous wars of the 20th century, our 'leaders' seem not to have learned that if we truly want peace and security, then we need to make some deep structural changes to our institutions and systems. We need to move from a debt-based money system that favours a small minority of rich and powerful people and corporations to a socially just system that favours all people and supports a sustainable environment. We need to promote global citizenship, not national interests. This book explores some of the issues that need to be addressed. It does so from a mostly UK perspective, centred around the abuse of power engendered by the continued reliance upon nuclear weapons and militarism.

In 2016 the UK government may finalise the decision to build a new nuclear weapons system to replace the present Trident set-up. The nuclear submarines that carry Trident are getting old, so the Government has pledged to finalise contracts to replace them in 2016 in order to build a new generation of nuclear weapons at an estimated cost of £76–100bn. At the same time, current planned public spending cuts amount to £81bn. If the contracts go ahead, the warheads would be designed and manufactured at AWE (Atomic Weapons Establishment) Aldermaston and Burghfield, in Berkshire, about 50 miles west of London.[1]

Such a replacement and modernisation of a nuclear weapon system would be illegal under international law, as it breaches the commitment to nuclear disarmament that nuclear weapons states made under the Non-Proliferation Treaty (NPT). The long delay in implementing Article VI of the NPT places the world in a perilous situation. As the UN Secretary-General Ban Ki-moon recently said:

> Delay comes with a high price tag. The longer we procrastinate, the greater the risk that these weapons will be used, will proliferate or be acquired by terrorists. But our aim must be more than keeping the deadliest of weapons from 'falling into the wrong hands'. There are no right hands for wrong weapons... I urge all nuclear-armed States to reconsider their national nuclear posture. Nuclear deterrence is not a solution to international peace and stability. It is an obstacle.[2]

It is not just the Secretary-General who is frustrated by the nuclear weapon states. The non-nuclear states, which are in an overwhelming majority, are now actively campaigning for an international treaty to ban all nuclear weapons: 'Three in four governments support the idea of a treaty to outlaw and eliminate nuclear weapons.'[3]

However, unless there is a massive movement by civil society, that includes nonviolent direct action, all the nuclear weapon states *will* modernise and replace their nuclear arsenals, more states will build their own, more accidents will happen and the unthinkable may happen. The bad example of the original five nuclear weapon states (USA, Russia, France, China and the UK) continuing to depend on nuclear weapons has not only encouraged Israel, India, Pakistan and North Korea[4] to acquire them, but is inciting ever more states to join in.

In the UK, anti-nuclear activists (including those who supported Trident Ploughshares and Faslane 365) helped galvanise public opposition to Trident. This succeeded to the extent that the present Scottish Government have promised to ban all nuclear weapons from Scotland if the Scots vote for independence in the Referendum (to be held in September 2014) and they come to power in a newly independent nation. It is important now that there is a special focus on the English dimension – the atomic weapon establishments at Aldermaston and Burghfield. If we succeed here, then the potential for worldwide disarmament is great. Once the UK abandons its reliance on nuclear weapons, we can expect a 'good domino' effect to cascade around the world.

A new grassroots campaign called Action AWE (Atomic Weapons Eradication)[5] has recently formed to take up this struggle and to combine the strengths of as many peace, justice and environmental groups as possible. European groups as well as UK groups are being asked to join this campaign. Action AWE is dedicated to halting nuclear weapons production at the Atomic Weapons Establishment factories at Aldermaston[6] and Burghfield. The campaign aims to encourage groups and individuals to undertake autonomous actions and events to raise awareness of the catastrophic humanitarian consequences of nuclear weapons. Now more than ever, we need to exert political pressure on Britain to end the production, replacement and deployment of Trident, and to join other countries in negotiating a global treaty to ban nuclear weapons.

This book has been produced to expose some of the structures and links that keep our world chained to a militaristic, exploitative and abusive system and helps point to some of the changes required if we wish to create a healthier, happier, more sustaining and moral world order.

The essays in this book have been freely written for Action AWE by a wide range of people including academics, researchers and activists, and will hopefully inspire us all to think more deeply about the impact that nuclear weapons, war and militarisation have on our society.

Paul Rogers' essay draws threads from around the world and provides an overview of the many problems facing us. He shows us the inter-relatedness of socio-economic inequality and environmental constraints, especially climate change. He comments on the greater global access to information leading to a 'revolution of frustrated expectations' amongst the growing majority of marginalised and dispossessed people. Exploring the folly and danger of nuclear weapons and wars, he urges the more hopeful application of sustainable transformation.

Philip Webber explains the effects of the use of nuclear weapons and presents evidence that the launch of the nuclear missiles of even just one Trident submarine could cause devastating climatic cooling. Not only would there be far reaching environmental effects, way beyond the immediate conflict area, but the economic impacts across the globe would also be severe.

Kevin Lister provides a bleak appraisal of the links between what he describes as the 'two existential threats, runaway climate change and nuclear war', describing them as the 'flip sides to the same coin: *industrialisation*'.

Mary Mellor's article demonstrates how finance, trade and military conflict are closely linked with war. She provides a historical overview of the money system and illustrates how 'the present globalised money system creates many areas of actual and potential conflict'.

Helena Paul provides a stimulating, thought-provoking insight into the present industrial agricultural system and how this intertwines closely with our militarised society.

Whilst pondering the money system, Tom Anderson investigates who is profiting from the Atomic Weapons Establishment, and Kaye Stearman discusses the specific arms companies involved in the UK.

Britain's colonial past and present involvement in wars has led to an increasing militarisation of our society, and this is tackled by Owen Everett.

Trevor Trueman gives us a short reminder of the impact that violence and war have on ordinary people and the resulting trauma of the refugees who try to survive the war machine.

Joanne Baker's essay exposes the use of radiological weapons, which are poisoning people and the environment and causing major birth defects. Uranium weapons, depleted or otherwise, are both radioactive and toxic. She reminds us that the half-life of uranium is 450 billion years. The uranium dust from the use of these weapons is neither containable nor easily cleaned up.

Pete Roche scrutinises further the links between the civil nuclear power system and the military, a link that the nuclear industry tries to cover up. He tells us about the spread of uranium enrichment technology – 'a route to proliferation' and that 'peaceful nuclear energy is a myth'.

John La Forge's detailed essay on military pollution is based mainly on research from the USA that he has been collecting over many years. The findings are relevant to everyone, as all the nuclear weapon states are implicated in similar experiments, to a greater or lesser extent, and the air, sea and earth connect the planetary environment. The sheer extent of the long-lasting contamination caused by the nuclear military industry is horrifying.

Siân Jones describes some of the ways that our civil liberties and rights to protest have been undermined by the use of police intelligence gatherers, undercover agents infiltrating the movement and by anti-terrorist legislation. The erosion of civil liberties in highly militarised nuclear states was foretold by the peace movement many decades ago. She also reminds us of the many creative acts of resistance that have taken place over the last decade.

Having noticed that the majority of the anti-nuclear activists that Siân used to illustrate her essay were women, it is pertinent to read Cynthia Cockburn's essay on the gendered dimensions of nuclear weapons.

Bruce Gagnon gives us a timely reflection on how the UK is closely tied into US plans for global domination through armed force, as shown through its hundreds of foreign bases, space technology, and the expansion of NATO. The build up of military might around China and the Arctic are especially dangerous.

A thoughtful essay by John Hull examines the ethical dimensions of a reliance on weapons of mass destruction, concluding that the denial that accompanies it leads to a deadening of the conscience and a repression of natural human kindness.

Rebecca Johnson explains the recent international approaches aimed at achieving a new international treaty to ban nuclear weapons that will bypass all the objections of the reluctant nuclear weapons states and 'fundamentally change the legal and political context within which nuclear-armed states and proliferators operate'.

Lastly, Paul Mobbs takes up many of the themes mentioned in the essays above in an examination of the use of technology and machines by the State to command and dominate, posing questions about civil democracy in a cybernetic world. He expresses his concern for society in general at 'the increasingly close links between the military and security services, defence and IT companies, and the wider body of corporate interests who those security companies service. As a result of these links the boundary between the military, the public and the private has becoming increasingly blurred'.

All of the essays stimulate us to think more deeply about the structural and moral distortions in our societies brought about by the desire for power and control over others and most clearly identified by looking at nuclear weapons, militarisation and war.

I hope that you will be motivated to take part in Action AWE events. Most especially that you and your friends and neighbours do not vote in the next general election for any prospective MP who supports the replacement of our nuclear weapons, but instead vote for those who are serious about nuclear disarmament. These next couple of years are vital. We have to change many of the institutions that are destroying our world and transform them into ones capable of engaging our humanity. This will be underpinned by a major transformation of our defence and security structures, starting with nuclear disarmament.

Notes

1   Action AWE: http://actionawe.org/awe-burghfield-maps-gates/.
2   Secretary-General Ban Ki-moon, 'Advancing the Disarmament and Non-proliferaton agenda: Seeking Peace in an Over-armed World', Address at the Monterey Institute of International Studies, 18 January 2013.
3   ICAN: [http://www.icanw.org/why-a-ban].
4   Nine countries spent over $100bn on nuclear weapons in 2011. Ban Ki-moon (Ibid.) stated: 'Disarmament cannot be considered in isolation from other global challenges. The world spends more on the military in one month than it does on development all year. And four hours of military spending is equal to the total budgets of all international disarmament and non-proliferation organizations combined. The world is over-armed. Peace is under-funded. Bloated military budgets promote proliferation, derail arms control, doom disarmament and detract from social and economic development... The profits of the arms industry are built on the suffering of ordinary people – in Mali, Syria, Afghanistan, the Democratic Republic of Congo. At the foot of the pyramid lie small arms. At the top are nuclear weapons.' This is $100bn they did *not* spend on climate, health, education, food, water, development...
5   Action AWE: http://actionawe.org/.
6   Rob Edwards, 'Secret UK uranium components plant closed over safety fears', *The Guardian*, 24 January 2013. 'A top-secret plant at Aldermaston that makes enriched uranium components for Britain's nuclear warheads and fuel for the Royal Navy's submarines has been shut down because corrosion has been discovered in its "structural steelwork", *The Guardian* can reveal. The closure has been endorsed by safety regulators who feared the building did not conform to the appropriate standards. The nuclear safety watchdog demands that such critical buildings are capable of withstanding "extreme weather and seismic events", and the plant at Aldermaston failed this test.'

CHAPTER TWO

Chances for Peace in the Second Decade – What is Going Wrong and What We Must Do

PROFESSOR PAUL ROGERS

Paul Rogers is Global Security Consultant to Oxford Research Group (ORG) and Professor of Peace Studies at the University of Bradford. He writes regular reports and monthly global security briefings. This briefing originally appeared on the website of the Oxford Research Group on 14 December 2012.

Where to Start?

WE SURVIVED THE Cold War, the most dangerous period in human history so far. Well, most of us did.

In reality, more than ten million people died and tens of millions more were wounded in proxy wars involving the superpowers – in Korea, Vietnam, the Horn of Africa, Central America, Afghanistan and elsewhere. Some places took decades to recover, others never have.

It is true that at least an all-out nuclear war was avoided, but there were huge risks, many accidents and some exceptionally dangerous crises. Put bluntly, we were very lucky to come through it without a catastrophe.

Moreover, for 45 years, massive amounts of money and immense human resources were diverted away from far more important tasks to fuel war machines which, at their peak, employed tens of millions of people, wasted billions of pounds, produced vast masses of armaments, including over 60,000 nuclear weapons and threatened worldwide destruction. The many millions of lives that were lost through poverty, disease and malnutrition across the world through this appalling waste are rarely acknowledged.

More than 20 years later, the nuclear dangers are still far from over, even if we are on something more like a slippery slope to a proliferated world, rather than staring over the edge of an appalling nuclear abyss, and there is still much to do to save us from our capacity for self-destruction.

Even so, in the early 1990s, after the end of the Cold War, there seemed the prospect of a more peaceful world order, but it disappeared in the face of deep and enduring conflicts, not least in the first Gulf War, and the bitter conflicts in the Balkans, the Caucasus and the African Great Lakes.

Bill Clinton's first CIA Director, James Woolsey, characterised the changed world in the mid-1990s as one where the West had slain the dragon of the Soviet Union but was now facing a jungle full of poisonous snakes.[1] The jungle had to be tamed to maintain stability, and this was an attitude that came to the fore in an extraordinarily robust response to the 9/11 atrocities. It failed to control political violence and led to two major wars and persistent conflict across the Middle East and South Asia.

These are trends of the immediate past and present, but the issues that will come most to dominate international conflict relate only partially to them. What is much more necessary is to recognise the underlying trends that could be at the core of insecurity and conflict in the decades to come, and to understand how we can avoid their becoming the drivers of conflicts that may dwarf the problems of recent years, including even the 'war on terror'.

Divisions and Constraints

There are two root issues that will increasingly interrelate – socio-economic divisions and environmental constraints, especially climate change.

1 Rich-Poor World

In the past 60 years, the world economy has experienced almost continual growth. Until 1980, that was largely on the basis of a mixed economy model competing with the centrally planned economies of the Soviet bloc and China. From the early 1980s, the trend was toward a much more neoliberal free market approach with privatisation of state assets across many countries, the freeing up of markets and less regulation of trade and financial markets.

Ideas of a more planned world economy linking fair trade with development had been proposed in the 1960s, especially by the UN Conference on Trade and Development (UNCTAD). They reached their peak with the intended New International Economic Order of 1974, which would have promoted integrated commodity agreements, tariff preferences and other processes designed to improve the trading and development prospects of the Global South. These progressive proposals withered away by the end of the decade in the face of a determined neoliberal economic agenda.

This was pursued, in particular, by the Reagan administration in the United States and the Thatcher Government in the UK, but was more generally embraced by other states and especially by international financial institutions, such as the World Bank and the International Monetary Fund, in what became known as the 'Washington Consensus'.

It was an outlook that got a boost with progressive deregulation of financial institutions in the late 1980s, especially the 'Big Bang' for the London's financial institutions in 1986. There was then a further boost because of the collapse of the centrally planned system of the Soviet bloc in 1990–91, even though Russia's subsequent embrace of unbridled capitalism actually set back its own economy by a decade or more, wrecked the lives of millions of people, and still leaves a legacy of bitterness.

Across the world, economic growth continued, albeit at a slower rate than 1950-80, but what became increasingly clear was that it was becoming more and more unbalanced, with the benefits of growth falling mostly into the hands of around one fifth of the global population. While the poorest people did not generally get poorer, levels of malnutrition actually increased substantially, but what was even more significant was that by the early 21st century, the great majority of all the world's wealth and annual income – close to 85 per cent – was shared by about 1.5 billion people out of a world population heading towards seven billion.

This division had become steadily more pronounced in the last two decades of the 20th century, but one major feature of the change was that it was no longer a matter of 'rich country/poor country' – more a very large trans-global elite disproportionately sharing the benefits due to the entire world community.

This now includes hundreds of millions of people in China, India, Brazil and many other countries across the South, even if the 'old rich' countries of the Atlantic alliance still dominate. On top of this is a very much smaller trans-global 'super-elite', including many thousands of multi-millionaires. At the same time, along with the marginalised majority of billions of people across the South, there is also a marginalised minority, sometimes of tens of millions of people, in the old rich states of the West.

This failure to deliver socio-economic justice is particularly evident in the fast-growing Asian development region. According to the Asia Development Bank's 2012 Asia Development Report, if there had been more even distribution of the fruits of growth, 'another 240 million people in the 45 countries that make up developing Asia would have moved out of poverty in the last two decades'[2].

What is insidious is that we are faced with a deep-seated trend, which is persistently disguised by the more obvious signs of economic development. City tower blocks, beach hotels, safari parks and many other accoutrements of partial economic success all too frequently disguise deep and enduring divisions, with richer people living and travelling in cocoons of wellbeing, not seeing the slums that ring the cities or the endemic rural poverty.

Because of the size of the successful elite – more than one fifth of the world's population – it acts as a self-contained, if large, global entity that benefits from material wellbeing that is largely taken for granted. Moreover, it is for the most part a community that persistently fails to recognise the endemic mal-distribution of world wealth and income.

Thus the minority world lives alongside the majority world but is hardly conscious of the very existence of the divide. Rarely does it acknowledge the sustained benefit gained from appalling low wages and working conditions of hundreds of millions of people producing cheap goods, nor the existence of a trading system dominated by transnational corporations and favouring production of low-cost commodities at the expense of poor farmers and miners across the world.

A Success with Consequences

At the same time, none of this should diminish the progress that has been made in some aspects of international development, not least education. Forty years ago, one of the greatest challenges facing the countries of the South was the impoverishment of education, with only a minority of children getting even four years of primary education. That has changed dramatically, and most children now get a basic education. Even the pernicious gender gap is slowly narrowing.

This success has been achieved mostly by determined efforts of peoples and governments and it has more recently been combined with huge improvements in communications. There are still many communities that are notably 'data poor', but the combination of improved education, literacy and communications has been one of the great development success stories of the past four decades.

Yet, there is a very powerful consequence of this in that far more people are aware of their own marginalisation. It is a phenomenon that particularly affects young people across the majority world who are educated at least to high school level but have few job prospects or hopes for a reasonable standard of living. With the current recession, this is also being experienced in rich states such as Greece and Spain, with eruptions of discontent and protest onto the streets as well as the 'Occupy' and other new social movements. It has certainly added greatly to the much more widespread frustration and anger with Middle East autocracies that has underpinned the Arab Awakening that started early in 2011.

In the 1970s, it was common in countries such as Britain to talk of a 'revolution of rising expectations' as the consumer society and economic growth always promised more. People would be reasonably content, because, whatever the particular problems of national economies, the overall picture was of a promise of economic growth and innovation delivering better material wellbeing. What is more likely in the early 21st century is a 'revolution of frustrated expectations' as people among the marginalised majorities become more aware of their own marginalisation, leading to despair, resentment and anger.

2 Environmental Limits

On its own, the problem of a socio-economically divided world is ethically unacceptable, as well as being potentially unstable. The more the divisions endure in an increasingly connected world, the more there is the risk of anger and revolts from the margins, but what is even more important is that these persistent divisions are working in parallel with global environmental constraints – the inability of the global ecosystem to absorb human impacts, especially the carbon emissions that are leading to climate change.

Environmental constraints are many, and they include major issues of water resource use, as well as competition and conflict over strategic minerals, especially in Central Africa. The buying up of land by foreign interests, not least in Africa and Latin America, is a further example. In terms of the world's non-renewable resources, the concentrated location of oil and gas is the most remarkable. More than 60 per cent of the world's readily accessible high quality oil is found in just five countries around the Persian Gulf – Iran, Iraq, Kuwait, Saudi Arabia and the UAE – with another 20 per cent in Russia, Kazakhstan and Venezuela. The concentration of natural gas is even more extreme, with over half the world reserves in just three countries – Russia, Iran and Qatar.

Such a narrow resource base for these energy reserves is at the root of the strategic importance of the Persian Gulf and does much to explain recent and current conflicts, but the even greater global concern stems more from the potential impact of climate change.

Put in its most basic form, huge fossil fuel reserves of coal, oil and gas were laid down over millions of years, mainly during the Carboniferous Era, and large quantities of the carbon locked up in these reserves are now being released into the atmosphere, not in millions or even thousands of years but in centuries and, to some extent, even just decades. Most of this carbon release is in the form of carbon dioxide and this gas increases the absorption of the sun's radiation in the atmosphere. The overall impact is one of increasing temperatures and that is already happening, but this is not a uniform process across the world.

Until about 20 years ago, climate research suggested that the most pronounced impacts of climate change would be felt in the temperate latitudes. For the most part, these were the wealthier regions of the world and might best be able to cope. That view has changed dramatically, and it is now clear that the impact of climate change will indeed be asymmetric, but not in the way originally thought.

It is true that the northernmost latitudes will probably be greatly affected, with the near-Arctic already seeing a substantial rate of change that is much greater than elsewhere, but there will also be dramatic effects on the tropical and sub-tropical land masses.

In overall terms, climate change looks likely to have relatively little impact in atmospheric temperatures over the world's oceans. By contrast, temperature increases across Central America, Amazonia, the Middle East, Central Africa and South and South-East Asia will be well above average. The impacts are likely to include the drying out of the tropical rain forests of the Amazon and South-East Asia, and the progressive loss of the 'reservoirs in the sky', the glaciers in the Himalayas, the Karako-rams and the Tibetan Plateau that feed the great rivers of southern Asia.

The overall impact is likely to be a substantial decrease in the ecological carrying capacity of the tropical and sub-tropical crop lands, making it far more difficult for the majority of the world's people to access affordable food. This is particularly serious, because these are precisely those parts of the world in which people have least material wealth and are least able to cope.

Consequences

If we stay for the moment with present trends, not with what will happen if we make many positive changes, then the outlook is bleak. Leaving aside for now the huge issue of environmental limits, the socio-economic divisions alone point to a very disturbed future. Nearly 40 years ago the economic geographer Edwin Brookes pointed to the circumstances we had to avoid of '... a crowded, glowering planet of massive inequalities of wealth, buttressed by stark force yet endlessly threatened by desperate people in the global ghettoes...'[3]

In many ways we can see Brooke's dystopian prognosis already becoming evident. The heavily protected gated communities increase in size and frequency in cities across the world, and more extreme protests are common. China now has a formidable problem of endemic social unrest to which the authorities respond with more heavily armed internal security forces. The Arab Awakening has many elements, but among the driving forces are the poor economic prospects and lack of opportunity facing millions of young people.

India will soon be the world's most populous country and has been enjoying impressive rates of growth, but economic development is hugely skewed in favour of a minority, with the country having to face up to a bitter and wide-ranging insurgency from the neo-Maoist Naxalites. They are active in close to half the states of India and stem from the marginal-isation of millions, especially as mining and industrial developments take little notice of peoples' rights.

These are early indicators of problems that arise from the existing organisation of the world economy, but the real issue is to add these to the growing impact of climate change. What we are therefore likely to face is not just Brooke's 'crowded, glowering planet', but a constrained planet leading to a degree of desperation that will transcend the problems we already face. There is a particular risk of mass migration as people become desperate in their own communities and seek something better, and we are talking about much greater pressures than are already apparent.

There is also a great risk of 'revolts from the margins' as people turn to radical action to try and ensure their survival.

A previous analysis, written more than a decade ago and pointing to 'markers of rebellion' put it this way: there is sufficient evidence from economic and environmental trends to indicate that marginalisation of the majority of the world's people is continuing and increasing, and that it is extremely difficult to predict how and when different forms of anti-elite action may develop. It was not predictable that Guzman's teachings in Peru would lead to a movement of the intensity and human impact of Sendero Luminosa, nor was the Zapatista rebellion in Mexico anticipated. When the Algerian armed forces curtailed elections in 1991 for fear that they would bring a rigorous Islamic party to power, few predicted a bloody conflict that would claim many tens of thousands of lives.

> What should be expected is that new social movements will develop that are essentially anti-elite in nature and draw their support from people, especially men, on the margins. In different contexts and circumstances they may have their roots in political ideologies, religious beliefs, ethnic, nationalist or cultural identities, or a complex combination of several of these. They may be focussed on individuals or groups but the most common feature is an opposition to existing centres of power. They may be sub-state groups directed at the elites in their own state or foreign interests, or they may hold power in states in the South, and will no doubt be labelled as rogue states as they direct their responses towards the North. What can be said is that, on present trends, anti-elite action will be a core feature of the next 30 years – not so much a clash of civilisations, more an age of insurgencies.[4]

'Liddism' Rules OK

More than a decade later, we can see that the expected impact of climate change will exacerbate these trends, and the problems we face in the future stem from this unique combination of a divided and constrained world. It is a predicament that leaves us, in its most basic form, with two possible choices – trying to maintain control or working to confront the challenges.

The first is 'liddism' – we keep the lid on the problems and maintain the status quo. We stay rigidly with the belief that the free market is the only economic system and that the world economic system as it has evolved is, without question, the only way to operate. When threats to this system arise, they are dangerous and must be countered. This means vigorous support for elite regimes facing revolts from the margins, it involves stringent control of migration, persistent intervention in failed and failing states when they threaten 'our' interests and extending even to the violent termination of regimes deemed to threaten the security of the established international system – 'our' world.

Economic migrants are after our jobs. Asylum seekers are scroungers, living on welfare paid by our taxes. If more than a thousand people drown in the Mediterranean trying to reach Europe in the early months of 2011, it is of little account and no concern of ours. If people riot in cities in the West, they are criminals pure and simple, and there is no need for any further discussion. If rebels oppose a friendly autocratic government in the South, they are terrorists, a dangerous threat to established order and to be repressed with all necessary force.

In short, it is a matter of taming Woolsey's 'jungle full of snakes', secure in the belief that the jungle can be tamed and order maintained.

Lessons from a War

In a very real sense, the response to the appalling 9/11 atrocities and the consequent war on terror are striking examples of this approach and provide strong markers for future behaviour. At the peak of that response, when Bush delivered his 'mission accomplished' speech on 1 May 2003, Afghanistan was thought to be transforming into a pro-western developing state with a geopolitically useful US military presence and enhanced influence in Central Asia. Al-Qaida was dispersed and degraded.

Under the guidance of the Coalition Provisional Authority, Iraq would become a shining example of a true free market economy, a pro-western beacon for the Middle East with, as in Afghanistan, a useful US military presence. The most dangerous threat, Iran, would be thoroughly constrained by this new regional order. More generally, the idea of a New American Century of an unrestrained free market world order, led by the United States, would be 'back on track'.

The 9/11 attacks were visceral in their effect and it was almost impossible for the Bush administration and its closest allies to see them as grievous examples of a grotesque transnational criminality. Instead, they could only be seen as the starting point for a war against Islamo-fascism that even came to include whole states that threatened the western world in an 'axis of evil' .

What happened was radically different to expectations. A three-week regime termination in Iraq turned into a bitter eight-year war, with the country even now in a deeply unstable state and with millions of people still displaced. Iranian influence in the region is actually stronger than before the war and that of the United States is diminished.

In Afghanistan, an 'eight-week campaign' against the Taliban is now in its second decade. Even the al-Qaida idea survives in a diffuse yet potent form, much dispersed but with affiliates active across the region, not least in Yemen, Somalia, Mali and Nigeria.

According to a report from the Eisenhower Research Project at Brown University in 2011: At a conservative estimate, the overall death toll in Iraq, Afghanistan and elsewhere, including civilians, uniformed personnel and contractors, is at least 225,000.

> There have been 7.8 million refugees created among Iraqis, Afghans and Pakistanis.
>
> The wars will cost close to $4 trillion dollars and are being funded substantially by borrowing, with $185 billion in interest already paid and another $1 trillion likely by 2020.[5]

In so many respects, the conduct of the war on terror was an example of what some call the 'control paradigm', the early recourse to re-gaining control with little attention given to the reasons for conflict. The human costs have been appalling. If no lessons are learnt from this experience, then there is every probability that 'taming the jungle' will be the order of the day – no doubt with prolific use of armed drones and Special Forces, but this will only make matters far worse. If the deep injustices of the present world economic and environmental order are not addressed, then the result will be greater suffering and instability, leading rapidly to more conflict. The idea that the elite world can close the castle gates is a myth – it is simply not possible in a globalised and highly connected world.

Choices

'Liddism' may be the first choice but the second is addressing the under-lying causes of future insecurity. In the simplest of terms it is straightfor-ward, but translating the obvious into the actual is far from easy. Severe climate change has to be prevented by a rapid transition to low carbon economies, with the main carbon emitters of the North decreasing carbon outputs by 80 per cent in less than two decades. Lesser emitters must be enabled to develop along economic paths that are truly sustainable, aided substantially by the states of the North that have been responsible so far for the great majority of emissions.

Such an environmental transition has to be paralleled directly by an economic transformation to a far more equitable and emancipated system, both transnationally and within states. For the Global South, this involves much greater debt relief and the linking of trade with development in a manner similar to what was advocated by UNCTAD nearly half a century ago but never implemented – a genuine New International Economic Order. Technological innovations may well help, not least in adapting to that level of climate change that is already inevitable, and a rapid transition to versatile renewable energy sources, often seriously localised, can readily enhance economic emancipation.

These two paragraphs summarise the changes needed, but they seem so vast that there is an immediate feeling of powerlessness. That may be understandable but needs to be met head-on with a sense of hope. Thirty years ago, in the early 1980s, there was a palpable fear of nuclear annihilation and doubts whether we would make it to 1990, yet we did. Thirty years before that, some far-sighted politicians sought European economic cooperation as a means of preventing a third European civil war. Whatever we think of the European Union, a Franco-German conflict is now hardly likely.

There are also many examples where events prompt action, even more so when the necessary thinking and planning is already there. Take just a few examples:

Municipal engineers like Sir Joseph Bazelgette were already working on plans for proper sewage disposal in the squalid and cholera-ridden London of the 1850s, but it took the 'Great Stink' of the 1858 summer to prompt sustained and effective action, with London leading the way for many other cities and resulting in sustained improvements in health.

A century later, 4,000 people died in 1952 in the four-day 'Great Smog of London', but this prompted radical improvements in air pollution control across Britain that were already being called for.

Atmospheric chemists and the UN Environment Programme were already pointing to the dangerous effect of CFC pollutants on the world's ozone layer in the late 1970s, and, partly because of this, the discovery of the extent of the Antarctic 'ozone hole' in 1983 prompted a rapid international response, with the global Montreal Convention signed just four years later.

Even at the height of the Cold War, the shock of the Cuban Missile Crisis of 1962 was a major factor in leading the US and the Soviet Union to a welcome process of trust building and some key agreements, including the Partial Test Ban Treaty, as well as leading to a political climate that helped bring about the Non-Proliferation Treaty.

On the big issues that face us we certainly have an urgent need for wise political leadership, but that may be far more possible, if there is a powerful sense of vision from within the realms of civil society. The world community faces challenges that are quite extraordinarily profound, and we need to think through the many challenges and how they might best be met. If we define prophecy as 'suggesting the possible', then we need a great deal of prophetic thinking, and we need it soon.

We may be aided by major events, and there are many other examples from recent history of individual incidents that have catalysed substantial change, not least because some people had recognised the underlying problems, anticipated the need for change and thought how to help bring it about. It may well be that extreme weather events – so-called 'global weirding' – may turn out to be advanced warnings of climate change, like the canary in the coal mine, and if there has been enough 'suggesting the possible', then the change can happen before excessive suffering.

Much good work is already being done and there are innumerable examples from right across the world. Take just three examples from the hundreds in Britain alone: the Centre for Alternative Technology's extensive work on renewables and energy conservation, the New Economics Foundation's Great Transition project, and Oxford Research Group's work on sustainable security. Don't forget, also, that there are close to a billion members of cooperatives in over a hundred countries.

We also need a broader sense of perspective. There is sound evidence that the 1990s saw more conflicts and loss of life worldwide than the first decade of the 21st century, in spite of the impact of the war on terror. More generally, if we look back over several centuries, there is a legitimate argument that, given the growth in the world's population, proportionally fewer people have been the victims of violence, including war, over the past 50 years than in similar periods in previous centuries.[6] This does not mean that there is even a remote case for complacency, especially given the increase in destructive power of weapons, and the threat to the whole global environment, but it does help give a sense of hope.

A Century on the Edge – and of Hope

As individuals we may feel thoroughly daunted in the face of the changes that need to be made, yet each of us may have skills, knowledge and abilities that lie in particular directions and can vary greatly. However modest we think our individual contributions may be, they still help and they really can add to the efforts of many others into something really powerful.

In this we need to remember three things. Any one person is part of a whole movement, and recognising the big picture while contributing to one part of it makes great good sense. The second is that knowledge really is power – it is ever so important that we learn from all the many sources of information and ideas that are now in circulation, a process made much easier by the new social media. This enables us to be much more effective in expressing what needs to be done, and to convince others. Finally, there is the essential need to maintain a sense of hope, even during times of pessimism. Indeed, on the matter of hope, there is a particular way of looking at things which can actually help.

We may, in our arrogance, always think that our own time of living is the most significant in human history, but there is a sense in which one particular century, from 1945 to 2045, may actually fulfil that definition.

Why 1945?

Well, that's easy. The first atom bomb was tested in July; two Japanese cities were destroyed the following month, and within a decade, the world was in the midst of an appallingly dangerous nuclear arms race that could have set our world community back centuries. We had, for the first time in millions of years of human evolution, developed the means to wreak utter destruction worldwide.

As was remarked back in the introduction, we avoided it largely by luck, and we are not out of the woods even now. Yet we may be learning slowly to cope with our capacity for self-destruction, even if we have many challenges to come, not least from the potential misuse of bio-molecular science and nano-technologies.

Why, then, 2045? That is not so straightforward but revolves around the idea that we now have the potential to cause huge damage to our environment, including diminishing prospects for our own wellbeing. That, too, can be overcome, and we need to be well on the way by 2045 – indeed the second decade of this century is the period in which serious change must start.

The Key Decade

If we succeed, then there is every chance that young children who are alive now will look back in their later life, perhaps even at the dawn of the 22nd century and recognise, happily, that there was enough wisdom, energy and commitment 80 or so years earlier to begin the changes that helped make the 21st century the most peaceful, just and sustainable period in human history. That is what makes this second decade of the 21st century so important. If we can really begin the transformation by 2020, and if that leads on to much greater progress in the 2020s, then we can approach the following years not just with hope, but with confidence, too.

Further Information

There is a mass of information available on the issues covered here, so the following sources are just a beginning. The Oxford Research Group is a helpful source on sustainable security and related issues [www.oxfordresearchgroup.org.uk] and [www.sustainablesecurity.org]

One of the best web journals covering a huge range of topics is Open Democracy [www.opendemocracy.net]. It is particularly good in terms of the wide range of people who write for it and the breadth of subjects covered.

Information on the New Economics Foundation's Great Transition project is available on the NEF website [www.neweconomics.org]

Of the groups campaigning on development issues, see especially the World Development Movement [www.wdm.org.uk/]

Carbon Brief provides copious information on climate change [www.carbonbrief.org/] A good source on renewables and energy conservation is the Centre for Alternative Technology in Mid-Wales [www.cat.org.uk]

A useful resource on international peace and security issues is Open Briefing [www.openbriefing.org]

One recent book that focuses on land-grabbing in the Global South and, in the process, says much about how the entire current system runs, is Fred Pearce's *The Landgrabbers: The New Fight Over Who Owns the Earth* (London: Eden Project Books, 2012).

Notes

1 James Woolsey, 'Statement at Senate hearings', February 1993.
2 Neena Bhandari, 'Rising Inequality Could be Asia's Undoing', *TerraViva-Inter Press Services*, 13 April 2012.
3 Edwin Brookes, 'The Implications of Ecological Limits to Development in Terms of Expectations and Aspirations in Developed and Less Developed Countries' in *Human Ecology and World Development* ed. by Anthony Vann and Paul Rogers (London: Plenum Press,1974).
4 Paul Rogers, *Losing Control: Global Security in the 21st Century* 1st edn. (London: Pluto Press, 2001).
5 'The Costs of War', a report from the Eisenhower Research Project of the Watson Institute for International Studies at Brown University, (2011), [www.costsofwar.org].
6 This is a point powerfully argued by Steven Pinker in his book, *The Better Angels of Our Nature* (New York: Viking Press, 2011).

CHAPTER 3

The Climatic and Humanitarian Impacts of the Use of the UK's Nuclear Weapons

DR PHILIP WEBBER

Philip Webber is Chair of Scientists for Global Responsibility (SGR). SGR promotes ethical science, design and technology that contribute to peace, justice and environmental sustainability. He has published books and reports on science and the military.

IT IS GENERALLY well known that nuclear weapons are extremely destructive. What is not well known is that the detonation of several nuclear weapons over typical city targets can cause severe climatic cooling. Climatic effects can follow the use of nuclear weapons because nuclear fireballs would set fire to fossil fuel stocks, chemical plants, buildings and cars across large areas in cities, especially if blast damage had already occurred from a previous detonation. The fierce up-draught from a nuclear fireball lifts vast quantities of black carbon (soot) high into the atmosphere, much higher than from a conventional conflagration, creating a high altitude 'smog', reducing sunlight as well as creating the characteristic mushroom cloud. The small particles stay aloft for several years, floating well above most clouds and rainfall. Such climate impacts from high altitude particles have been observed following volcanic eruptions.

Climate effects from nuclear war: early studies

The possibility that a nuclear conflict could cause climate effects was first thought about in the 1980s. Three climate modelling studies – by two US research groups and one Russian – were especially important.[1] They showed that a full-scale nuclear war – with some 1,000 nuclear warheads exploded over cities and fuel-laden targets such as oil refineries – would cause reductions in surface temperature, rainfall, and energy from sunlight at the Earth's surface so large that the climatic consequences could be

described as a 'nuclear winter'. The effect would last a year or more and
lead to 'darkness at noon' and other severe climatic disturbances. The
stratospheric ozone layer would be destroyed, resulting in a major increase
in the dangerous ultra-violet radiation reaching ground level. There would
be major extinctions of wildlife, and most people on the planet would be
in danger of starvation. The modelling predicted a significant effect if more
than a few hundred nuclear weapons were detonated. The political response
to these calculations was intense, as these findings were seen as undermining the concept of nuclear deterrence. Some opponents coined the term
'nuclear autumn' in an attempt to discredit the work.[2]

In recent years, as the nuclear threat has seemed to recede, attention
has shifted to climate change as a result of carbon emissions from fossil
fuel burning. Combined with massive improvements in computing power,
climate models have markedly improved.

Nuclear Winter confirmed

In 2007, several new studies were performed using the latest models running
on supercomputers at the NASA Goddard Institute of Space Science, by
several leading US climate scientists and published in the scientific litera-
ture.[3] These studies also considered new work on the incendiary effects
of nuclear weapons. For example, fire-storms may be created, where hur-
ricane-force winds feed an intense fire that kills even those sheltering, by
consuming the oxygen in the air, as took place in Dresden in the Second
World War. This could increase the extent of fires and the volumes of soot
produced. Three new scenarios were considered: an India-Pakistan conflict
involving about 100 Hiroshima sized weapons (1500kT), a conflict using
US, Russian and Chinese weapons on high alert (launch on warning –
1,300,000kT); and a full scale nuclear conflict (5,000,000kT).[4] These three
scenarios would produce 5, 50 and 150 million tonnes of black smoke
respectively as shown in Figure 1.

At the upper end of the spectrum, the two higher scenarios strengthen
the basic conclusion that a large scale nuclear conflict would have devastating climatic consequences. An average cooling effect of 3.5–8°C is
predicted, equivalent to moving into a new Ice Age, with the maximum
temperature drop lasting three to four years and temperatures returning
to normal over seven more years. Global average summer temperatures
would drop by 20–30°C. In two key crop growing areas, Iowa and

Climatic changes caused by nuclear conflict

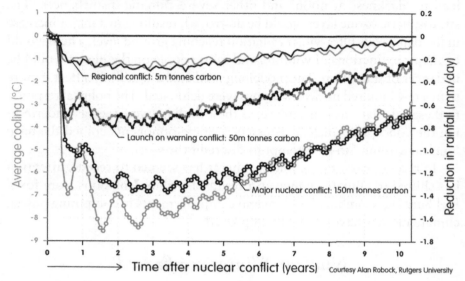

Figure 1: Nuclear cooling produced by regional, launch on warning and major nuclear conflicts [10]: Robock 2007].

Ukraine, detailed simulations show temperatures below freezing for two years and a halving of the growing season respectively, combined with a drought due to rainfall being 50–70 per cent of normal. The Indian, African and North American Monsoon seasons would likely be wiped out.

In 1983, the Scope study[5] estimated that the longer term impacts upon the climate would mean that all survivors of nuclear attacks would have to depend upon food stocks for at least one year. Even assuming that the remaining food was distributed between survivors, the resulting casualty figures were extremely stark. Assuming no food production for one year and minimal food storage, deaths of approximately 90 per cent of the global population were estimated. The only exceptions, in this scenario, were areas in latitudes 20–30° South, which includes Australia, New Zealand and parts of southern Africa and South America, where the nuclear winter effects were somewhat less severe and there could be up to 30 per cent survivors.

But the 2007 calculations mean that survivors would have to rely on stored food for several years, not one. Virtually all farming would cease for over two years, with a dramatically shorter growing season (if any) due to sharply reduced rainfall for around a decade. Worse still, today, world food stocks stand typically at only 80 days' supply of grain or rice.[6] To compound matters, there would also be major shortages of fertilisers, fuel for machinery, pesticides (but not pests) and seeds, coupled with periods of darkness during daytime, unpredictable frosts, widespread radioactivity and toxic chemicals, and a food distribution system in chaos.

It is hard to overstate the level of global catastrophe that this would represent.

These results alone need to be brought before the public eye as a shocking reminder of the sheer folly and longer term devastation that a major nuclear conflict would bring, not just to the attacker and the attacked, but to every country and region on the planet.

Climatic effects of a regional nuclear conflict

If the results of a large scale nuclear conflict were not shocking enough, research simulating the effects of a 'regional conflict' realistically involving 100 Hiroshima-sized nuclear weapons (1500kT in total) concluded that even this could cause significant cooling for several years across the Northern Hemisphere.[7] The results show a global cooling for ten years, peaking at 1.3°C. This would still be a major climatic change, especially given the speed at which it would occur. Such a conflict would thus have far reaching environmental effects, far beyond the immediate conflict area. One would have to assume that economic impacts across the globe would also be severe.

In the conflict area, casualties from blast, fire and radiation due to the nuclear weapons are themselves very severe – up to a total of 20 million if 'super cities' such as Delhi or Mumbai are included in the target list. Such super cities have very large populations and high population densities with many millions of people living in structures that are very vulnerable to blast and fire.

What are the implications for nuclear weapons policy?

The fact that about 100 'small', Hiroshima/Nagasaki-sized nuclear weapons could cause climatic effects should have major implications for nuclear weapons policies. Basic nuclear weapons in the possession of India and Pakistan are around 15kT in size: so 100 make a total of 1500kT. This is a very small fraction – about 0.1 per cent – of the nuclear arsenals of the US or Russia, who each have over 1,000,000kT in their nuclear arsenals[8]. The major nuclear powers typically have nuclear weapons with a much greater destructive power in the 100–200kT range. What this means is that plans to use any more than a small fraction of these large major nuclear arsenals would not only be extremely destructive for the country targeted, but would be tantamount to a suicidal act by the launch country as the severe climatic effects would spread across the entire northern hemisphere with no respect for national boundaries. Or to put it another way, more than one or two dozen 100kT nuclear weapons could simply not be used to gain any kind of military advantage, but would only contribute to a global situation where everyone had lost with devastating adverse global effects. It should be stressed that this longer term climatic effect would be on top of huge casualties caused by the direct effects of blast and fire on targeted cities and a collapse of the world economy. In today's highly interconnected world, even the economic impact of a nuclear conflict would be extremely serious – much worse than any world depression – and long-lasting.

Climate Implications for UK nuclear policy?

The UK has long deployed intercontinental range nuclear weapons in a fleet of Vanguard submarines, known as the Trident nuclear weapons system.

The Vanguard submarine and the nuclear warhead are built in Britain. The Trident missile is made and maintained by the US. The UK has 'co-mingled' access to 58 Trident missiles from the USA, who maintain and refit them from a random selection on a rotating basis from a large US Trident missile stockpile at Kings Bay naval base Georgia, Tennessee (rather like hailing a cab from an approved rank).

The debate about this weapons system usually focuses upon its costs, whether it should be kept or upgraded and its usefulness to be part of the UK's defence posture.

However, the latest research shows that use of Trident, whilst not at the scale of a major nuclear conflict, would have a greater impact than the

THE CLIMATIC AND HUMANITARIAN IMPACTS OF THE USE OF THE
UK'S NUCLEAR WEAPONS

'small' – by nuclear standards – regional conflict scenario. Each UK Trident submarine carries 40 x 100kT nuclear warheads (making 4000kT destructive power in total), each of which can be independently targeted, i.e. against up to 40 cities (or more typically up to 20 cities targeted with 2–8 warheads each), carried on ten intercontinental range ballistic missiles (actual range 7,000 miles).

This is an immense fire power. The total explosive power of all the explosives used in World War Two, including the two nuclear weapons exploded over Japan, is estimated at around 3000kT,[9] so, rather astonishingly, one Trident submarine alone has a greater destructive power than this, and the UK normally has twice this fire power available from the one submarine on patrol and one in reserve from its total fleet of four submarines.

Numerically, one Trident submarine has a fire power 2.7 times the regional conflict scenario of the Robock study above. But the effects of fire and blast do not scale in a linear way, so after correcting for this, we find that the smoke-producing capability of one Trident submarine is 1.6 the size of the regional scenario. What this means is that Trident would cause climatic cooling effects somewhat more serious than a regional nuclear conflict. From the published data it is possible to estimate that Trident used against city targets or inflammable infrastructure such as fuel storage, chemical plant etc would cause swift climatic cooling of 1.5–3°C lasting for two years, with less severe effects persisting for up to a decade.[10]

This finding alone is completely in conflict with the UK Government's stance that Trident is a minimum deterrent. In fact, its use would reduce crop yields over the entire northern hemisphere including the US and Ukraine grain harvests and cause severe food supply problems for many years. Its use would impact upon neutral states and the UK's allies. Even at the most limited scale of impact, food shortages upon an already stressed global food supply system could cause deaths from famine of about two billion[11] outside of the areas targeted. Even such a 'limited' use would cause severe economic consequences. World markets would crash due to fears of nuclear escalation, people would not trust that money held electronically was safe, causing a run on the banks, and food, gold and important commodity prices would dramatically increase.

These consequences would follow from the use of just one Trident boatload, would constitute a very serious case of genocide, a crime against humanity involving weapons of mass destruction and be quite inconsistent with the UK's stated moral and political position.

So, for climate impact reasons alone, any major use of Trident would have totally unacceptable consequences. But the Trident system, along with most other nuclear weapons, is actually *designed* to create maximum amounts of damage, deaths and injury and is *designed* to be targeted against major centres of population, such as large cities.

UK *Trident – a* WMD *designed to kill millions*

The Trident system – or more specifically the missile and warhead system – was designed and conceived at the height of the Cold War in the 1980s with countermeasures (for example dummy warheads) to penetrate the anti-missile system that ringed Moscow. The requirement for the UK 'deterrent', according to government papers released under the 30 year rule, was to kill at least 40 per cent of Moscow's 11 million inhabitants and severely damage the city's physical infrastructure.[12] Moreover, because of the 7,000-mile range of the missile and warhead system, combined with the global reach of the submarine, this destructive power could be unleashed against any continent, country or city anywhere in the world.

Nuclear weapons in an air burst are set to explode at several thousand feet over a target such as a city. The altitude is chosen to maximise the area of damage and the level of human deaths and injury. In deterrence, a centre of population is deliberately targeted to cause maximum casualties. In the case of a ground burst – an explosion at ground level – the weapon is aimed at a target such as a command centre or a major centre of industry. Because of the wide-area effects of nuclear weapons, it is virtually impossible to avoid civilian casualties, even if one was trying, and it has long been an accepted part of nuclear doctrine that nuclear weapons are targeted against people. This is known as a counter-value strategy, or

---

What is Trident?

4 x large submarines • 'up to' 8 missiles per sub
'no more than' 40 warheads per sub

'deterrence'. Trident is also capable of being very accurately targeted – for example, with accuracy of as little as a few metres. This design feature makes possible its use against military targets in what is known as counterforce. However, most major cities contain counterforce targets such as centres of administration and political control. An attack on these would also kill large numbers of civilian populations who live in the same area within the enormous damage radius of even a small nuclear warhead.

The UK Government factsheet states that 'the missiles are not targeted at any country'.[13] Whilst this may be true in a narrow sense, target lists still have to be drawn up so that the missiles are available for use. Missile launch requires authorisation from the submarine commander, executive officer and weapons officer after direct orders from the Prime Minister. Also, after a period of conflict and a breakdown in communications, the submarine can act independently on the basis of sealed 'letters of last resort' from the Prime Minister written for such a situation.[14]

The 2010 Strategic Defence & Security Review (SDSR) states that 'the UK will not use or threaten to use nuclear weapons against non-nuclear weapon states parties to the NPT'.[15] It is interesting to note that this careful wording means that targets in India, Israel, North Korea or Pakistan are not covered by this assurance – as well as, of course, other nuclear weapons states, specifically Russia and China. The SDSR goes on to say: 'we reserve the right to review this assurance if the future threat, development and proliferation of these weapons [Weapons of Mass Destruction] make it necessary'.[16] This means that targets would be considered in Iran, for example, or other states if they became possessors (or alleged possessors) of nuclear weapons or other weapons of mass destruction as was the case for Iraq.

The immense explosive power of a nuclear weapon means that large areas would be destroyed and those living in them killed and injured by a combination of a fierce fireball, massive blast pressure, intense winds, fires, conflagrations and fire storms. In addition, for a ground burst, intense radioactive fallout extending downwind or in rainfall beyond the areas of immediate destruction renders large areas dangerously radioactive for several years. Communications and electronics systems such as the internet, the electrical grid, water supplies and vehicle engine management systems would be inoperative due to the nuclear electro-magnetic pulse (EMP). Literally millions of people would be maimed, burned, blinded or poisoned by the weapons effects. Organisations of physicians are clear that the consequences of the use of even one warhead – let alone 40 – would overwhelm the capacity of a country's health and medical services.[17] The casualties caused depend mainly on the population density and would range from ten million in typical European and Russian cities, up to around 20 million if world super cities in the Indian sub-continent, China or Asia were targeted.

So, one Trident submarine with its combined enormous capability for immediate devastation and death and longer term climate damage, has the power to literally unleash a global apocalypse.

Conclusions

Use of the US or Russian missiles in an attempted first strike (or retaliation) would be suicidal as well as genocidal. Use of the smaller Chinese, French, Indian, Pakistani, Israeli or UK Trident arsenals would have terrible consequences both for the targeted and targeter alike. The uncomfortable realities of the effects of nuclear weapons make their use in numbers above a few dozen a suicidal risk because of longer term environmental impacts upon world food supplies and economy.

For the UK, the reality is that Trident does not increase the country's security. Trident poses the risk that its use would cause devastating harm to the UK itself as well as to many non-targeted non-nuclear states across the globe. Its continued deployment and the UK Government's deterrence stance promote a dangerously misleading view of the scientific reality, and undermine realistic attempts to reduce nuclear weapon numbers in the nuclear weapon states. Existing Trident warheads should be taken off deployment and into verifiable storage as part of measures to build confidence and understanding of the need to negotiate a nuclear free world. Plans to replace the system should be cancelled.

Notes

1 P. J. Crutzen and J. W. Birks, 'The atmosphere after a nuclear war: twilight at noon' in Ambio, vol. 11 (United States: 1982) pp. 115–125; V. V. Aleksandrov and G.L. Stenchikov, 'On the modelling of the climatic consequences of the nuclear war' in Proc Applied Math. Computing Centre (Moscow: USSR Academy of Sciences, 1983); R. P. Turco, O. B. Toon, T. P Ackerman, J. B. Pollack and C. Sagan, 'The climatic effects of nuclear war' in Scientific American, vol. 251 (United States: August 1984), pp. 33–43.

2   S. L. Thompson and S. H. Schneider, 'Nuclear winter reappraised' in *Foreign Affairs*, vol. 64 (United States: Summer 1986), pp. 987–988 of 981–1005.

3   A. Robock, L. Oman and G. L. Stenchikov, 'Nuclear winter revisited with a modern climate model and current nuclear arsenals: still catastrophic consequences' in *Journal of Geophysical Research*, vol. 112, no. D13, D13107 (United States: 2007); O. B. Toon, R. P. Turco, A. Robock, C. Bardeen, L. Oman and G.L. Stenchikov, 'Atmospheric effects and societal consequences of regional scale nuclear conflicts and acts of individual nuclear terrorism' in *Atmospheric Chemistry and Physics*, vol. 7, no. 8 (United States: 2007), pp. 1973–2002; A. Robock, L. Oman, G. L. Stenchikov, O. B. Toon, C. Bardeen & R. P. Turco 'Climatic consequences of regional nuclear conflicts' in *Atmospheric Chemistry and Physics*, vol. 7, no. 8 (2007), pp. 2003–2012.

4   Nuclear weapon units
    The explosive power of a nuclear weapon is measured in tonnes of TNT equivalent. Even the smallest nuclear weapon, such as the ones detonated over Hiroshima and Nagasaki in the Second World War, have explosive powers of at least 10,000 tonnes of TNT usually described as 10 kilo-tonnes or 10kT. Many modern weapons are even larger, with explosive powers in the millions of tonnes. One million tonnes of TNT equivalent is a Megatonne – one MT. 1MT=1000kT. Russia and the USA both have around 2,000 long range nuclear missiles with warheads of 100kT or over, on land, in submarines, and on bombers.

5   R. Turco, B. Toon, T. Ackerman, J. Pollack and C. Sagan, 'Nuclear winter: global consequences of multiple nuclear explosions' in *Science*, vol. 222 (US: 1983), pp. 1283–1292. Further information can be found at: SCOPE ENUWAR Committee, 'Environmental consequences of nuclear war: an update – severe global-scale effects of nuclear war reaffirmed' in *Environment*, vol. 29, no. 4 (US: 1987) pp. 4–5, 46.

6   Grain indicator data. *Earth Policy Institute*, (2013): [http://www.earth-policy.org/indicators/C54].

7   O. B. Toon, R. P. Turco, A. Robock, C. Bardeen, L. Oman and G. L. Stenchikov, 'Atmospheric effects and societal consequences of regional scale nuclear conflicts and acts of individual nuclear terrorism' in *Atmospheric Chemistry and Physics*, vol. 7, no. 8 (United States: 2007), pp. 1973–2002; A. Robock, L. Oman, G. L. Stenchikov, O. B. Toon, C. Bardeen and R. P. Turco 'Climatic consequences of regional nuclear conflicts' in *Atmospheric Chemistry and Physics*, vol. 7, no. 8 (2007), pp. 2003–2012.

8   [http://ploughshares.org/world-nuclear-stockpile-report].

9   [http://www.nucleardarkness.org/globalnucleararsenal/globalarsenal-graphic/].

10 Philip Webber, 'The climatic impacts and humanitarian problems from the use of the UK's nuclear weapons': [http://www.sgr.org.uk/sites/sgr.org.uk/files/SGR_climatic_impacts_Trident_Feb2013.pdf], also 'Forecasting nuclear winter', *Bulletin of the Atomic Scientists*, vol. 63, no. 5 (US: September/October 2007), pp. 5–8.

11 Ira Helfand [http://www.psr.org/resources/two-billion-at-risk.html].

12 Kristan Stoddart, 'Maintaining the Moscow Criterion: British Strategic Nuclear Targeting 1974–1979' in *Journal of Strategic Studies*, vol. 31, no. 6 (London: December 2008) p. 909; John Baylis, 'British Nuclear Doctrine: The 'Moscow Criterion' and the Polaris Improvement Programme', in *Contemporary British History*, vol. 19, no. 1 (Spring 2005).

13 UK Government, 'Defence White Paper 2006, Factsheet No. 4'.

14 R4 Today Programme, BBC, 2 December 2008.

15 UK Government. '2010 Strategic Defence & Security Review section 3.7', pp. 37–38.

16 Ibid.

17 International Committee of the Red Cross, 2011: http://www.icrc.org/eng/resources/documents/resolution/council-delegates-resolution-1-2011.htm]; Reaching Critical Will: [http://www.reachingcriticalwill.org/disarmament-fora/others/hinw]; O. Greene, B. Rubin, N. Turok, P. Webber and G. Wilkinson, London After the Bomb: what a nuclear attack really means (Oxford: Oxford University Press, 1982).

CHAPTER FOUR

Why Climate Change and Nuclear Disarmament Talks Must be Linked

KEVIN LISTER

Kevin Lister is an environmental activist who has campaigned against the military industrial complex and climate change. He stood as a candidate for the Green Party in the 2010 general election.

THE WORLD NOW stands on the edge of the abyss, facing two existential threats: runaway climate change and nuclear war. These are the flip sides to the same coin: industrialisation.

It has only taken 150 years of industrialisation to cause atmospheric CO_2 to exceed the safe limit to avoid runaway climate change. This is two average human life spans, an immeasurably small time period compared to the millions of years of relative climatic stability that led to our evolution. Today, atmospheric CO_2 is increasing so rapidly that within a very few years it will be far above the levels appropriate for us to sustain our civilisation and quite probably for the planet to sustain life. Despite the clarity of the scientific evidence, despite the evidence on the ground from crop failures to super storms, 19 rounds of international climate change talks with all the best intentions have resulted in 19 failures. To think the 20th or the 21st will succeed is naivety.

Industrialisation has also brought the military industrial complex. There is a symbiotic relationship between the two. You cannot have a military industrial complex without industrialisation and industrialising nations need a military industrial complex to secure resources and markets. The apex of this is the possession of nuclear weapons. As our planet becomes more unstable due to the climate change caused by industrialisation, governments around the world will seek and are seeking protection by nuclear weapons. The grand intentions of the 1967 Nuclear Non Proliferation Treaty, which obligated existing nuclear powers to disarm at the earliest possible time and non-nuclear armed nations to remain as such, have all but collapsed. Instead, all five of the UN permanent member states and the new nuclear weapons states such as Israel, India, Pakistan and North Korea are either upgrading or expanding their nuclear weapon systems.

It is against this dangerous backdrop of nuclear weapons proliferation that we debate the causes of climate change. Depending on what particular vested interest someone has, it can be argued that cow methane, cars, planes, China or anything else is the biggest cause. But these are all manifestations of global industrialisation and we need to de-industrialise. While the world's major economic blocks remain at locked horns with highly complex and expensive nuclear weapons systems requiring large scale industrial bases, this cannot happen. The industrial competition in which we are forced to participate by nuclear weapons and the military industrial complex makes these the biggest cause of climate change. In the UK, Trident is thus our biggest culprit.

The damage that this industrial competition has done to our ecosystem is already so severe that the world will never be as good a place to raise children as it was only one generation ago. To put this into context, prior to industrialisation, atmospheric CO_2 had remained in equilibrium at below 280ppm for nearly one million years.[1] To avoid runaway climate change, it needs to be below 350ppm. Today it is at 400ppm and increasing super exponentially.[2] This exceeds the worst case scenario of the 2007 IPCC report[3] and will lead to the loss of virtually all life on the planet unless urgent action is taken.

Instead of taking action on this reality, we continue to force our ecological systems closer to collapse, which stresses the global systems of governance to a similar state of collapse. The results are self-evident. Wars and financial collapse are now the order of the day, destroying millions of lives. One erupting fault line is Syria. It suffered a protracted drought over a three year period, killing 85 per cent of all its livestock and converting the Middle East's major wheat producer into a wheat importer at the mercy of world food prices.[4] This war has little to do with Assad being evil and nasty, instead it is an evil and nasty climate change war.[5] It is a warning of what lies ahead for other societies as they become destabilised through climate change. The fact that Syria is a dictatorship simply means it goes to the front of the queue for collapse as its government has little legitimacy either externally or internally.

As the realisation of impending collapse dawns, government decisions on all things from aviation to energy policy are caveated with the statement that we need major policy changes to tackle climate change. However, none ever dare talk of the policy changes needed. By contrast, policy is actually set to ensure business as usual continues, irrespective of the damage caused. To support this, governments feed their populations the tempting idea that an economy addicted to intensively using fossil fuels can be easily transformed into a zero carbon economy with no changes to the philosophies and economic systems that govern us. They are successful at this as the majority of people hear what they want to hear and disregard the rest, and what they want to hear is good news. It is also what the most powerful corporations that governments have become beholden to want to hear. This failure to engage with the reality of the climate change crisis at the national level drives the failure of the international climate change conferences and the substantial CO_2 cuts we need do not happen.

As time is running out, we should acknowledge that this façade has to stop and that the process is structurally flawed. Unless we do this, we will destroy our planet.

The structural flaw is simple and obvious. Our planet is divided into nation states that compete militarily and economically for survival. Any nation that decides not to compete faces an existential threat. Barring a couple of World Wars, this competitive engagement served humanity reasonably well when there was space for economies to continue growing and some great achievements resulted, such as getting man to the moon. However, once limits to growth are imposed and nations continue to implement economic policies that require exponential growth, competitive engagement between nation states is doomed to become deadly.

The ultimate limits to growth are climate change and peak oil. In the near total absence of viable technical solutions, the only response to these limits is painful and difficult mutual sacrifices which can only be achieved through cooperation. This is the antithesis of our competitive environment, so nations are trapped between the devil and the deep blue sea. If a nation takes action on climate change by unilaterally slashing its economy to reduce energy consumption and greenhouse gases it *might* be destroyed by its increasingly desperate competitors as they face climate change disasters of their own and who will be stronger if they have not made similar sacrifices. However, if all nations continue to compete they will definitely be *destroyed* through climate change. It is not really a great choice, but cooperating to fight climate change on balance is a slightly better bet if you can improve the odds by eliminating competition. It is game theory's prisoners dilemma made more serious by many countries competing together across the multiple games of climate change, nuclear disarmament and economic competitiveness.

The problem is that the cooperation needed becomes a more distant prospect as nations react to emerging insecurity by becoming increasingly competitive. This becomes the objective of government, irrespective of the party in power, and the press act as their mouthpiece. Hence our corporations that succeed in securing contracts and resources from abroad are extolled by the press and government. Nationalistic flag waving events such as the 2012 Queen's Diamond Jubilee and the Olympics are covered from front pages to back with happy smiling children and no critique. In the middle of these celebrations the government announced the decision to proceed with a £1 billion contract to start building the nuclear reactors for the new Trident class submarine, the ultimate in nationalistic flag waving. The press, not wanting to ruin a series of good parties, remained virtually silent and despite the prospect of deep spending cuts across the country, there was not even a murmur of protest on the streets.

By contrast, the idea of cooperating on mutual threats is deemed by the press, politicians and much of the public to be subversive and dangerous. As such it receives no serious debate. Yet the move to a cooperation based global society is essential to our survival and requires the biggest and boldest change of mindset mankind has ever made. If we fail we will be trapped in a zero sum game where pre-emptive attacks by the strongest before they are weakened through economic contraction becomes a reality. We will also force our competitor nations to play the same game.

The ultimate competitive statement a nation makes is with its military. The apex of this is the ability to terrify any potential competitor by the possession and deployment of nuclear weapons along with a credible threat to use them. The inherent failure of this strategy is that nuclear weapon systems require massive energy hungry military industrial complexes to build both the nuclear weapons systems and the conventional forces to defend them. In turn, this needs an expanding economy that must consume to excess to raise the necessary taxation and governments must lie to their populations about the inherent danger of doing this. Any competitor nation must make the same calculations and protect the same falsehoods, irrespective of being a dictatorship or a democracy.

The industry needed to build weapons of mass destruction always ends up as a strategic industry that must be protected and nurtured. This is done by feeding it with a continual stream of new contracts. The Russians did this in the 1990s when they continued building the Akula class attack submarines despite the nation being bankrupt. The UK and the USA are about to do the same with the Trident replacement programmes. The initial gate document[6] which was submitted to parliament and gave the go ahead for early procurement of long lead items for Trident components is remarkably open and honest about this. It states that the objective of proceeding is that: We must retain the capability to design, build and support nuclear submarines and meet the commitment for a successor to the Vanguard Class submarines.

In other words, we will build Trident submarines simply to continue building Trident submarines. By this logic, we and our competitor nations will continue building nuclear submarines forever, irrespective of the environmental costs.

In 2012, I challenged the Department of Energy and Climate Change (DECC) to provide a carbon budget for building, operating, defending and funding the Trident missile system.[7] This request was made in accordance with the Government's Low Carbon Transition Plan which stated, 'every major decision now needs to take account of the impact on the carbon budget', and no decision is more major than replacing Trident. Yet, the UK Government resolutely refused to even contemplate quantifying the carbon budget for Trident. Instead we eventually received a facile comment from DECC that 'the Government believes that the operation of Trident and the combating of climate change are consistent with each other'.[8] It was a claim made with no back up or validation. So we explored the possibility of doing the budget ourselves.

Like the Government, we failed. We failed because the Trident industry's huge tentacles reach into so much else. It needs a functioning steel industry, shipbuilding industry, aviation industry, nuclear industry, electronics industry, chemical industry, etc, etc, etc. To maintain a 'credible at sea deterrent', the industry of a whole industrialised country is needed, which means the high carbon industries must be kept competitive and intact by continually fuelling them with increasingly scarce energy and mineral resources through new contracts. It does not matter if the Government goes for the politically correct option of operating a minimum deterrent or not, as the industrial overhead is the same irrespective of having

100 or 1,000 nuclear weapons on deployment. The only difference is the amount of times you can destroy the planet.

Thus the decision to preserve a nuclear deterrent forces all sides into a race to grab the last available resources on the planet and to ignore the science on climate change. Government response is to fall back on the use of long plausible words to disguise their inability to tackle our climate change crisis.

To run this race, nations must raise taxes over and above that needed to pay off the increasing interest burden on government debt. This can only be done by maintaining exponential economic growth. This further destabilises global security, strengthening the case made to populations for nationalistic nuclear weapons development and arms build ups.

It is a race to the bottom. The three per cent economic growth needed to maintain economic stability and raise taxes causes a nation's economy to double in size every 23.5 years. During this doubling period, a nation will consume the same amount of resources as it has ever consumed since its inception. It will also create the same amount of pollution as it has ever created. It will do this at a time when wars are already being fought for the last remaining global resources and when the climate is already crashing through the greenhouse gas overload.

This race to destruction has forced worldwide spending on nuclear weapons to reach a new height of at least $1 trillion per decade,[9] nearing the levels of the Cold War. It is impossible for any government caught up in this madness to agree to cooperate on climate change talks. It also makes it impossible for governments not caught up in it to do so as they will always be under threat from the voracious appetites of those that are.

This is a death spiral that we are being forced down by a dangerous combination of national pride, ignorance and the vested interests of the world's military industrial complex. To stop it, we must unequivocally link the failure of nuclear disarmament with the failure to address climate change.

History warns us of the dangers. Leading up to the First World War, Britain and Germany strained their economies to breaking point in the race to build the biggest super Dreadnought battleship fleet. The instability it caused hastened the race to war as a weakened Germany was forced to pre-emptively attack before its economy was weakened further. The result was the death of millions.

If the First World War was not enough of a lesson, history obliged again with another repeat example, this time in Iraq. In the calculus of

Tony Blair and George Bush, they knew that delaying the start of the war was not possible, as their economies would be weakened by rising oil prices and Sadam Hussein's would be strengthened, so they struck when they still has the strength to do so.

Tony Blair acknowledged this in the Chilcott enquiry. He said of the decision to justify a first strike that:

> It is at least surely arguable that [Sadam Hussein] would have not changed, been there [remaining in control of Iraq] with a lot of money [as the price of oil rose] and the same intent.[10]

The dynamics of a zero sum game forced the decision for a disastrous preventative war. It was a risk they had to take in order to maintain economic growth and raise the taxes for Trident and the other overheads of nation state competition. To put this in perspective, the Trident System replacement will cost the UK over £100 billion,[11] and unlike any other form of public spending, it offers absolutely no societal benefit. Crudely, this will require a nearly bankrupt nation to create nearly £500 billion of unnecessary economic activity to raise sufficient taxes, and this needs cheap fossil fuel. This can only be obtained by the desperate use of force and further catastrophic damage to the environment. In the ensuing Iraq war, the American Petroleum Institute calculated that in the first three weeks, the allied forces used the same amount of fuel as was used by the allies in the whole of the First World War, making it the most energy intensive war ever. In addition, the large scale use of depleted uranium rendered large parts of the country uninhabitable.

World Oil Prices and the road to the second Iraq War

The possession of nuclear weapons and the implicit assumption they make about retaining competitive dominance is the most powerful statement any nation can make to the rest of the world that it is not prepared to make sacrifices or cooperate on climate change. It says that they intend to preserve the destructive status-quo of economic growth and militarisation irrespective of the cost to the planet. It is no coincidence that the repeated annual fiasco of the Climate Change Conference (COP) revolves around the positions of the nuclear armed nations, namely the

Oil Price

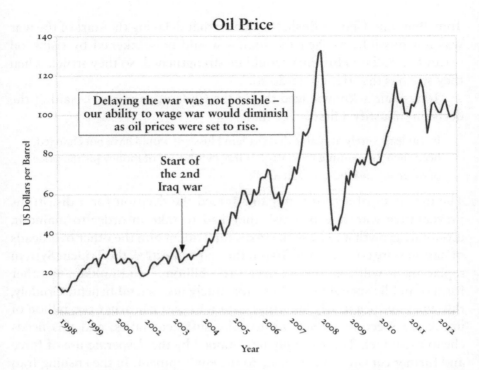

USA, China, India, the UK, Russia and France. Each refuses to commit to the CO_2 cuts necessary to minimise the worst effects of climate change. Instead, they offer bogus protestations of virtue about how they are committed to finding a global solution, or how they will pay the developing nations to make cuts on their behalf through carbon trading or how they will support agreements that are ineffective or unenforceable.

Possession of nuclear weapons is thus the ultimate Faustian bargain mankind could ever envisage. This is why negotiations for nuclear disarmament and climate change must be brought together – Britain must put its nuclear weapons on the climate change negotiation table, and persuade others to do the same. Only then will we have the security to start the process of de-industrialisation. Maintaining Trident as the UK does to 'allow us to punch above our weight' is wholly incompatible with working as an equal to tackle climate change. By contrast, in offering our nuclear weaponry in climate change negotiations, we say to the world that we are more concerned about global cooperation than national self-interest. By so doing, we offer all players in the world a chance to inclusively build a new paradigm.

Within this new paradigm, the opportunities to implement genuine alternatives to our destructive capitalist system become possible, such as the introduction of carbon rationing or carbon taxation. This stops the absurdity of our current economic system where the top five per cent of society are responsible for about 30 per cent of greenhouse gas emissions through their excess consumption.[12] At the other end of the income scale, the bottom 30 per cent of society is responsible for only five per cent of emissions, whilst simultaneously being exposed to increased risk of hardship as global resources tighten.

Thus an intimate and circular relationship exists between the three big campaign issues of today – climate change, nuclear disarmament and social equity. Climate change requires mutual sacrifice at all levels of our global society. This requires a rationing based economy. A rationing based economy is essential to social equity in the zero sum world we are moving towards. But a rationing based economy cannot be implemented when economies are forced to compete and raise taxes for nuclear weapons programmes. One campaign cannot be won without winning all three simultaneously. To win these battles, we must start by attacking the control that the military industrial complex has over our society and the power that it gives the most powerful governments. We must recognise that the military and the arms industry that once freed us from tyranny have become a tyranny that is destroying us all.

So the young people of today are faced with three future scenarios.

The first scenario is the 'Easter Island Scenario'. In this scenario the planet becomes largely uninhabitable through climate change by 2050. The last survivors are the crews of the nuclear submarines that are cruising the world's oceans targeting abandoned cities with their missiles. There will be no economic resources to decommission these and they will forever remain as a deadly liability for anyone that survives. In this scenario the Trident submarines become the modern day equivalent of the Easter Island statues – ridiculous statements of political vanity and hubris built in the face of clear evidence of total collapse. This is the strategy that the governments of the world's most powerful nations are actively, but unintentionally, pursuing.

The second scenario is that the nuclear build up continues amid increasing international tensions brought about by climate change and the stealth characteristics of modern weapons systems. In this new environment battlefield commanders have seconds to make critical decisions in environments that are becoming increasingly stressful. They can easily find themselves making an inadvertent premature launch decision provoking large-scale nuclear war. The radioactive nuclear winter the planet will be plunged into will temporarily halt catastrophic global heating but will also mean that what little food can be grown will be too poisonous to eat. After a few years, once the dust settles, heating will resume. The weakened survivors will succumb and our once beautiful planet will be devoid of life.

The third scenario is that the organisations committed to environmental and social stability globally dominate and overturn the power that big corporations and the military industrial complexes have over their governments. Having done this they are able to implement an economic system that allows the distribution of resources against the background of a globally heated planet and implement plans for survival.

This final scenario draws its inspiration from the Christmas Day truce in the First World War, where the participants met to play football. In the horrors of trench warfare, they took the first opportunity they could to communicate directly with each other to stop the fight and cooperate for their survival. In spite of this, they were forced to continue fighting to the death by the power interests of the military industrial complex that equally dominated both sides. They lacked the communication infrastructure, knowledge and organisation to continue their fight for survival. Today the internet gives the global community all three. There are some encouraging signs, Facebook groups such as 'Israel loves Iran'[13] shows the people in both countries finding more in common with themselves than with their governments' attempts to steer them to war.

Like all fights, there is never any guarantee of success. If nuclear weapons can be forced into climate change agreements, it does not guarantee escape from climate change catastrophe. However, if the worldwide nuclear weapons build up is allowed to continue, it does guarantee our extinction.

Notes

1   '650,000 years of greenhouse gas concentrations', Real Climate: [http://www.realclimate.org/index.php/archives/2005/11/650000-years-of-greenhouse-gas-concentrations/].
2   A. D. Husler and D. Sornette, 'Evidence for super-exponentially accelerating atmospheric carbon dioxide growth', (Zurich: March 2011) [http://arxiv.org/pdf/1101.2832.pdf].

3   'Updating the world on the latest climate science', *Copenhagen Diagnosis* (2009), Figure 1: [http://www.copenhagendiagnosis.com/].
4   Khaled Yacoub Oweis, 'Environmental disaster hits eastern Syria', *Reuters*, Nov 2010: [http://www.reuters.com/article/2010/11/15/us-climate-syria-idUSTRE6AE2BT20101115].
5   Patrick Seale, 'The destruction of Syria', *Agence Global*, 24 July 2012: [http://www.agenceglobal.com/index.php?show=article&Tid=2840].
6   'The United Kingdom's Future Nuclear Deterrent: The Submarine Initial Gate Parliamentary Report' [http://www.mod.uk/nr/rdonlyres/7f9f5815-c67b-47b1-b5c4-168e8ab50dc3/0/submarine_initial_gate.pdf].
7   Kevin Lister, 'Request for carbon budget of Trident Submarine replacement programme', [http://kevsclimatecolumn.blogspot.co.uk/2012/02/uk-low-carbon-transition-plan-says-make.html].
8   'Refusal by DECC to provide a carbon budget for Trident, letter to George Farebrother', *Institute for Law, Accountability and Peace* [http://kevsclimatecolumn.blogspot.co.uk/2012_02_01_archieve.html].
9   Bruce G. Blair & Matthew A. Brown, 'Global Zero Technical Report: Nuclear Weapons Cost Study', June 2011, [http://www.globalzero.org/files/gz_nuclear_weapons_cost_study.pdf].
10 Tony Blair, transcript at Chilcot Iraq inquiry [http://www.iraqinquiry.org.uk/media/50865/20110121-Blair.pdf].
11 Greenpeace, 'In The Firing Line: An investigation into the hidden cost of the super carrier project and replacing Trident', 2009, [http://www.greenpeace.org.uk/files/pdfs/peace/ITFL_trident_report.pdf].
12 Kevin Lister, 'Presentation given on Trident and Climate change', see slides 34 and 35: [http://media.wix.com/ugd/1741a6_18f78d8452c641039ff-78c68a2ac9df1.pdf].
13 Facebook group, 'Israel loves Iran' started by Ronny Edry: [https://www.facebook.com/israellovesiran].

CHAPTER FIVE

Finance, War and Conflict

PROFESSOR MARY MELLOR

Mary Mellor is Emeritus Professor in the Department of Social Science and Languages at Northumbria University Newcastle upon Tyne.

Finance and the Arms Race

THE MOST OBVIOUS link between finance, war and conflict is a long-standing public-private partnership – the arms trade. It was a republican president, Dwight D. Eisenhower, who coined the phrase 'the military-industrial complex' to describe this relationship, although it long precedes industrialism. What industry has such a range of products and conditions, from hand guns and instruments of torture to drones and nuclear arsenals? It does not matter if the products are used or not: time and technology will make them obsolete. It does not matter which side is being supplied as long as there is profit to be made. The source of finance is also both public and private, from arms suppliers to the National Rifle Association to the commissioning and manufacture of Trident submarines. Over a trillion and a half dollars are spent on the military each year with most suppliers coming from the developed nations led by the United States, with many recipients coming from the developing nations, often contributing to the indebtedness of the latter.

War and Trade

Trade, finance and militarism have been closely linked in European history. The era of mercantilism that dominated Europe until the emergence of industrialism was based on military support of trade with foreign colonies and the calculation of a nation's wealth by its ownership of precious metal bullion. European countries fought with each other to safeguard trading posts and trade routes. Spanish treasure ships from the New World were closely guarded by warships. Any less well protected merchant ships were harassed by official and unofficial pirates. The aim of mercantilism was to amass as much precious metal (particularly gold) as possible and establish trading monopolies and trading empires. A problem arose when areas of the world with desirable goods such as China refused to trade in return (nothing has changed in that regard!). In the early 19th century, British silver piled up in China through its exports of silk, porcelain and tea. Britain retaliated by launching the Opium Wars to force China to continue to import Indian opium.

Banking Systems and War

The emergence of the modern banking system has also been closely linked to war and conquest. The early Italian bankers such as the Medici linked economic, military and political power. Alongside mercantilism, Europe was beginning the process of consolidation into what would become nation states. Disputed land was the basis of local wars, skirmishes, fortifications and standing armies. This cost a lot of money and local rulers often borrowed from rich merchant bankers if their tax receipts or precious metal holdings were not sufficient to fight wars. Repayment was often through some form of tax or trading monopoly or licence. A major origin of international banking was the crusades. Proto-banking networks such as the Knights Templar arranged the transport and international settle-ment of payments and debts to follow the route of the crusades. Equally the Rothschild banking empire was built during the Napoleonic wars.

War and Money are not necessarily linked

Most human societies have experienced forms of conflict and most societies have had a form of money (stones, shells, hieroglyphs, clay tablets) but the invention of gold coin has played a particular part in European history.[1] Money, banking and conflict all go back thousands of years but money as precious metal coinage is much more recent, invented in 630 BCE in present day Turkey. This led to the belief that money itself was valuable, rather than merely representing value as in a hieroglyph, clay tablet or stone. A gold coin may have the same value as a bank note, but one can be melted down and sold as a commodity, the other would just burn. One is purely social and political, a product of trust, authority and agreement, the other is made of something which many societies (but not all) see as precious. Economics textbooks will claim that precious metal coinage emerged from the needs of trade. It is asserted that prior to the invention of coinage trade was based on barter, which was very inconvenient. This totally misrepresents the history of coinage, also, there is no historical evidence for the barter story. Precious metal coinage emerged as a product of political authority, not through trade. It was originally used mainly in the pursuance of empire building, that is, coinage was a mechanism of power. The right to coin money has always been heavily guarded by rulers.

Money, Conquest and Tax

Alexander the Great used the appeal of precious metal and the pressure of power in his military conquests. Empire-building relied heavily on mercenaries, who were paid in silver coin. This was used by the soldiers to pay their way. While armies did rape and pillage, they also built economies as their coinage circulated among the camp followers who provisioned the soldiers. Why would local communities provision a conquering army? The political answer was taxation. As well as directly commandeering resources, Alexander could demand that a tax be paid in coinage. This was a less violent way of making people part with their crops and resources. In order to pay the tax they needed to supply the soldiers in exchange for the coins.

Tax has been a major instrument of imperialism and colonialism, the Roman Empire behaved in much the same way. As not all the coinage was extracted as tax (British colonies extracted around 60 per cent of the coinage they issued through tax) coinage based economies grew and economic imperialism gradually replaced direct military force. This was less successful in Britain: when the Romans withdrew, the use of coinage also disappeared for a considerable period. Even when silver and gold coins circulated widely, such as across Europe during the reign of Charlemagne (742–814), it was still a coinage for the elite rather than the mass of the people who used base metal or records of debts such as tabs, notched sticks or personal trust.[2]

Coinage and Nationhood

While coinage was an instrument of empire, it was also a symbol of nationhood. One of the drivers in the American War of Independence was the refusal of the British to allow the settlers to create their own currency. Finance was also a major factor in the American Civil War. The South funded itself by issuing bonds based on the cotton trade. This was thwarted when the North blockaded Southern ports and the cotton bonds could not be redeemed. The North funded itself in a very modern way by issuing thousands of 'greenbacks' the forerunner of the modern dollar. This was secured on nothing but people's trust in the broad economic capacity of the North. The modern dollar is backed by the same economic trust. While historically paper currency was based on a notional Gold Standard, since 1971 there has been no monetary link to precious metal.

National Banking and the National Debt

Although rulers monopolised the production of coin, the strength of their political power rested on their ability to tax it back, find new sources of precious metal, or get suppliers to take royal credit instruments such as tally sticks.[3] Many early banks were ruined by rulers defaulting. The Bank of England was set up in 1694 to finance the war with France. As the merchants who set up the bank did not trust the King to repay his debts, they demanded that Parliament take on the £1.2 million loan as a National Debt. Ever since, the national budget has been a combination of coining, taxation and borrowing. As currency (coins and notes) have become less important as a form of money, the state is left with only taxation and borrowing. In reality, the state is perfectly capable of issuing new money electronically as in the case of Quantitative Easing, but neoliberal ideology demands that any such new money must only be issued as debt through the banking system. This stranglehold of the private sector over money supply has led to a new form of conflict, social breakdown as the state is 'rolled back' and the people are forced into austerity and impoverishment.

War and Money

Competition over colonial and military power culminated in the horrors of World War One and the unsustainable nature of the post war reparations leading to the collapse of the German money system were major contributing factors leading to World War Two. Following the experience of war and the Great Depression, a more sensible post-war settlement and the adoption of Keynesianism led to a period of economic stability in most of the combatant countries. However, there was little chance to reap the Peace Dividend as colonialism and inequality continued, and a new enemy was found in the Cold War to justify huge expenditure on conventional and nuclear weapons.

The Gold Standard and its Demise

As the rapid expansion of leading global political and economic systems easily outstripped the production of precious metal, most payments were made in promissory form, that is, as credit or bank notes. In fact, throughout history most money has not been valuable in itself, but represented social agreements of trust. The use of precious metal did not need to take account of social and personal trust, so how were bank and credit notes to be regarded in the modern era? Launched in 1717 by Isaac Newton as head of the Royal Mint, a Gold Standard was proposed based on the promise to redeem bank notes for precious metal at the value of the time. It is arguable how far the Gold Standard really worked. It was suspended when more paper money was needed, particularly to fight wars. Its re-establishment in 1925 had a drastic impact on the British economy and it was finally abandoned in the 1930s. The United States maintained a dollar-based Gold Standard until 1971, but this only applied to payments between central banks.

It was war, in this case in Vietnam, that finally destroyed the notion of a Gold Standard. In 1971 Nixon had to acknowledge that central banks around the world could no longer exchange dollars for gold. This did not stop the United States dominating the world economy, but trading countries started building up reserves of dollars, rather than gold.[4] At first this was mainly the oil exporting nations as oil was traded in dollars. (Many people see the threat of Iraq to price its oil in euros as the real reason for the second Iraq war). OPEC price rises in the 1970s led to a surge in dollars which were recycled in loans to developing countries as banks sought profitable outlets for this growing 'money market'. An irony was that one of the major innovators in lending dollars held in Europe (so-called Eurodollars) was a Soviet bank, Narodny, which had taken its dollars out of the United States in 1956 in case they were frozen by the US after the invasion of Hungary.

Money and Third World Debt

The notional Gold Standard had allowed nations to control exchange rates and the movement of finance around the world. As national controls broke down, a flood of globalised finance swept around the world looking for profitable opportunities. Western banks found themselves swamped in currency with no ready source of investment. Most western economies had been stagflating after the years of post-war reconstruction and could take no more investment. Instead, a debt explosion was triggered in the Majority world. Many Majority nations had recently been liberated from colonialism and were keen to modernise their economies and build up national prestige projects as well as build up military forces. In fact, many had experienced coups and become military regimes. New elites also emerged and corruption was rife. Loans were made at relatively cheap interest rates. However, within ten years, as monetarist theory replaced Keynesianism, interest rates rose sharply and many countries found themselves with unsustainable debt. Repayments began to outstrip the original loan schedules. Campaigners eventually managed to get some loans to the poorest countries cancelled, but much of the debt had been sold to so-called 'debt vultures' who demanded payment of the whole original sum.

The Globalisation of Finance

The financial expansion of the 1970s exploded in the 1980s as governments such as those in Britain and the US acknowledged that they could no longer control financial movements and relaxed their regulations. This was described as 'Big Bang' in the UK. In particular, floating exchange rates saw an exponential growth in finance trading, particularly derivatives. These are purely financial gambles, largely related to movements of currency. In the run up to the 2007–8 crisis, derivative trading outstripped global production by ten to one. As the financial crisis has shown this has led to global instability. Apart from the neoliberal push for austerity, private speculation (hot money) has undermined currencies around the world. Hot money has also led to sharp rises in commodity prices, which has caused social unrest and which many argue was a major factor in the Arab Spring.[5] Conflict in itself is not a bad thing if people are struggling for their freedom and political and economic rights, but globalised finance does not separate progressive from oppressive regimes. It will destroy both if a profit is to be made.

Currency Wars?

One of the major potential sources of instability is a new form of mercantilism. Instead of fighting each other to accumulate gold, countries are fighting each other via and even within their currencies.[6] Witness the crisis in the Eurozone, with disputes across states but within a currency, and the debate over the value of China's currency as against the dollar. As a result of the globalisation of production, countries with major resources or high levels of production are storing up reserves of other currencies, particularly the dollar. Sixty-four per cent of reserves across the globe are held in dollars, a good proportion by China. China has reinvested much of this in US government debt, but is also using its reserves as a Sovereign Wealth Fund to buy up resources and land around the world.

At one level, countries using and holding each other's currencies could be seen as a good thing, fulfilling the promise of neoliberalism by turning the world into one large economy. On the other hand, a nation's currency reflects a potential call on its labour and resources. Holding a nation's currency is very different from holding gold, which is a commodity in itself. A fiat currency (i.e. a currency not made of, or backed by, a commodity) is a promise, a debt. As with all fiat currencies, the backing for that promise is the goods, services, resources, possessions of the people in whose name that currency was issued. Given that globalised trading and finance has produced almost unlimited amounts of money designated in national currencies, it is the people in those nations who will have to honour that debt. This is the message of the financial crisis – the people have had to pay in austerity for the activities of privatised finance. Their wages and benefits are being cut and they are being asked to sell off (privatise) their national assets.

Who Controls Money?

If the global flow of money is in danger of causing currency wars, if not actual war, or causing social breakdown, fundamental questions need to be asked about the ownership and control of money. National currencies, or electronic or paper promises made in their name, do not come from nowhere. Modern money has two sources, the national mint/central bank (historically notes and coin, but now also electronic quantitative easing) or bank issued 'credit' through loans or overdrafts. The main difference between the two forms of money is that historically (but not so much recently) state issued money was spent into the economy and reclaimed by taxes whereas all new money issued by banks is created as debt, it must all be repaid with interest. Economic text books will argue that only state money is 'real' money while bank money is only a form of credit. They will also claim that banks are merely acting as a link between savers and borrowers. Neither is true. As the banking crisis showed, central banks have had to rescue all forms of financial institutions and accounts. Also, bank deposits hugely outstrip the issue of currency by 97 per cent as against only three per cent in the UK.

Every time someone takes out a mortgage, a small company increases its overdraft, or a hedge fund borrows millions to make a split second gamble (so-called leverage), they are creating money. All the new debts are designated in a national currency and the people of that nation are responsible for honouring that money as it is spent into circulation. Issuing the money supply of a nation through debt is also highly unsustainable. Firstly all that money has to be paid back with interest, and as the only source of new money (or at least 97 per cent of it) is debt, more debt must be taken out if there is to be sufficient money in circulation to pay previous debts with interest. This also drives economic growth, people have to work harder, use more resources, find some means of making a profit, driving down wages, standards etc. Eventually people can take no more debt and the whole money supply starts to unravel, as in the credit crunch and the financial and economic crisis that followed. Paper promises have been allowed to flow around the world and the people in whose name they are made have had no say in the economic choices that have been made. Equally they have no say in the conflictual positions created by profit-seeking companies which often have to be rescued by military intervention. In particular there is likely to be conflict in the ever-increasing scramble for resources in a resource-limited world.[7]

Peaceful Solutions?

After the calamities of two World Wars there was a concerted attempt to find a structure within which economic relations between nations could proceed. At the Bretton Woods Conference of 1944, Keynes's solution was to have a buffer currency in which global trade would be conducted, which he proposed to call a 'bancor' (bank gold). Countries would be penalised if they went too far into deficit – but also if they went too far into surplus. The world economy, like a national economy, cannot work if it gets too imbalanced. The solution in national economies is to channel money or economic stimulus to poorer parts of the country – Liverpool is not expected to be as successful as London. This is a lesson that has not been learnt in the Eurozone. From a Keynesian perspective, markets should be seen as a relationship, not a competitive struggle to the death. Unfortunately Keynes was defeated by a US proposal to make the dollar the main global currency. This enabled the US both to support and dominate global post-war reconstruction.[8]

A major problem in the international context is the relationship between reserve and non-reserve currencies. Put brutally, the United States, as it controls the world's dominant currency in which many commodities are priced (particularly oil), can issue as many dollars as the world will stand, to buy the goods and services it needs. Non-reserve countries have first to earn one of the major currencies (dollar, euro, yen) before it can buy goods on the international market. In the absence of a global currency (like a global euro) or a buffer currency as Keynes suggested, whichever country has control of the dominant currency can consume the world's goods effectively for free. The disadvantage is that the countries supplying the dominant economy with goods are storing up that currency which is a call on future goods, services and assets of the dominant economy. Where major currencies have effectively let the profit-based financial sector gain control of the nation's money supply, it is profit seeking companies who have gained control of the world's resources. Around 40 per cent of global trade is conducted entirely within single transnational corporations, with all the opportunity for tax and price manipulation that presents.

Given the experience of the euro, we are a long way from having a global currency or a buffer currency as Keynes suggested. This leaves action at the national level in relation to national currencies. The most important reform would be to stop the financial sector creating new money – in other words, controlling the money supply. This would mean that banks could only lend money that is put on long term deposit, that is, do what the text books claim they do, act as a link between borrowers and investors/savers. Ordinary bank deposits would be administered separately to enable transfer payments etc. Control of money supply would return to public issue under democratic control which, hopefully, would not give a priority to armaments. This money would be spent into circulation on public services, be allocated to development banks to provide credit for businesses or be given directly to the people, for example as a basic income.[9] Taxation would be used to manage the overall money supply, penalise anti-social or resource wasteful activities and redistribute wealth.

A major reform would be to demand that transnational trade should be conducted by each nation in its own currency. For example, a US company selling to Nigeria would be obliged to accept payment in Nigerian currency. However this would not overcome the inequality between currencies. There would still be need for an international buffer between currencies, as Keynes suggested. If no currencies traded directly with each other, this would immediately remove the basis of most financial speculation through derivatives. The critical question would then be the exchange rate at which each currency would 'buy' the global buffer currency. My suggestion would be that the exchange rate for each currency should have a social base, such as a measure of income/labour as against the buffer currency. This would equalise the purchasing power of each currency and remove the benefit of shifting production to cheap labour countries. It would also mean poorer countries would pay less for global goods. A US person would buy a product for a global price set in the buffer currency related to her rate of pay (100 globals = 100 x $ hourly rate); equally, a Nigerian could buy the same product at her rate of pay (100 globals = 100 x Naira hourly rate). I prefer to call the buffer currency globals, as Keynes' concept of bancor (bank-gold) implies a link to gold.

Historical evidence shows that finance, trade and military activity are closely intertwined. War is good for finance: it unleashes massive demand even as it destroys environments and lives. The present globalised money system creates many areas of actual and potential conflict. Let us hope that nations will be able to find national and global financial structures that will allow them to settle their trading and financial obligations to each other in peaceful, ecologically sustainable and socially just ways.[10]

Further Sources

Mary Mellor, 'Bringing Economics Down To Earth'
  [http://www.youtube.com/watch?v=9F-DuD6T_io]
Mary Mellor 'Just Banking'
  [http://www.youtube.com/watch?v=uAhxDsmoeZE]
Mary Mellor 'Understanding Money 1: What is Money?'
  [http://www.youtube.com/watch?v=5IZRWQn5jgk]
Mary Mellor 'Understanding Money 2: Money and Banking'
  [http://www.youtube.com/watch?v=8wpbnYZZaG4]
Mary Mellor 'Understanding Money 3: The Crisis'
  [http://www.youtube.com/watch?v=PoIRCHq7Cr4]
Mary Mellor 'Understanding Money 4: The Future of Money'
  [http://www.youtube.com/watch?v=argEb1tWtto]

Notes

1 Glyn Davies, *A History of Money* (Cardiff: University of Wales Press, 2002); Geoffrey Ingham, The Nature of Money (Cambridge: Polity, 2004); Mary Mellor, *The Future of Money: From Financial Crisis to Public Resource* (London: Pluto Press, 2010).
2 Glyn Davies, *A History of Money* (Cardiff: University of Wales Press, 2002).
3 Ibid.
4 Michael Rowbotham, *Goodbye America! Globalisation, Debt and the Dollar Empire* (Charlebury: Jon Carpenter, 2000).
5 World Development Movement, 'Broken markets: How financial regulation can help prevent another global food crisis', (2011): [http://www.wdm.org.uk/sites/default/files/Broken-markets.pdf]
6 James Rickards, *Currency Wars: The Making of the Next Global Crisis* (London: Penguin, 2011).
7 Costas Panayotakis, *Remaking Scarcity: From Capitalism Inefficiency to Economic Democracy* (London: Pluto Press, 2011).
8 Yanis Yaroufakis, *The Global Minotaur* (London: Zed Books, 2011).
9 Joseph Hanlon, Armando Barrientos and David Hulme, *Just Give Money to the Poor: The Development Revolution from the Global South* (Sterling VA: Kumerian Press, 2010).
10 Ariel Salleh (ed.) '*Eco-sufficiency and Global Justice: Women Write Political Ecology*' (London: Pluto Press, 2009).

CHAPTER SIX

Ploughshares into Swords: Industrial Agriculture as Warfare and the Need for a Paradigm Shift

HELENA PAUL

Helena Paul is a researcher, writer and co-director of EcoNexus, focusing on the impact of corporate power and new technologies: on ecosystems, biological and cultural diversity.

IT IS EASY TO overlook the violence implicit in many modern technologies: we so rapidly become used to them and many of us are never truly confronted with their violent aspects. The aim of this brief essay is to reveal some of the violence embedded in modern industrial agriculture. It will only touch on a few aspects, inviting readers to think further on the proposition. A whole essay could be written, for example, on the use of food as a weapon, when, for example, heavily subsidised grain is dumped on local markets in the global south in the guise of aid, but instead it destroys the livelihoods of local farmers. It's worth remembering that Rafael Mariano, chairperson of the Peasant Movement of the Philippines, noted in 2000: 25 years ago USDA Secretary Earl Butz told the 1974 World Food Conference in Rome that food was a weapon, calling it 'one of the principal tools in our negotiating kit'.[1]

There are many other examples: the impacts of mechanisation and monocultures; the dependence on fossil fuel; the animal welfare and environmental impacts of the intensive pig industry in the US, Mexico, Poland, China and many other countries around the world;[2] the impacts, particularly on women in the global south, of using pesticides without adequate advice or protective clothing; the suicides of farmers in many parts of the world that can be attributed to the multiple pressures of industrial agriculture and increasing corporate control; the impacts on forests and peoples of the rapid spread of industrial palm oil production in Asia and increasingly in Africa. Here we confine ourselves to first looking at a few of the links between research in agriculture and weapons and then move on to consider the destructive impacts of genetically modified herbicide tolerant crops, primarily soya, first introduced from 1995 onwards.

We begin briefly with language, as a key indicator. The language used by proponents of modern industrial methods frequently involves phrases such as 'winning the war on pests', 'new weapons in the old war on pests', 'eliminating pests', 'waging war on weeds'. Metaphors are powerful shapers of thought, making it appear that agriculture is a constant war against nature, rather than collaboration with nature. The idea has deep roots in western culture, for example in Genesis where God says to Adam: 'Cursed is the ground for thy sake, in sorrow shalt thou eat of it all the days of thy life. Thorns also and thistles shall it bring forth to thee...' – hardly an auspicious beginning to his new life outside the garden, for which agriculture is presented as a future war of attrition. When looking at the flattened and cowed landscapes of intensive farming or the long sheds in which thousands of animals, pigs, chickens, turkeys or cows are locked away for brief and brutalised lives, the signs of violence become clearer. The metaphor is reinforced by the names given to chemicals used in these wars on pests, which include, for example: fusillade, skirmish, bullet, revolver, rifle, striker, throttle, conqueror, broadside, invader.

From metaphor to reality: the link with war

Synthetic nitrogen

It is not only a metaphor, however: two of the main props of modern industrial agriculture, synthetic fertilisers and pesticides (both herbicides and insecticides) emerged from the two World Wars of the 20th century. Guano, is excrement, mainly of birds and bats. It is rich in nitrates and has probably been used as a fertiliser for hundreds of years by Andean peoples, whose Quechua name for it is the source of the word guano. In the 19th century, it became a major trade item, sourced from seabirds living on islands off the coast of South America, and was in high demand both as a fertiliser and as a basic ingredient in the manufacture of explosives. However, early in the 20th century, the Germans realised that in the increasingly likely event of a war with Britain, they would be cut off from access to this essential ingredient for their war effort.

The German chemist Fritz Haber, meanwhile, had discovered a process for producing ammonia from atmospheric nitrogen, which is still in use and still bears his name. The synthetic ammonia so produced was used for the production of nitric acid, employed for making explosives and munitions in the absence of guano. The chemical company BASF purchased the process and employed Carl Bosch to scale up the process to industrial levels. By 1913 this had been achieved, using what is still the major source of nitrogen fertiliser, the Haber-Bosch process. Its hunger for energy means that currently it consumes some three to five per cent of global natural gas production.[3] The process continued to be used for weapons production until the end of World War Two, when the enormous stocks and production capacities developed for war efforts were turned to the application of synthetic nitrogen to the soil.

Since then the use of synthetic nitrogen fertiliser has expanded massively, with major negative impacts on the global nitrogen cycle. Unfortunately, most of the nitrogen applied is not actually taken up by the crops for which it is intended. The excess runs off, polluting water and soil, destroying marine ecosystems (eutrophication) and creating multiple 'dead zones', such as that in the Gulf of Mexico. Unabsorbed nitrogen also becomes nitrous oxide, helping to make industrial agriculture a potent emitter of climate-forcing greenhouse gases, because the Global Warming Potential (GWP) of nitrous oxide is 310 times that of CO_2.[4]

It leads to elevated levels of ozone, with negative implications for human health and agricultural productivity. It also eliminates many soil micro-organisms and their beneficial action, thus reducing the availability of other minerals in the soil. It has a negative effect on many useful wild plants and varieties of crop. At the same time it has enabled us to increase industrial agricultural production and led to the breeding of varieties that are actually dependent on high inputs of synthetic nitrogen. This in turn has helped to generate a major global livestock industry. Sixty per cent of EU cereal production is used as animal feed in an industry that is both unsustainable and inhumane.[5] A 2011 UN Food and Agriculture Organisation report said:

> When livestock are raised in intensive systems, they convert carbohydrates and protein that might otherwise be eaten directly by humans and use them to produce a smaller quantity of energy and protein. In these situations, livestock can be said to reduce the food balance.[6]

The implications are obvious: synthetic nitrogen is causing major damage to the ecosystems we all depend on, but the dominant model of industrial agriculture has become dependent on it and so therefore has our current energy dense model of development. It is just one of many factors indicating that we need a complete change of approach to agriculture.[7]

Organophosphates

During the 1930s, a chemist working for the German conglomerate IG Farben, which counted Bayer and BASF among its member companies,[8] began to experiment with the potential use of organophosphates as insecticides because of their lethal impact on the nervous system of insects. It was a short step from this to the realisation of their potential as chemical weapons, to which the research effort was then switched as war loomed. It should be noted that the British were also researching chemical weapons and later produced some lethal ones of their own. The German effort resulted in the production of several compounds, the best known of which is sarin. Although the Nazis did not employ them, they have since been used as chemical weapons several times by others, most recently in Syria. After World War Two, US scientists used information they obtained about the German effort to produce organophosphate pesticides such as parathion and malathion. Even though these insecticides are less lethal to humans than sarin gas, they cause a wide range of symptoms, including vomiting, breathlessness, dizziness, blurred vision, convulsions and coma.[9] They are also endocrine disruptors and have been linked to neurological disorders such as Parkinsons disease.[10] Their acute toxicity is now well recognised, but it took far longer for the impacts of low level, long term exposure to be acknowledged.

It is therefore disturbing to read that although it was recommended as early as 1951 in the UK that organophosphates should be labelled as deadly poison, containers were only labelled in 1976 and no directions or cautions about safe use were included. Later, during the 1980s and 1990s, many farm workers reported symptoms ranging from memory loss and depression to fatigue, joint and muscle pain and generalised weakness. They attributed this to low level exposure to organophosphates over many years, especially through (mandatory) sheep dips. Soldiers returning from the Gulf War reported similar symptoms, subsequently called Gulf War Syndrome, but the Ministry of Defence has never acknowledged its existence as such. If the government were to acknowledge the problems, they would be exposed to claims for compensation both from victims and from the companies producing organophosphates for loss of market. They therefore say that they are safe if used properly, but there is little understanding of what 'safe use' really means. In 2012, a paper was published showing that organophosphates definitely do affect cognitive function, most obviously memory.[11]

In December 2011, the Permanent Peoples Tribunal indicted six major pesticide producers, Monsanto, Dow Chemical, BASF, Bayer, Syngenta and Dupont for violating human rights to life and health, and destroying biodiversity.[12]

Herbicides

2,4-D (2,4-Dichlorophenoxyacetic acid) was discovered during World War Two when:

> ... both United States and England scientists initiated secret biological warfare research on plant growth regulators with the objective of destroying enemy crops. Kraus at the University of Chicago had observed since 1936 that certain growth regulators were phytotoxic (28). Kraus was aware of the inadequacy of existing herbicides, and in 1941 he was first to propose that growth regulators might work as herbicides, because they often killed test plants.[13]

Like its more potent relative, 2,4,5-T, 2,4-D is a synthetic auxin, or plant hormone, that acts as a selective weedkiller. In November 1942, the United States Army began developing Camp Detrick (later renamed Fort Detrick) in Frederick, Maryland, as the center for research and testing of chemicals for biological warfare with special emphasis on crop destroying chemicals.[14]

This research, authorised by the US Chemical Warfare Service, included investigating the use of 2,4-D and 2,4,5-T to destroy crops.[15]

Later these two chemicals, produced by Monsanto and Dow Chemical, were used in combination as Agent Orange and massively sprayed in Vietnam to defoliate the forests; they also had the effect of destroying small-scale agriculture. As we now know, the 2,4,5-T was contaminated with dioxin, leaving a terrible legacy of birth defects and disease.[16]

What is the impact today of these developments?

The above examples show in brief how the synthetic fertiliser and pesticides that are so crucial to modern industrial agriculture are linked with wars. It is now time to look at how industrial agriculture is currently affecting environments and people around the world. We confine our focus to the rolling out of genetically modified herbicide tolerant crops, mainly soya, mainly for animal feed and fuel, in South America and the US. GM soya, engineered to tolerate applications of glyphosate, the basic ingredient of RoundUp, Monsanto's proprietary herbicide, is a product that has from the outset been dominated by that one company. The soya boom is driven by markets, mainly for animal feed, in the form of soya meal or cake, and biodiesel from soya oil. The demand for feed and fuel is apparently limitless as meat consumption and car ownership increase, so soya represents a rewarding investment, which helps to explain its extremely rapid spread.

South America: Herbicide tolerant crops in Argentina and Paraguay

The cultivation of herbicide tolerant crops in Argentina began in 1996 with GM soya and spread swiftly through the country.

> The model was based on the political decision that Argentina, which had once been the grain basket of the world and a producer of healthy and high-quality foods, would be transformed into a producer of animal forage, firstly, to provide fodder for European livestock, and then for livestock in China.[17]

At first, herbicide tolerant crops seemed to simplify the farming process, especially for larger mechanised farms. Instead of skillful weed management plans, farmers simply applied massive quantities of the herbicide glyphosate, mainly from the air. Additionally, there were large pools of investors involved in driving GM soya production. Small farmers could not compete and many left or were driven off their land by armed groups using threats of violence that they were all too often able to carry out with impunity. Hundreds of thousands of people left the land for towns and cities. In this process, which is continuing, they lose their food sovereignty and become food insecure consumers, not producers; while people who remain in the countryside and the small towns find themselves bombarded from the air with increasingly complex mixtures of pesticides (both herbicides and insecticides), intended to combat the problem of growing weed resistance and other problems generated by the 'simplified' farming process. Although GM crops were promoted as a means to reduce levels of pesticides used, pesticide use in Argentina has increased massively, 'from nine million gallons (34 million litres) in 1990 to more than 84 million gallons (317 million litres) today'.[18]

In 2008, a group of towns that had experienced crop spraying and related impacts made a declaration that described the broad array of illnesses they consider to have been caused by the imposition of this agriculture model, including cancers, birth defects and disorders of the immune, hormonal and nervous systems.[19] In 2010, following a decade of mounting harm and protests, the Faculty of Medical Sciences from the National University of Cordoba called a first meeting for doctors working in the crop-sprayed towns in several provinces of Argentina, during which they would examine and discuss evidence.

> The physicians stressed that they have been serving the same populations, in general, for over 25 years, but what they found in recent years was quite unusual and strictly linked to systemic sprayings of pesticides. For example, Dr Rodolfo Páramo, a paediatrician and neonatologist at the public hospital of Malabrigo, a Northern city in Santa Fe, highlighted the alarm he experienced when he found 12 cases of birth defects in newborns, out of 200 births per year in 2006. This situation is analogous with the four cases of stillbirths due to birth defects in the small town of Rosario del Tala, in Entre Ríos, both areas characterised by massive pesticide spraying.[20]

Since that meeting, reports of illness caused by agrochemicals have continued to accumulate, along with evidence of major failures to apply any rules about spraying, or to inform people about the dangers.

Unfortunately the fate of rural populations is increasingly invisible, due to ongoing urbanisation processes, often forced, as we saw above.

> The consequences of the compulsive urbanisation which confuses urban living with supposed progress is responsible for marginalisation, social fragmentation, extreme insecurity, poor nutrition, rising levels of disease, people trafficking, aid programmes, and narco-power in the shanty towns.[21]

The lack of political influence amongst the marginalised populations means that little action has so far been taken on their behalf. Their numbers are dwindling in a landscape of industrial monoculture crop production that needs almost no people. The impact of aerial sprayings of agrotoxics on local food production by small food providers still on the land has been equally serious, with the destruction of crops and animals and a range of health problems. The impacts on biodiversity, water courses, soil micro-flora and fauna, worms, frogs and other crucial elements of a functioning ecosystem are also intense, especially as aerial spraying is carried out without consultation or consideration of people or environment. This is the collateral damage of the agricultural war and it is not acceptable.

Meanwhile GM crops continue to expand in Argentina, covering some 24 million hectares, some two thirds of the total arable land available.

Paraguay

Paraguay has suffered similarly devastating impacts, starting a little later than Argentina.[22] Land distribution has long been hugely unequal. Soya production began in the 1970s, with many Brazilian farmers taking over large tracts of land. Gradually after 1996, GM soya seeds were smuggled in for planting until finally four varieties were approved in 2004. At that time, only 24 per cent of soya producers were Paraguayan. Brazilian, German, Japanese and Mennonite producers, supplying agribusinesses including Cargill, Archer Daniels Midland and Dreyfus, made up the rest.[23] Repression and displacement, often violent, of remaining rural popula-tions, illness, falling local food production have all featured in this picture. Indigenous communities have been displaced and reduced to living on the capital's rubbish dumps. This is a crime that we can rightly call genocie – extinguishing entire Peoples, their culture, their way of life and their environment.

Forest loss in Argentina and Paraguay

Both Paraguay and Argentina have lost large areas of forest since 2004, with GM soy considered to be a major driver, accelerating a process that was previously much more gradual. Bulldozers with chains between them can clear vast areas very quickly and the investment going into the process has steadily increased – from the investment pools mentioned above and others. In South America, we are used to thinking mainly in terms of the Amazon rainforest, but Paraguay has lost nearly a million hectares and Argentina nearly two million hectares of forest since 2004 alone.[24] The impacts of the loss of these unique and little understood forests are many: biodiversity loss, including many endemic species found nowhere else, and displacement of indigenous peoples, some not previously contacted, to say nothing of impacts on soils and water, regional and local climate change and changes in rainfall. This is shortsighted destruction driven by short-term profits, and it is criminal – both ecocide and genocide.

Brazil – the largest agrochemical user in the world

Brazil, Uruguay and Bolivia have been similarly affected by the spread of soya since 1970, greatly accelerated by GM soya starting in 1996. In a special interview, a Brazilian agronomist, Leonardo Melgarejo, who represents the Ministry of Agrarian Development at the country's GMO regulatory body, makes a key point: that GM crops are weakening the social fabric that is essential if people are to be able to flourish in rural areas. One could extend this point and say that GM agriculture also weakens the environmental fabric on which we all depend. He also notes that Brazil, where GM crops are grown on 36 million hectares, has become the largest user of agrochemicals in the world. This might be good for business, but not for people. It is leading to a vicious circle of weed resistance requiring the use of ever more, and more toxic, herbicides. To address this, Brazil is now considering the introduction of a GM crop that tolerates 2,4-D.[25]

In 2013, Brazil began an ongoing process to consider a bill that would overturn the national and international moratorium on Terminator technology, the name popularly given to Genetic Use Restriction Technologies (GURTs). The aim of this technology is to prevent seeds from germinating. In some cases, the addition of a chemical is proposed to enable germination in order to produce a harvest, but saved seed will not grow, thus the nickname 'suicide seeds'. The excuses given for developing such a technology are to prevent contamination by GM crops, and as a means to protect patents on crops, but it seems clear that the real purpose is to prevent seed saving.

This conclusion fits well with, for example, new EU draft seed legislation and the G8's New Alliance on Food Security and Nutrition, which is designed to prevent the saving of what the latter calls 'unimproved' or unregistered seed. This strategy to prevent farmers and communities from saving, exchanging and breeding seed would outlaw many varieties informally bred and improved over millennia by farmers. Together with attempts to produce seed that cannot germinate, this is a clear example of violence as defined for the purposes of this essay, as it strikes against justice, equity, diversity, the right to food and the life of the seed itself.

The US – more of the same

Here, 'RR crops [RoundUp Ready – resistant to Monsanto's proprietary herbicide] were rapidly adopted because they provided farmers a simple, flexible, and forgiving weed management system'. As a result, herbicide use increased in the US by an estimated 239 million kilograms between 1996–2011, 'with HR [herbicide resistant] soybeans accounting for 70 per cent of the total increase across the three HR crops [soya, maize, oilseed rape/canola]. Rising reliance on glyphosate accounted for most of this increase.'[26] Gradually during this time, news of the appearance of several different kinds of weed resistant to glyphosate began to emerge, increasing year on year until now some 20–25 million hectares may be affected. The response has been to use older and more toxic herbicides such as 2,4-D in tank mixes of agrotoxics and to develop new 'stacked' GM seeds with several traits for resistance to different herbicides.

Proposing 2,4-D resistant crops, stacked crops and more

Now Dow Agrosciences, the company that originally produced 2,4-D, seeks to release genetically engineered soyabean and corn resistant to 2,4-D in Brazil, Argentina and the US. In their petitions seeking 'nonregulated' status for these crops in the US, they cite many problems with glyphosate.[27] It is worth noting that 2,4-D, first marketed in 1944,[28] is long out of patent protection. Producing a crop resistant to it opens up the opportunity, thoroughly exploited by Monsanto, to retain control of the system by creating packages of products and restrictive grower contracts that place the onus entirely on the grower, limiting the liability of the company, and increasing profits and control. Violation may lead to legal action and severe financial sanctions.[29] Dow's proposed crops are stacked with traits for resistance to other herbicides as well, including glufosinate and glyphosate.[30] Perhaps this is not surprising, considering that there are already weeds in the US that are resistant to 2,4-D.[31] Monsanto is also producing genetically engineered seed stacked with multiple traits, notably resistance to the herbicides dicamba and glufosinate.[32] It is legitimate to ask how these new traits are meant to address weed resistance effectively, especially in the long term. It is estimated that releasing the 2,4-D products could increase the volume of herbicide sprayed, possibly by up to by 50 per cent,[33] and 2,4-D has negative impacts on crops, ecosystems, animals and people.[34] The same is true of dicamba.[35] Both are also implicated in the growing number of cases of pesticide drift and destruction of other farmers' crops.

Conclusions: a paradigm shift is required

This essay has attempted to begin a process of reflection on the violence implicit in many aspects of modern industrial agriculture, the way this violence breeds further violence, and its consequences for us all. We have looked briefly at some instances of the close relations between research into weapons of war and agricultural weapons in the form of synthetic fertilisers, herbicides and insecticides. The description of fertiliser as a weapon might seem overstated, but the negative impacts of synthetic nitrogen fertiliser, hardly more than hinted at above, justify the description. The abiding image is one of seeking to dominate and control natural systems and compel them to comply with a certain model, using methods that are the property of commercial companies that derive large profits from their products. If a system of control should break down, this provides an opportunity to create or use a new product, creating a toxic treadmill. Thus the emergence of herbicide resistant weeds is an opportunity to which companies are responding by engineering crops with multiple traits and resistance to more herbicides, which in turn means farmers are applying more and more toxins, with impacts on us all.

The fact that we do not understand the complexities of the natural systems we are trying to control is rarely mentioned. We are repeatedly told that the only way forward is through up-scaling industrial agriculture, and any other path leads to starvation. However, an increasing number of people – including scientists – are questioning that assumption, ranging from small-scale food providers to people who have been brought up inside an industrial food system and barely know anything different, but are troubled by what they see and feel.

Move away from agriculture as war on people and the land

The destruction of biodiverse ecosystems and indigenous cultures, the contamination of soil, water and air, the impacts on climate and the planetary nitrogen cycle, the impacts on human health and wellbeing, all to produce animal feed for industrial livestock and biofuel for cars, is surely a form of short term thinking we should all reject. So what are the alternatives?

There are many: we all need to take far more heed of the sources of our food and recognise that small farmers around the world are still the main source of food for the human population, in spite of the pressures they face.[36] Instead of marginalising them and driving them off the land into slums, we should be developing policies to support them and the organisations that represent them, such as La Via Campesina, the international peasant movement that has 164 member organisations in 79 countries, representing some 200 million farmers around the world with a steadily increasing membership.[37]

Slowly but surely, support for diverse ways of farming other than industrial monocultures is strengthening around the world. Agroecological approaches to food production, which include organic farming, biodynamic agriculture and permaculture, have been constantly sidelined by the publicity around industrial approaches despite their capacity for high yields. We are constantly told that inter-cropping, companion-planting and other mixed cropping systems are not viable because they are not amenable to large-scale mechanical production and nothing else is acceptable these days in developed countries, where no one wants to get dirt under their fingernails.

Hopefully looking at the fundamental violence of the dominant system will contribute to accelerate this change in thinking. We need to marginalise industrial agriculture and food production and adopt agroecological approaches appropriate to different regions and cultures around the world. If we tackle the violence of modern industrial agriculture, we can also begin to tackle multiple injustices and major inequalities linked to it. We can more clearly reveal the cartels that dominate seed, chemicals, food processing and transport.[38] We can also highlight the 'collateral damage' caused by this model of industrial agriculture, but it requires thought, action and commitment from each one of us.[39]

Notes

1   Quoted in 'Chapter 1', Hungry Corporations: [http://www.econexus.info/sites/econexus/files/ENx-HC-Ch1.pdf].

2   [http://www.pigbusiness.co.uk/].

3   Wikipedia equates 3-5 per cent natural gas with (~1–2 per cent of the world's annual energy supply): [http://en.wikipedia.org/wiki/Haber_process].

4   [http://epp.eurostat.ec.europa.eu/statistics_explained/index.php/Glossary:CO2_equivalent] See also: Crutzen *et. al* 'N2O release from agro-biofuel production negates global warming reduction by replacing fossil fuels', *Atmospheric Chemistry and Physics*. 8: 389–95 (2008): [http://www.atmos-chem-phys.net/8/389/2008/acp-8-389-2008.html].

5   [http://www.ciwf.ie/education/CIWFUnsustainabilityPaper_Dec2012.pdf].

6   'World Livestock 2011: livestock in food security: UN Food and Agriculture Organisation', p. 21: [http://www.fao.org/docrep/014/i2373e/i2373e00.html].

7   Sources for nitrogen information include: [http://www.motherjones.com/tom-philpott/2013/04/history-nitrogen-fertilizer-ammonium-nitrate].
[http://ngm.nationalgeographic.com/2013/05/fertilized-world/charles-text].
[http://e360.yale.edu/feature/the_nitrogen_fix_breaking_a_costly_addiction/2207/].
[http://en.wikipedia.org/wiki/Fertilizer].

8   See 'Chapter 3', *Hungry Corporations* [http://www.econexus.info/publication/hungry-corporations].

9   [http://toxipedia.org/display/toxipedia/Organophosphates].

10 [http://www.panna.org/resources/organophosphates].

11 [http://www.politics.co.uk/reference/organophosphates]; Exposure to organophosphates harms memory, say scientists: [http://www.fwi.co.uk/articles/03/12/2012/136539/exposure-to-organophosphates-harm-memory-say-scientists.htm].

12 [http://www.downtoearth.org.in/content/international-peoples-tribunal-indicts-monsanto-dow-chemical-and-others-pesticide-deaths-inj].

13 Orvin C. Burnside, 'Chapter 2: The History of 2,4-D and Its Impact on Development of the Discipline of Weed Science in the United States', in *Phenoxy Herbicides* [http://www.24d.org/abstracts/chapter2.pdf].

14 Ibid.

15 Archives Search Report Findings for Field Testing of 2,4,5-T and Other Herbicides, Fort Detrick: [http://www.detrick.army.mil/responsible/ArchivalReport2012.pdf].

16 Tom Fawthrop, 'Agent Orange Victims Sue Monsanto', *Corp Watch*, 4 Jan. 2004, [http://www.corpwatch.org/article.php?id=11638]; 'The Legacy of Agent Orange', [http://home.clara.net/heureka/gaia/orange.htm].

17 Grupo Reflexion Rural, a letter to Pope Francis, April 2013, Argentina, English version: see item 2 at [http://www.gmwatch.org/index.php/news/archive/2013/14881-cardinal-turkson-say-no-to-gmos] see also: 'Argentina: A Case Study on the Impact of Genetically Engineered Soya'; [www.econexus.info/publication/argentina-case-study-impact-genetically-engineered-soya].

18 Michael Warren & Natacha Pisarenko, 'Argentines link health problems to agrochemicals', *Associated Press/Aurora Advocate*, 18 October 2013: [http://www.auroraadvocate.com/ap%20financial/2013/10/18/argentines-link-health-problems-to-agrochemicals].

19 'Declaration of Caroya', 13 September 2008: [http://semillasdeidentidad.blogspot.com/2008/09/paren-de-fumigar.html].

20 'Report from the 1st NATIONAL MEETING OF PHYSICIANS IN THE CROP- SPRAYED TOWNS, 27-28.8.2010': [http://www.reduas.fcm.unc.edu.ar/report-from-the-first-national-meeting-of-physicians-in-the-crop-sprayed-towns/].

21 Grupo Reflexion Rural, a letter to Pope Francis, April 2013, Argentina, English version: see item 2 at [http://www.gmwatch.org/index.php/news/archive/2013/14881-cardinal-turkson-say-no-to-gmos].

22 See for instance: Paraguay Sojero by Grupo Reflexión Rural, Argentina [http://www.grr.org.ar]; document available at [http://lasojamata.iskra.net/en/node/12].

23 Jane Monahan, 'ibid and Soybean fever transforms Paraguay', BBC, 6 June 2005: [http://news.bbc.co.uk/1/hi/business/4603729.stm].

24 [http://www.argentinaindependent.com/socialissues/environment/terra-i-mapping-latin-americas-disappearing-forests/].

25 [http://www.ihu.unisinos.br/entrevistas/520591-a-transgenia-esta-mudando-para-pior-a-realidade-agricola-brasileira-entrevista-especial-com-leonardo-melgarejo]. Google translation into English: [http://bit.ly/15HNY1q].

26 Charles M. Benbrook, 'Impacts of genetically engineered crops on pesticide use in the US – the first sixteen years' [http://www.enveurope.com/content/24/1/24].

27 [http://www.aphis.usda.gov/brs/aphisdocs/11_23401p.pdf], p.17.

28 [www.pan-uk.org/pestnews/Actives/24d.htm].

29 Example of a fairly typical grower agreement: [http://www.dowagro.com/na/usa/en/traitstwd/das_tech_use_agreement.pdf].

30 [http://www.aphisvirtualmeetings.com/24d_about.html].

31 Charles M. Benbrook, 'Impacts of genetically engineered crops on pesticide use in the US – the first sixteen years', [http://www.enveurope.com/content/24/1/24].

32 [http://www.aphisvirtualmeetings.com/dicamba_about.html].

33 Charles M. Benbrook, 'Impacts of genetically engineered crops on pesticide use in the US – the first sixteen years', [http://www.enveurope.com/content/24/1/24].

34 [http://www.pan-uk.org/pestnews/Actives/24d.htm].

35 [http://www.pesticideinfo.org/Detail_Chemical.jsp?Rec_Id=PC32871].

36 See for example: [http://www.twnside.org.sg/title2/susagri/2013/susagri276.htm].

37 [http://viacampesina.org/en/].

38 'Agropoly: a handful of corporations control world food production', (2013), [http://www.econexus.info/publication/agropoly-handful-corporations-control-world-food-production].

39 Mark Bittman, 'How to feed the world', *New York Times*, 14 October 2013, [http://www.nytimes.com/2013/10/15/opinion/how-to-feed-the-world.html?pagewanted=1&_r=1].

CHAPTER SEVEN

Who profits from the Atomic Weapons Establishment?

TOM ANDERSON

Tom Anderson is a writer and researcher for Corporate Watch.

'THE CORPORATION'S... legally defined mandate is to pursue, relentlessly and without exception, its own self-interest, regardless of the often harmful consequences it might cause to others.'[1]

Corporations have attained an unprecedented power within our societies. Our health, the clothes we wear, work, time off, government policies and political influence, the food we eat and the culture and values we absorb, military policies, surveillance and security are all increasingly controlled and mediated by the needs of profit-driven corporations and the ideology of the primacy of the pursuit of profit .

The expansion of corporate power requires an increased militarisation of society. From new wars over natural resources to imperial interventions to neuter popular uprisings, the corporate driven militarisation of national and international politics continues apace. Corporations benefit from state military and colonial policies, profiting from the contracts created by military operations and by providing security technology and services for an increasingly militarised world. Military ventures prompt the development of new technologies of repression which can be marketed and sold for profit. Our fears and insecurities are utilised in corporate marketing rhetoric to sell new military, surveillance and security technologies.

The militarisation of society is changing the face of modern warfare. Drone technology has allowed the US and Israel to wage war in Gaza, Yemen, Somalia and Pakistan without ever needing to set foot on enemy soil.[2] The same drone technology has been used to protect corporate assets, for example Chevron's oil fields in Angola. Weaponry developed in the context of military occupation and on the battlegrounds of the WAR ON TERROR is increasingly pervading everyday life in the Global North. Non-lethal weaponry developed by international companies and tested against social movements in Palestine in the context of military occupation[3] have been used against anti-corporate protesters in the US[4] and marketed for use against rioters in the UK.[5]

Nuclear weapons are another comparatively new and constantly developing technology which has fundamentally changed the balance of global politics. These weapons have the capacity to kill hundreds of thousands of people indiscriminately and render natural environments uninhabitable. However their manufacture, deployment and development is done for private profit.

The development of nuclear weapons technology has been internationally condemned. After the bombings of Hiroshima and Nagasaki, which caused the deaths of over 200,000 people, social movements in Japan began to call for a ban on nuclear weapons.[6] In the UK, grassroots movements have been resisting the development of nuclear weapons technology since the first peace marches to Aldermaston almost 55 years ago.[7] In 1996 the United Nations asked the International Court of Justice (ICJ) for its opinion on whether nuclear weapons were legal. The resultant ICJ judgement stated that nuclear weapons could never be used legally within international law and that to threaten the use of thermonuclear weapons was illegal within international humanitarian law.[8] Despite this, nuclear weapons continue to be deployed. Nuclear weapons technology and the expansion of nuclear weapons facilities have proven a lucrative market for private corporations. In the UK further opportunities for corporate profit from nuclear weapons were created by the privatisation of the Atomic Weapons Establishment (AWE) in 1993.[9]

AWE is managed by the Ministry of Defence but is currently subcontracted to AWE Management Ltd (AWE ML), which, in turn, contracts to AWE PLC. AWE ML was awarded a ten year contract to manage AWE in April 2000. This was extended in 2003 and is now set to run until March 2025.[10] The company manages three sites at Aldermaston, Burghfield and Blacknest.[11]

AWE PLC is a consortium of private companies which manufactures and maintains the warheads for the UK's nuclear weapons system, Trident. Since 2008, the consortium has been made up of Serco, Jacobs Engineering and Lockheed Martin UK who hold an equal share.[12] The government of the UK holds a golden share in the company.[13]

Serco[14] is a British company specialising in providing services under government contract. They have been a major beneficiary of successive

British government's drive to privatise public services and contract out functions previously carried out by the state. Serco currently hold contracts in the military, healthcare, leisure, prisons, local government and education sectors.[15]

With regard to the military, Serco doesn't just manage the Aldermaston Atomic Weapons Facility, the company also facilitates naval access to, and operates vessels at, Faslane, Devonport and Portsmouth Naval Bases, where nuclear weapons are deployed ready for use. It also provides services to several military bases across the UK including RAF Fylingdales, where it maintains the UK's 'Anti Ballistic Missile Warning System' and the joint RAF/US Department of Defence operation at Menwith Hill.[16] In 2007 the Government announced that Menwith Hill would become part of the US' Missile Defence System.[17] Thus Serco is, in effect, directly involved in maintaining the UK and US's illegal threat of a nuclear strike and, consequently, in maintaining military hegemony through the threat of offensive action.

Lockheed Martin UK[18] is a subsidiary of the US firm Lockheed Martin, the world's largest arms company operating in 75 countries[19] with annual military sales of close to $40 billion.[20] Lockheed Martin specialises in military aircraft, missiles and munitions. The company operates nuclear weapons systems in the US and the UK.[21]

Lockheed Martin's slogan is "'we never forget who we're working for', and it's not hard to see who that might be, as the company is the largest recipient of US defence contracts and does 60 per cent of its work for the US Department of Defence.[22] The company manufactures the F-16 and is developing the new F-35 fighter planes, which are being supplied to human rights abusers like the Israeli[23] and Turkish[24] governments, the US[25] and UK.[26] In 2009 it received 7.1 per cent of total Pentagon funding.[27]

In 2011, anti-militarist campaigners refused to participate in the UK national census due to the decision to award the £150 million government contract to Lockheed Martin.[28] The company has also been involved in running census programmes in the US.[29]

Jacobs Engineering is a US company engaged in construction, engineering and provision of services to governments with annual revenues in excess of $10 billion.[30] Jacobs is the newcomer in the AWE PLC consortium buying out British Nuclear Fuels Ltd (BNFL) in 2008. The sale prompted concern that AWE is now majority controlled by US corporations.[31]

All three members of AWE PLC are profiting from producing and maintaining nuclear warheads which are used to maintain a constant threat that they could be used with the aim of ensuring military dominance by those states which possess nuclear technology over those which do not. The operations of these three companies can be resisted. For instance SERCO runs public services across the UK and campaigners could disrupt its capacity to continue obtaining profitable local government contracts while it remains a partner in AWE PLC.

Notes

1   Joel Bakan, *The Corporation*, (2004), pp. 1–2.
2   See, for instance [http://www.thebureauinvestigates.com/category/projects/drones/].
3   [http://corporateoccupation.wordpress.com/2011/01/03/1080/].
4   [http://www.corporatewatch.org/?lid=3443].
5   [http://www.wired.co.uk/news/archive/2011-08/12/water-cannon?page=all].
6   Jim Falk, *Global Fission: The Battle Over Nuclear Power* (1982), p. 98.
7   [http://www.cnduk.org/information/info-sheets/item/437-the-history-of-cnd].
8   John Mayer, *Nuclear Peace: The Story of the Trident Three* (2002), pp. 1–2.
9   [http://www.hse.gov.uk/nuclear/awe/awe00-03.htm].
10 [http://www.awe.co.uk/aboutus/the_company_eb1b2.html].
11 [http://www.awe.co.uk/aboutus/our_sites_92e5c.html].
12 [http://www.awe.co.uk/aboutus/the_company_eb1b2.html].
13 A golden share is a nominal share which is able to outvote all other shares in certain specified circumstances.
14 A map of Serco's business in the UK can be found at [http://www.serco.com/markets/index.asp].
15 [http://www.serco.com/markets/index.asp].
16 [http://www.serco.com/markets/defence/].
17 [http://www.raf.mod.uk/organisation/rafmenwithhill.cfm]; [http://www.cnduk.org/campaigns/no-to-us-missile-defence/menwith-hill].
18 A map of some of Lockheed Martin's UK locations can be found at: [http://www.caat.org.uk/resources/mapping/organisation?name_search=lockheed+martin] and [http://www.lockheedmartin.co.uk/uk/who-we-are/Locations.html].
    For more info on Lockheed Martin see: [http://www.crocodyl.org/wiki/lockheed_martin].
19 [http://www.lockheedmartin.com/us/who-we-are/global.html].

20 [http://www.caat.org.uk/resources/companies/lockheed-martin/] and [http://www.crocodyl.org/wiki/lockheed_martin].
21 [http://www.lockheedmartin.com/us/who-we-are/organization.html].
22 [http://www.guardian.co.uk/uk/2011/mar/18/lockheed-martin-targeted-census-protesters].
23 See [http://www.jpost.com/Defense/Article.aspx?id=279106] and [http://www.f-16.net/f-16_users_article7.html].
24 [http://www.turkishweekly.net/news/141212/turkey-to-buy-two-planes-in-second-f-35-shipment.html] and [http://www.globalsecurity.org/military/systems/aircraft/f-16-fms.htm].
25 [http://www.airforce-technology.com/projects/f16/].
26 [http://www.raf.mod.uk/equipment/f35jointstrikefighter.cfm].
27 [http://www.motherjones.com/politics/2011/01/lockheed-martin-shadowing-you].
28 See [http://www.guardian.co.uk/uk/2011/mar/18/lockheed-martin-targeted-census-protesters] and [http://www.indymedia.org.uk/en/2011/11/488424.html].
29 [http://www.motherjones.com/politics/2011/01/lockheed-martin-shadowing-you].
30 [http://www.jacobs.com/].
31 [http://www.guardian.co.uk/world/2008/dec/20/british-nuclear-fuels-sells-awe-management-stake].

CHAPTER EIGHT

Arms Companies, Nuclear Weaponry and the Military

KAYE STEARMAN

Kaye Stearman works with the Campaign Against Arms Trade (CAAT) to end the international arms trade.

A global business

THE ARMS BUSINESS is a global one, reaching across borders and affecting peoples' lives thousands of miles away. While the USA has by far the world's largest arms industry, the UK remains a major manufacturer and exporter of weapons. It is home to one of the world's largest arms companies, BAE Systems, as well as other significant players, such as Rolls-Royce, Cobham, QinetiQ, GKN and Chemring.

In addition, non-UK arms companies play a significant role: Italian arm giant Finmeccanica owns Agusta Westland helicopters, and Lockheed Martin, Thales and EADS have substantial businesses based in the UK.

Arms companies, nuclear weapons and the military establishment go hand in hand. Take BAE Systems as an example. One of its proudest boasts is that it is building a new generation of Astute class nuclear-powered attack submarines for the Royal Navy at its shipyards in Barrow-in-Furness. While BAE routinely showcases the submarines as a triumph for British technology and innovation, the programme has consistently run late and over budget, a cost that is paid by the taxpayer.

BAE is heavily involved in the development of the Trident replacement submarines, though supposedly no decision has yet been made on Trident. In May 2012, BAE was handed the lion's share of a MOD contract worth £350 million to build the next generation of nuclear armed Successor submarines, which will replace the Vanguard submarines which currently carry Trident.

BAE is not the only arms company working on the nuclear submarine programme. Rolls-Royce engines and Thales sensors are used in construction. Babcock International Group, the largest supplier of services to the Ministry of Defence, is involved in the construction of both the Astute and Vanguard nuclear submarines. Each Vanguard has the capacity to carry 16 Trident missiles, manufactured by American arms giant Lockheed Martin, containing up to 192 nuclear warheads (currently 48 warheads). Rolls-Royce and Babcock also share in the new Successor submarine contract.

In September 2012, BAE proposed to merge with EADS, whose military interests include manufacturing Eurofighter military helicopters and military transport aircraft, to form the world's largest arms and military services company. A few weeks later, the merger collapsed. However, the two companies were already collaborating in some areas and will continue to do so, most prominently in the enormously expensive Eurofighter Typhoon project and MBDA Missiles.

MBDA *Missiles*

BAE and EADS each owns 37.5 per cent of MBDA Missiles, with Italian weapons manufacturer Finmeccanica holding a further 25 per cent. The name MBDA is not well known, yet it is the second largest manufacturer of a wide range of guided missiles, both conventionally armed and nuclear, for Eurofighter, Gripen and Rafale aircraft. It has long been responsible for supplying France's nuclear missile programme.

One country that bought MBDA Missiles was Colonel Gadaffi's Libya who agreed to buy 1,000 Milan anti-tank missiles for £168 million in August 2007. The deal was agreed soon after the then Prime Minister Tony Blair, accompanied by Guy Griffiths of BAE/MBDA, visited Libya and signed an 'Accord on a Defence Cooperation and Defence Industrial Partnership'.

In 2011, UK forces were using MBDA Brimstone missiles in air strikes against the Gaddafi regime. By 2012 MBDA was rejoicing at a full order book from the Royal Air Force to replace the depleted missiles. Meanwhile, UK Trade & Investment Defence and Security Organisation (the Government's arms sales body) was organising a new arms trade mission to Libya – a 'floating arms fair' took place when a British warship docked at Tripoli in 2013.

Justifications

How does the Government justify their involvement in such dangerous and controversial activities, such as arming repressive regimes or facilitating a nuclear threat? Usually they cite two factors – national security and employment.

The Government, the military and the arms industry defines 'national security' in narrow military terms. It sees the answer to external threats, however unspecific or distant, as increasing military numbers, weaponry and/or reach. Yet even the Government's 2010 Strategic Defence and Security Review sees conventional military threats as much less likely than non-military ones. It identifies major 'Tier 1' threats as natural disasters, international terrorism, cyber attacks and an international military crisis between states drawing in the UK and other parties. Yet, the stated response of the review is to 'project power' through military might.

As for protecting British jobs, the numbers of jobs in the arms and related nuclear industry have been declining for many years and will continue to do so. Most of the arms industry workers will find their skills and expertise in high demand in other industries, including renewables. Even if other employment is not readily available (and it nearly always is), the idea that government should subsidise the arms industry in order to provide employment is wasteful in the extreme.

Former Lib Dem defence minister Nick Harvey recently commented:

> The idea that you should produce weapons of mass destruction in order to keep 1,500 jobs going in the Barrow shipyard is palpably ludicrous. We could give them all a couple of million quid and send them to the Bahamas for the rest of their lives, and the world would be a much better place, and we would have saved a lot of money.

Military spending in western countries is in decline, even though it is still far too high and has so far escaped the harshest budget cuts. The UK still spends £39 billion a year on the military and arms – the fourth highest military spending in the world. Rather than protecting the military budget we should cut it further – cancelling the Trident replacement, stopping government subsidies to arms companies and directing investment towards more useful and beneficial technologies, such as renewables. Such moves would enhance our national security and provide a stable base for creating new jobs and industries.

CHAPTER NINE

Nuclear Weapons and Militarisation in the UK

OWEN EVERETT

Owen Everett was heavily involved in environmental and anti-arms trade activism at university. After graduating in 2012, he was a one-year Quaker Peace and Social Witness Peaceworker at Forces Watch and War Resisters' International.

Militarisation in the UK generally

'MILITARISATION' means the ways in which the presence and approaches of the military (typically state armed forces and Defence Ministries) are normalised in a society. Military solutions are prioritised, and the military is privileged in various ways.

A society has to be militarised for a government to justify the development and maintenance of nuclear weapons to its citizens; militarisation creates a culture of acceptance. It popularises military euphemisms such as 'Defence', 'Security', and – particularly relevant to nuclear weapons – 'Deterrent', and makes it hard to for those challenging these to be seen as credible.

The indicators of militarisation used in the Bonn International Centre for Conversion's Global Militarisation Index 2012 are comparisons of: military expenditure with gross domestic product (GDP) and health expenditure; the total number of (para)military forces with the total number of physicians, and with the total population; and the number of 'available' heavy weapons with the total population.[1] The UK was ranked 63rd out of 135 states, based on data from 2011.[2] However, its expenditure on military activities (including Armed Forces and Ministry of Defence [MOD] personnel, operations, procurement, maintenance, and research and development) was the fourth highest in the world at $62.7 billion (3.6 per cent of the global total, although not all of this was for its own military: at least £9.95 billion – around $15.5 billion – worth of military equipment was exported in the same year).[3]

However, the Index's range of indicators is quite limited. In addition to overlooking other commonly-acknowledged indicators of militarisation such as the role of the military in government, and whether or not conscription exists, it does not examine the role of the military in everyday life.

It is in this latter sense that the UK is militarised. Military personnel may have little visible influence in government, and apart from during the two World Wars we have only had conscription between 1945–1960, yet the military and its values have been noticeably promoted in many areas in the last five years. This perpetuates the UK's self-perception that it has a special military status – 85 per cent of the public believe that our Armed Forces are the best in the world, and 86 per cent believe that we need strong Armed Forces – which is required for sustaining the claim that our continued possession of nuclear weapons is necessary and justifiable.[4] Our military expenditure and capability are disproportionate to our economic standing; Germany and Japan – with far bigger GDPs – and Brazil and Italy (with similar ones) don't have nuclear weapons. In 1954, Foreign Secretary Anthony Eden remarked during cabinet discussions in which the government decided to make its first nuclear bomb, that the 'possession of [atomic] weapons is now [a] measure of power & influence in the world'.[5] Although largely unstated, the aspiration to retain world power status probably remains central to the decision to replace Trident.

How is the UK becoming more militarised?

Many will have noticed the growing presence and influence of the military in UK society in recent years. Positive images of the military are promoted through policy and in the media. We are all being asked to support the Armed Forces through charitable giving and local community initiatives. The growing prominence given to the military was written into government policy five years ago. The 2008 report *National Recognition of Our Armed Forces*, written by Quentin Davies MP, Bill Clark (MOD), and Martin Sharp (RAF) for then-Prime Minister Gordon Brown, stated (based on surveys of the public) that the Armed Forces had 'become increasingly separated from civilian life and consciousness', which could inhibit their 'motivation and effectiveness', potentially endangering 'the society they are defending'.[6] It asserted that 'The Government therefore needs to make a continued effort to explain the rationale for the Armed Forces to the public', and made 40 recommendations for 'increasing visibility', 'improving contact', 'building understanding', and 'encouraging support', including, respectively:

- encouraging members of the Armed Forces to wear their uniforms in public, making local authorities responsible for homecoming parades, and supporting the call for an Armed Forces Day
- holding open days at military facilities
- greatly expanding the Cadet Forces in state schools, and by introducing an Armed Forces element to the Citizenship curriculum
- introducing special discounts for Armed Forces personnel.

Almost all of these recommendations have been implemented, some under the Armed Forces Covenant, the legal formalisation in May 2011 of the supposed (but unwritten) contract between civilians and members of the Armed Forces, which 'recognises that the whole nation has a moral obligation to members of the armed forces and their families and it establishes how they should expect to be treated.'[7] The Armed Forces covenant encompasses the Community Covenant, which encourages local support for and interaction with Armed Forces personnel. Half of the UK's local authorities had officially signed the Community Covenant as of the end of 2012; since then several more have signed.[8] A recent example of a Community Covenant initiative is the call by Labour Party shadow ministers for more streets to be (re)named after Armed Forces personnel killed in combat, which the London Borough of Barking and Dagenham have already started doing.[9]

The recommendations in the 2008 report are mostly about increasing the presence of the military in everyday life, seen in the statement: 'If military uniforms become more commonplace the Armed Forces will increasingly be seen as a normal part of society.'[10] Other developments, particularly in the way that the military is giving access to young people within education and local communities, not only utilises the presence of the armed forces in the everyday life of young people to create positive influence over them and interest potential recruits but increasingly seeks to use military approaches as a solution to perceived social problems.

The militarisation of young people in particular

The 2005 Strategy for Delivery of MOD Youth Initiatives stated that:

The principles underpinning the youth policy are:

a. to integrate Armed Forces Youth Policies with wider Government youth policies, particularly those aimed at capability building, social inclusion and citizenship;

b. to provide appropriately resourced university, combined and single service cadet units so that all youths have a reasonable opportunity to participate in cadet activities;

c. to provide an environment which maximises awareness of the Armed Forces among both young people and their gatekeepers in order to create the conditions in which recruiting flourishes.[11]

The 2012 summary of the 2011 *Youth Engagement Review* reiterated that the most significant benefits of running activities for young people are to defence rather than the young people themselves – 'the two most important benefits to the MOD are awareness and recruitment', and 'there is a definite benefit to the MOD of young people and the UK population as a whole being aware of the Armed Forces'.[12]

The military's physical presence and its values are growing in schools: in addition to armed forces visits, lesson plans, and sixth form scholarships for potential officers, the Department for Education (DfE) is rolling out a 'military ethos and skills' programme in schools, which includes the £10.85 million expansion of the cadets in state schools (recommended in the 2008 report), and alternative provision for vulnerable, disengaged pupils, such as Challenger Troop – a full-time military-uniformed programme for 10–16 year olds, which is due to be greatly expanded.[13] It is striking that whereas the MOD frames the outcomes of its youth policy in 'defence' terms, the DfE frames them as social outcomes.

There is considerable overlap between militarising initiatives in schools and in universities; there are university equivalents to the school scholarships, cadet forces, and recruitment stalls. Military-oriented research and teaching are quite common in universities' Engineering, Science, and Technology departments, and also feature in some more surprising areas.[14] The militarisation of research is particularly concerning. Approximately 17 per cent of the UK's current Research and Development (R&D) budget is allocated to military R&D. Although only a small fraction of this funding is channelled into universities, it 'can shape the research priorities' of the departments where it is particularly concentrated.[15] The Sussex University academic Anna Stavrianakis frames this as the 'instrumentalisation' and 'militarisation' of higher education by the state and by corporations, where national interest and competition are emphasised, and the rightful public benefit and 'autonomous space' of higher education are overlooked.[16] She has argued that:

> University involvement with arms companies [and, by extension, with the MOD] sees the privileging of military concerns in the allocation of time and resources, which orients scientific and engineering research towards weapons production, encourages students to pursue militarised careers (such as engineering jobs with arms-producing companies), and discourages investment and innovation in the development of alternative technologies, all of which also contributes to the privileging of force as a means of resolving conflict and ordering social relations.[17]

A Campaign Against the Arms Trade (CAAT) analysis of how nuclear weapons fit into the arms industry indicates the possible links with university-based research: 'Arms companies, nuclear weapons and the military establishment go hand in hand... BAE is heavily involved in the development of the Trident replacement submarines'.[18] Indeed, although a lot of the designing and building of Trident components seems to take place in industry rather than universities because of the security issue, a 2007 report by CAAT and Fellowship of Reconciliation revealed that AWE PLC funded 46 military projects in the 26 UK universities it investigated (2 per cent of the total number of projects).[19] A forthcoming Nuclear Information Service report will describe the range and nature of collaboration between AWE and a significant number of UK universities.

There are various other youth initiatives which specifically relate to Trident. The Atomic Weapons Establishment (AWE), which 'on behalf of the Ministry of Defence' manufactures and maintains Trident's nuclear warheads, runs science demonstrations and competitions for secondary school students. Is there any mention of the horror of nuclear warfare during these events? The closest thing to it in recent press releases are references to the benign *'vortex cannons'* and trebuchets that pupils get to use and design.[20] AWE school visits' emphasis on non-military applications of science is similar to the problematic concept of 'dual use' – research which is essentially civilian but that can be used to develop and exploit military applications; it is difficult to criticise because its main purpose is civilian. Another example of encouraging the uncritical acceptance of Trident among young people are work experience placements with the Defence Fire Fighters at the Clyde naval base, site of the Trident submarines when they are not at sea.[21]

In the academic year 2011–12 the Defence Technical and Navy under-graduate bursary schemes, which commit students to a minimum of three years' service after graduation, involved 28 Navy Technical students, and four Navy Engineers.[22] Some of them may end up working on Trident; although it is unclear how much nuclear weapons research and develop-ment occurs at universities, AWE does actively seek to recruit talented Engineering, Physics and Chemistry graduates, and as usual the interest-ing science and opportunities are emphasised and the nuclear warheads are only mentioned fleetingly.[23]

One of the most objectionable things about many of the militarising initiatives explored in this essay is that they do not give an honest impres-sion of what war – the ultimate focus of militarism - is really like; neither school-based cadets, nor undergraduate Armed Forces bursars, nor any of the other young people involved, seem to be informed about the awful destruction that armed conflict causes. In the Trident-specific examples above, nuclear warfare appears to be ignored in the same way.

The visibility and influence of the military in everyday life in the UK has increased significantly in the last few years, and this looks set to continue. A public which is sympathetic towards the military, and accept-ing of military approaches, is less likely to be critical of our possession of nuclear weapons. The most recent public opinion poll on Trident, in 2010, suggested that 63 per cent of people would back the non-renewal of Trident in order to reduce the national deficit – a slight increase on similar surveys in 2009 and 2006 – but it is not a very big majority, and the concern is the financial cost.[24] Would a 2013 poll show less opposition to Trident, given that a lot of the initiatives described above have been rolled out since 2010?

The movement against the renewal of Trident could be strengthened by encouraging debate about militarisation in the UK.

Notes

1   Jan Grebe, 'Militarisation Index 2012', Bonn Centre for Conversion, 2012. [www.bicc.de/fileadmin/Dateien/pdf/press/2012/Update_GMI_2012_Fact_Sheet_e_neu.pdf].

2   Global Militarisation Index Ranking Table, Bonn Centre for Conversion, 2012. [http://bicc.de/old-site/index.php?page=ranking-table].

3   Stockholm International Peace Research Institute, 'The 15 countries with the highest military expenditure in 2011'. [www.sipri.org/research/armaments/milex/resultoutput/milex_15/the-15-countries-with-the-highest-military-expenditure-in-2011-table/view]; Campaign Against Arms Trade, UK Arms Export Licenses, 13 June 2012. [www.caat.org.uk/resources/export-licences/date?date_to=2011-12-31&date_from=2011-01-01].

4   MOD, 'MOD Annual Report and Accounts 2011-12' (2012) [www.gov.uk/government/publications/mod-annual-report-and-accounts-2011-12].

5   Cited in Cabinet Secretary Norman Brook, notebook account of 1954 cabinet meeting: [http://nationalarchives.gov.uk/releases/2007/november/weapons-part2.htm].

6   Quentin Davies MP, Bill Clark (MOD), and Martin Sharp (RAF), 'National Recognition of Our Armed Forces' (May 2008) [www.ppu.org.uk/ref/recognition_of_our_armed_forces.pdf].

7   MOD, 'The armed forces covenant': [https://gov.uk/the-armed-forces-covenant].

8   MOD, '2012 Community Covenant Conference', 12 November 2012: [www.gov.uk/government/news/2012-community-covenant-conference]; MOD, 'Nottingham commits to supporting the Armed Forces', 29 January 13: [www.gov.uk/government/news/nottingham-commits-to-supporting-the-armed-forces].

9   BBC News, 'Labour urges councils to rename streets after war heroes', 21 February 2013: [http://bbc.co.uk/news/uk-politics-21530095].

10 Davies, Clark, and Sharp, 'National Recognition'.

11 Directorate of Reserve Forces and Cadets, 'Strategy for Delivery of MOD Youth Initiatives', 2005: [http://webarchive.nationalarchives.gov.uk/20121026065214/http://www.mod.uk/NR/rdonlyres/DCA0B266-5CA4-47AA-8172-85DA92892C52/0/drfc_modyouthstrat.pdf].

12 'Youth Engagement Review: A Summary and Way Forward', 2012: [http://armycadets.com/uploads/documents/YER/20120712Youth_EngReview_WayForward-U.pdf].

13 Emma Sangster, 'Militarising Education', 27 December 2012: [http://forceswatch.net/blog/militarising-education].

14 ForcesWatch are publishing a report on the military's presence and influ-

ence in UK universities on their website, [www.forceswatch.net], around June 2013.

15 Stuart Parkinson, 'Military-university collaborations – an update on the UK situation', Scientists for Global Responsibility, 19 September 2012: [http://www.sgr.org.uk/resources/military-university-collaborations-update-uk-situation].

16 Anna Stavrianakis, 'In Arms' Way: Arms Company and Military Involvement in Education in the UK', ACME, 8:3 (2009): [http://acme-journal.org/vol8/Stavrianakis09.pdf], pp. 505–520.

17 Anna Stavrianakis, 'Call to arms: the university as a site of militarised capitalism and a site of struggle', Millenium (2006) [http://sro.sussex.ac.uk/1729/1/Call_to_Arms.pdf].

18 Kaye Stearman, 'Arms companies, nuclear weaponry and the military': [http://actionawe.org/arms-companies-nuclear-weaponry-and-the-military/].

19 Martha Beale, Tim Street, and Jo Wittams (CAAT/FoR), 'Study War No More: Military involvement in UK universities', (October 2007): [www.studywarnomore.org.uk/documents/studywarnomore.pdf].

20 AWE news, (October 2012): [www.awe.co.uk/shownews_402b11d.html]; [www.awe.co.uk/shownews_5985bd6.html]; and [www.awe.co.uk/shownews_c55eba8.html]. See also the third photo down at [http://tinyurl.com/cz6pd76] which illustrates this.

21 Royal Navy news, 22 January 2013. [www.royalnavy.mod.uk/sitecore/content/home/news-and-events/latest-news/2013/january/22/130122-hermitage-pupil-learns-what-it-takes-to-become-defence-fire-fighter].

22 'Freedom of Information request response', Royal Navy, 24 January 13: [www.whatdotheyknow.com/request/145827/response/353271/attach/3/20130124%2016%2001%202013%20131127%20009%20Everett%20Reply%20u.pdf].

23 Graduate-jobs.com, 'AWE graduate jobs': [http://graduate-jobs.com/training_scheme/AWE_graduate-jobs/]; Warwick Chemistry, Opportunities Portal, 'Atomic Weapons Establishment': [http://www2.warwick.ac.uk/fac/sci/chemistry/chemintra/placements/warwickstudents/news/?newsItem=094d43a23b4bc65f013b614deb04697b].

24 Campaign for Nuclear Disarmament, 'Opinion polls': [http://cnduk.org/campaigns/no-to-trident/opinion-polls].

CHAPTER TEN

Refugees and Asylum Seekers: Human Debris of the West's War Machine

DR TREVOR TRUEMAN

Trevor Trueman trained as a GP. After three visits to Sudan, involving cross-border visits to Ethiopia, training health workers from 1988 to 1991, he started reporting human rights abuses. This was because the new regime in Ethiopia was killing, detaining, torturing and disappearing friends and people he had trained. He then set up the Oromia Support Group (becoming its Chair) and continues to monitor and report on the human rights abuses and atrocious treatment of refugees by the UK Border Agency. www.oromo.org/osg

MY TELEPHONE RINGS twice one Friday morning in September. Anxious Oromo refugees and asylum seekers in Hargeisa, Somaliland, report beatings and refoulement back to Ethiopia. A young woman with a history of detention and rape is refused asylum in the UK and reports tearfully from Yarlswood Immigration Removal Centre that she is due for deportation to Ethiopia in a few days.

Ordinary people are in extraordinary circumstances because of tyranny in one country and hostility and xenophobia in another. Is this misery, fear and abuse related to militarism and the West's military-industrial complex? Let's look more closely at Ethiopia.

Respect for human rights is both foundation and mortar in the building of a developed, democratic society. Despite international plaudits for economic growth and its proclaimed meeting of Millennium Development Goals, the one-party state of Ethiopia abuses its citizens and has formalised its hobbling of civil society and media with three laws passed since 2008.[1]

There has been some ritual clucking from foreign donor states, but no effective criticism. The main reasons for Ethiopia's huge financial and moral support from the USA, UK and the EU, once it jettisoned the Albanian communist ideology of its ruling elite, are its commercial and ideological cooperation, most notably in the 'war on terror'.

To secure a toe-hold of influence in the Horn of Africa, the West has sacrificed its token regard for human rights as a foreign policy objective. Political killings, arbitrary detention, disappearance, torture and rape – tools of repression routinely and daily practised in Ethiopia – are ignored, despite the ritual categorisation of abuse in yearly State Department reports on the country.

With US encouragement, Ethiopia invaded Somalia at the end of 2006. Atrocities committed against civilians during Ethiopia's destruction of the Islamic Courts Union,[2] responsible for the first semblance of law and order in Somalia since 1991, spawned a backlash – the murderous insurgency led by al-Shabaab, which now destabilises the region.

Ethiopia's cooperation with the West goes further. In return for training and supplying the Ethiopian army, the US is permitted to launch drone attacks from the Ogaden against al-Shabaab militants in Somalia.

In receipt (mostly from the USA and UK) of $3 billion per year in aid, a third of its annual budget,[3] Ethiopia has built one of the largest and best equipped armies in Africa. Yet, millions of its people are still in need of food aid.

Ethiopia therefore is a crucible in which the military-industrial complex competes with and supplants economic development and the growth of civil society. Food security and human rights are relegated to the bottom division, despite politically correct nods in their direction from western donors.

Ethiopia's abusive and suffocatingly restrictive regime produces as many refugees as Iran.[4] Only Colombia and the Democratic Republic of Congo surpassed Ethiopia as sources of asylum seekers awaiting refugee status determination at the end of 2011.[5]

The UN refugee agency's league tables show the clear relationship between conflict and human rights abuse and the exodus of refugees and asylum seekers. At the end of 2011 there were 42.5 million displaced people. Over 26 million were displaced within their country of origin. More than 15 million were refugees; 4.8 million Palestinians and 10.4 million under the care of UNHCR elsewhere.[6]

The role of conflict and abuse, both the results of militarism benefiting from the exploits of the European and American military-industrial complex,[7] is clearly apparent from UNHCR figures. Over 60 per cent of the refugees cared for by UNHCR come from five countries – Afghanistan, Iraq, Somalia, Sudan and the Democratic Republic of Congo – all synonymous with conflict and abuse. Those lower down the league table are similarly embroiled in war and human rights violations.[8]

And the refugee burden does not fall on Europe or America, contrary to the scaremongering of political parties and the racist British press:[9] only 17 per cent of refugees live outside their region of origin and four out of five live in developing countries, those least able to afford to provide help.[10]

In the 12 months up to the end of June 2012, there were only 19,959 asylum applications in the UK. Decisions were made in 16,729: 10,922 (65 per cent) were refused. There were 15,014 forced removals from the UK in that 12 month period (with the help of Group 4 Securicor – a security satellite of the military-industrial complex).[11]

Western hypocrisy in redefining 'economic migrant' as a derogatory term contrasts with the welcome extended to educated professionals, the middle class of developing countries, while those remaining in war zones are 'starved, stunted and deprived of education'.[12] Vijay Mehta has written persuasively about the role of western militarism in further impoverishing the developing world:[13] how our 'military-industrial complex has promoted an international cycle of war and poverty.'[14]

The USA's and other countries' insistence on their 'fifth freedom' – to have unfettered access to the world's resources and markets – is the central tenet of foreign policy strategy. State violence against uncooperative citizens, committed by cooperative and kleptocratic elites, is made possible with the awesome physical power of industrial scale militarism, sold to those elites by the West.

The millions who seek sanctuary from conflict and state violence are a predictable consequence of the West's prioritising profit over people, in the nourishment of its military-industrial complex. The culpability of western 'democracies' in this waste of human lives and resources is compounded by their refusal to shoulder a proportionate burden of the human consequences.

Notes

1   The Press Law was introduced in 2008 (US State Department (2011) 2010 Human Rights Reports: Ethiopia. 8 April 2011, Section 4).
    'The restrictive Anti-Terrorism Proclamation (adopted in 2009) has been used to justify arrests of both journalists and members of the political opposition' (Human Rights Watch World Report 2012: Ethiopia, Events of 2011: [http://www.hrw.org/world-report-2012/Ethiopia]).
    'The restrictive Charities and Societies Proclamation, adopted in 2009, which prohibits organizations receiving more than 10 percent of their funding from abroad from carrying out human rights and governance work, continues to severely hamper basic rights monitoring and reporting activities.' (Ibid.)

2   'Human Rights Watch World Report 2008: Ethiopia, Events of 2007, Abuses Relating to the Conflict in Somalia'.

3   30–40 per cent of Ethiopia's spending is from foreign assistance. Human Rights Watch World Report 2012. Op. cit.
    Ethiopia receives $3 billion annually in aid. Human Rights Watch, 'Development without Freedom: How Aid Underwrites Repression in Ethiopia.' New York. October 2010. Summary, p. 4.

4   At the end of 2011, there were 70,670 refugees from Ethiopia and 72,000 from Iran. UNHCR Global Trends 2011 (May 2012), [www.unhcr.org/4fd6f87f9.pdf]

5   DRC – 52,119; Colombia – 42, 569; Ethiopia – 38,755. Ibid.

6   Ibid.

7   Vijay Mehta. *The economics of killing: How the West fuels war and poverty in the developing world.* (London: Pluto Press, 2012).

8   UNHCR, Op. cit.

9   For example, 'Stronger curbs on immigration are needed before our communities explode, David Cameron was warned yesterday.' Immigration debate is on. *Daily Star*, 7 September 2012, p. 2.

10 UNHCR, Op. cit.

11 Home Office Immigration Statistics April-June 2012. [www.homeoffice.gov.uk/publications/science-research-statistics/immigration-asylum-research/immigration-q2-2012/asylum1-q2-2012]

12 Vijay Mehta. Op. cit. p. 4.

13 Ibid. pp. 32–35.

14 Ibid. p. 40.

CHAPTER ELEVEN

The Use of Radioactive Material in War

JOANNE BAKER

Joanne Baker is a human and environmental rights campaigner. She is co-founder of the charity Child Victims of War and co-author of Uranium in Iraq: the poisonous legacy of the Iraq wars.

THE USE OF uranium by the military began with the discovery of the fission process and led to the nuclear programmes in Germany, the US and Britain during the Second World War. In 1945 atomic bombs were dropped on the cities of Hiroshima and Nagasaki in Japan. The US was also concerned that the Germans might use radioactive material as a ground and lung contaminant and US military planners began looking for radioactive material with high gamma and beta radiation and short half-lives which would have an immediate effect on the target population. A declassified US military document of 1943 states: From consideration of the possible effects and uses of radioactive material in warfare, it is evident that considerable experimentation with actual field trials would be necessary to determine the optimum conditions under which radioactive dusts could be disseminated with lung contamination and ground contamination.[1]

The use of uranium as a radiological weapon never materialised, but by the 1950s the US were experimenting with the use of depleted uranium (DU), in anti-tank munitions. A product of the Cold War, it was used in anti-tank penetrators to cut through heavily armoured Soviet tanks. DU trials began in the UK in the 1960s at Eskmeals in Cumbria, although full scale firing did not take place until 1980. DU is a waste product of the enrichment process and the DU used by the military has included uranium extracted from reactor fuel.[2] Its military advantage is that it is a very dense, heavy metal (similar to tungsten) which self sharpens when it hits a hard surface and spontaneously ignites, burning at around 3,000–6,000 C.

DU penetrators were first tested on the battlefield by the Israelis in the Yom Kippur war of 1973.[3] Their first extensive use was in the Gulf war of 1991 by the British and US. It was estimated that between 300 and 800 tons of DU were used during the six weeks of the Gulf war, releasing possibly tens of millions of grams of DU oxide into the environment. DU was used again by the US in Bosnia in 1995, Kosovo, Serbia and Montenegro in 1999, and continuously in Iraq and Libya in 2011. It is also believed to have been used by the Israelis in Palestine, in Lebanon in 2006 and by the US in Somalia in 1993.

The Mystery – from depleted to un-depleted and enriched uranium?

Since the war of terror began in 2001, independent scientists have been travelling to war zones to collect human and environmental samples and testing them for uranium. Mass spectrometry results show that samples collected from bomb craters, air filters, soil samples and urine contain un-depleted or slightly enriched uranium, not depleted uranium.

After the bombing of Afghanistan in 2002, a team from the Uranium Medical Research Centre in Canada took urine samples from civilians suffering symptoms of 'fatigue, fever, musculoskeletal neurological alterations, headaches and respiratory impairment'. Soil and water samples were also taken from the bombed sites. The mass spectrometry results showed no DU, but high levels of un-depleted uranium, 100 times that of the normal range. Seven residents of Kabul were also contaminated with U–236 which meant that although the uranium had a similar isotopic ratio to natural uranium, it could not have come from a natural source.[4]

In 2006, samples taken from bombed areas in Lebanon and tested at the Atomic Energy Research Establishment at Harwell and the School of Oceanographic Sciences, University of Wales Bangor, again showed no DU but slightly enriched uranium.[5]

A recent study analysing hair samples from parents in Fallujah whose children had been born with congenital anomalies showed that they had been exposed to significant amounts of enriched uranium in 2004.[6]

The Weapons?

It is no secret that DU has been used in tank armour, anti-tank penetrators and some types of landmine. *Jane's Defence Weekly* has also confirmed the use of DU in shaped charge liners and in 2001 the MOD website mentioned

British/French trials of DU in shaped charge liners at Aldermaston.[7] US patents cite depleted uranium or uranium metal as a preferred metal in a number of weapon systems including bunker busters and cruise missiles. In 1999, a Decalogue warned troops in Kosovo to 'avoid any medium or material suspected of being hit by munitions containing depleted uranium or Tomahawk Cruise missiles'[8], and unofficial US military sources have stated its use in large bunker busting weapons such as the GBU–28,[9] 500 of which were shipped to Israel for use in Lebanon in 2006. There is also suspicion that uranium could be used as a reactive metal in thermobaric weapons.[10]

The discovery of un-depleted and slightly enriched uranium indicates a novel use of uranium in undeclared weapon systems. This should be of major concern to the international community because we no longer know what we are dealing with. The international campaign to ban 'depleted' uranium weapons is growing apace, but the disturbing and undisclosed use of uranium in other weapons systems by the US and Israel is going unchallenged. The use of uranium in larger weapons would mean it had a more widely contaminating effect. The plumes go high into the atmosphere and are picked up by the air streams. Air filters from Aldermaston showed significant radiation peaks after the Tora Bora bombing in Afghanistan, 2002, and the shock and awe bombing of Baghdad in 2003. In both cases the National Oceanic and Atmospheric Administration (NOAA) showed air currents travelling from these regions to the UK.[11]

Uranium weapons, depleted or otherwise, are both radioactive and toxic. The half-life of uranium is 450 billion years. Whereas an atomic bomb releases huge amounts of external radiation, uranium weapons create the risk of internal radiation. Uranium burns at high temperatures creating minute ceramic particles which can be inhaled or ingested. Exposure to uranium dust is known to cause oxidative stress, genomic instability, chromosome damage, neurological problems and kidney dysfunction. Children are particularly at risk from cancers and congenital deformity. In Fallujah, Iraq, 15 per cent of children are now born with congenital malformations, worse than the aftermath of Chernobyl or Hiroshima. Congenital heart defects have the highest incidence, followed by neural tube defects.[12] As Dr Malak Hamdam, co-author of two scientific papers on Fallujah, writes:

> This extraordinary discovery of a new uranium weapon should serve as
> a wake-up call to the entire world. It is as if the military were at war with

humanity, secretively winning their battles with what is effectively a kind of delayed-action radioactive poison gas. They cannot keep denying that these radioactive weapons can discriminate in their effects between military and non-military targets.

Notes

1   Doctors James B. Conant, Chairman, A.H.Compton, and H.C. Urey, (1943) Use of Radioactive Material as a Military Weapon – summarised from a report by the Subcommittee of the S-1 Executive Committee; US Information Paper on Depleted Uranium: [http://www.nato.int/du/docu/d010123a.htm].
2   R. Brown, 'Depleted Uranium Munitions and Assessment of the Potential Hazards DERA Protection Services', 19 January 2000, p. 6 para.17.
3   A. Durakovic, 'New Concepts in CBRN Warfare in the Light of the Gulf War Experience and Current Reality of Global Terrorism', *The Third GCC Conference of Military Medicine and Protection Against Weapons of Mass Destruction*, (Doha, Qatar: October 2002).
4   [http://umrc.net/wp-content/uploads/2012/06/Uranium-Contamination-of-Afghanistan-Tedd-Weyman-2003.pdf].
5   [http://www.greenaudit.org/papers/evidence-of-enriched-uranium-in-guided-weapons-strikes-on-le].
6   S. Alaani, M. Tafash, C. Busby, M. Hamdan, E. Blaurock-Busch, 'Uranium and other contaminants in hair from the parents of children with congenital anomalies in Fallujah, Iraq' in Conflict and Health (2011): [http://www.conflictandhealth.com/content/pdf/1752-1505-5-15.pdf].
7   D. Williams, 'Under the radar: identifying third-generation uranium weapons'.
8   M. Zucchetti, 'Cruise missiles with depleted uranium on Libya' [http://www.voltairenet.org/Cruise-missiles-with-depleted].
9   J. Shaft, 'US Colonel Admits 500 Tons of D.U. Were Used in Iraq': [http://www.thecbdf.org/en/cbdf-news/34-press-releases/86-us-colonel-admits-500-tons-of-du-were-used-in-iraq].
10 D. Williams. 'Under the radar: identifying third-generation uranium weapons'.
11 Busby, C. Morgan, S. 'Did the use of Uranium weapons in Gulf War 2 result in contamination of Europe?': [http://www.greenaudit.org/papers/did-the-use-of-uranium-weapons-in-gulf-war-2-result-in-conta].
12 Four Polygamous Families with Congenital Birth Defects from Fallujah, Iraq: [http://www.unidir.ch/pdf/articles/pdf-art2759.pdf].

CHAPTER TWELVE

Civil Nuclear Power and Nuclear Weapons Proliferation

PETE ROCHE

Pete Roche is an energy consultant based in Edinburgh and policy adviser to the Scottish Nuclear Free Local Authorities, and the National Steering Committee of UK Nuclear Free Local Authorities. He was a nuclear campaigner for Greenpeace UK for 13 years, until 2004, and a member of the Government's Committee Examining Radiation Risks of Internal Emitters.

Introduction

WHEN THE QUEEN opened Britain's first nuclear reactor, Calder Hall (at Sellafield), in 1956 its primary role was to produce plutonium for British bombs, demonstrating from the start the inextricable link between civil and military nuclear power.[1]

The International Atomic Energy Agency (IAEA) and the Non-Proliferation Treaty (NPT) embody a fundamental contradiction – both seek to promote the development of 'peaceful' nuclear power at the same time as trying to stop the spread of nuclear weapons. Since the NPT came into force in 1970, Israel, India, Pakistan and North Korea have all obtained nuclear weapons and Iran, Iraq and Libya have confirmed the connection between nuclear weapons and power – illustrating that the current non-proliferation regime is doomed to fail.

Fissile material

Manufacturing a nuclear bomb requires fissile material – either uranium-235 or plutonium-239. The problem is that most nuclear reactors use uranium as a fuel and produce plutonium during operation.

In natural uranium only around 0.7 per cent consists of the 'fissile' uranium-235 which can support a chain reaction. The rest is uranium-238.

Most modern reactors need the proportion of uranium-235 in the fuel to be increased to around two or three per cent – a process known as enrichment. A nuclear bomb requires the proportion of uranium-235 to be around 90 per cent. Anyone with uranium enrichment technology for manufacturing nuclear fuel simply needs to increase the enrichment level to manufacture a nuclear weapon. A bomb only needs around 20 kilograms of Highly Enriched Uranium (HEU).

When a nuclear reactor is operating, the non-fissile uranium-238 in the fuel is transmuted into plutonium-239. Given the right equipment to chemically separate out this plutonium from the waste, a reactor operator can also make a nuclear bomb. In a nuclear reactor, other plutonium isotopes will be produced as well. To make an efficient and predictable nuclear weapon you would want to maximise the proportion of plutonium-239. But any grade of plutonium can be used to make nuclear weapons, if you are not too worried about yield and efficiency.[2]

Proliferation – the uranium route

So the first major challenge to nuclear proliferation controls is the spread of uranium enrichment technology. Nothing better illustrates how so-called peaceful nuclear technology can be used for military purposes than the activities of the Khan network. Abdul Qaadeer Khan was able to build a global nuclear information network and business which had access to supposedly secret uranium enrichment technology. Using a mixture of legal and illegal transactions involving businesses all over the world, ultracentrifuge enrichment technology was exported to Libya, North Korea and Iran.[3] Despite being a signatory to the NPT, Iran established a uranium enrichment programme without informing the IAEA.

Proliferation – the plutonium route

Another major challenge is the impossibility of adequately safeguarding a plutonium separation or reprocessing plant. Commercial reprocessing plants handle large amounts of plutonium – typically about seven or eight tonnes of plutonium a year. A nuclear weapon could be made with as little as three or four kilograms of reactor grade plutonium. To ensure the timely detection of the diversion of such a small amount of plutonium in a plant where so much plutonium is handled requires much more precision than is achievable with today's technology, so the IAEA has an impossible task.[4]

'Proliferation Resistant' Reactors – a misconception

It is a misconception that conventional nuclear reactors are somehow proliferation resistant, if a nuclear operator doesn't have access to uranium enrichment or reprocessing technology. Separating plutonium from spent nuclear waste fuel does not require a large industrial-scale reprocessing facility. A quick and simply designed plutonium separation facility could be in operation four to six months after the start of construction.[5]

Spread of civilian technology

Although the Fukushima Daiichi nuclear accident has affected nuclear power in some countries, a new report by the OECD Nuclear Energy Agency (NEA) and the IAEA estimates that world nuclear electricity generating capacity will grow from 375 GW (at the end of 2010) to between 540 GW and 746 GW by 2035.[6]

A global expansion of nuclear power will require a proportional expansion of uranium enrichment capacity. Brice Smith looks at a scenario which involves nuclear power capacity expanding to 1,000 GW by 2050. If just one per cent of the enrichment capacity required to power a nuclear programme this size were diverted to weapons, this would be enough to make between 175 and 310 bombs every year.[7]

Nuclear expansion would probably also lead to an expansion of reprocessing too. The scenario looked at by Brice Smith would require 17 new plants the size of the THORP reprocessing plant at Sellafield. 155.3 tonnes of plutonium would be separated annually. If just one per cent of this plutonium were diverted it would be enough to make 194 bombs every year.[8]

The spread of civil nuclear reactors risks the possibility of multiple mini cold wars around the globe.[9] About 60 countries were reported to have approached the IAEA in 2012, expressing an interest in starting nuclear programmes.[10] Thirteen countries in the greater Middle East expressed an interest in 2008, according to the International Institute for Strategic

Studies (IISS). Some of these countries appear to be moving down the nuclear path in reaction to Iran's determined pursuit of uranium enrichment, raising the prospect of a Sunni/Shia arms race.[11] Kuwait[12] and Bahrain[13] both announced they were abandoning plans for new reactors in 2012. But other countries such as Saudi Arabia and the United Arab Emirates (UAE) are continuing. The United Arab Emirates (UAE) has become the first new country in 27 years to launch a nuclear power programme.[14] The UAE accepted a $20 billion bid from a South Korean consortium to build four commercial nuclear power reactors (5.6 GWe) by 2020. Construction of the first unit started in July 2012, and the second in May 2013.[15] Saudi Arabia plans to construct 16 nuclear power reactors over the next 20 years at a cost of more than $80 billion, with the first reactor coming on line in 2022.[16] Senior Saudi Arabian diplomats have reportedly stated that 'if Iran develops a nuclear weapon, that will be unacceptable to us and we will have to follow suit', and officials in Riyadh have said that the country would reluctantly push ahead with their own civilian nuclear programme.[17]

The IAEA also expects Vietnam[18], Bangladesh[19], Turkey[20], and Belarus[21] to start building their first nuclear power plants in the next few years. According to the IAEA, Jordan and Nigeria have also taken the decision to introduce nuclear power.[22]

Conclusions

The history of the IAEA and the NPT demonstrate that peaceful nuclear energy is a myth. Promoting 'peaceful' nuclear power has accelerated nuclear weapons proliferation. The United Nations needs a body leading the way in tackling the twin threats of climate change and nuclear proliferation, promoting a nuclear phase out and sustainable energy which can foster world peace rather than threatening it.

Notes

1   S. Durie & R. Edwards, Fuelling the Nuclear Arms Race, (Pluto Press, 1982).

2   US Department of Energy, 'Nonproliferation and Arms control Assessment of Weapons-Usable Fissile Material Storage and Excess Plutonium Disposition Alternatives', (1997), p.37, excerpted in [http://www.ccnr.org/plute.html].

3   Joop Boer, Henk van der Keur, Karel Koster, Frank Slijper, 'A. Q. Khan, Urenco and the proliferation of nuclear weapons technology: The symbiotic relation between nuclear energy and nuclear weapons', Greenpeace International May 2004: [http://www.greenpeace.org/international/press/reports/a-q-khan-urenco-and-the-prol].

4   M. M. Miller, 'Are IAEA Safeguards on Plutonium Bulk-Handling Facilities Effective?', Nuclear Control Institute, (Washington, DC: August 1990): [http://www.nci.org/k-m/mmsgrds.htm]; P. Leventhal, 'IAEA Safeguards Shortcomings: A Critique', Nuclear Control Institute, (Washington, DC: 12 September 1994): [http://www.nci.org/p/plsgrds.htm].

5   Shaun Burnie and Tom Clements 'The end of KEDO: Why supplying a nuclear reactor to North Korea would have increased proliferation risks in East Asia', Greenpeace International, May 2006: [http://www.greenpeace.org/international/en/publications/reports/the-end-of-kedo/]; V. Gilinsky, M. Miller & H. Hubbard, 'A fresh examination of the proliferation dangers of Light Water Reactors', Nonproliferation Policy Education Center, (Washington: October 22nd 2004). [http://npolicy.org/article_file/A_Fresh_Examination_of_the_Proliferation_Resistance_of_Light_Water_Reactors.pdf].

6   'Global Uranium Supply Ensured for Long Term, New Report Shows', IAEA Press Release, 26 July 2012 [http://www.iaea.org/newscenter/pressreleases/2012/prn201219.html].

7   'Insurmountable Risks' by Brice Smith, IEER, 2006. (Section 3.1): [http://www.no2nuclearpower.org.uk/reviews/review01.php].

8   Ibid section 3.2.

9   Niall Ferguson, 'Fast forward 10 years... and there are cold wars everywhere', *Sunday Telegraph*, 14 May 2006: [http://www.telegraph.co.uk/comment/personal-view/3624969/Fast-forward-10-years-and-there-are-cold-wars-everywhere.html].

10 'New Countries go Nuclear Despite Fukushima,' Nuclear Power Daily, 24 February 2012: [http://www.nuclearpowerdaily.com/reports/New_countries_go_nuclear_despite_Fukushima_UN_official_999.html]. See also Froggatt and Schneider, 'World Nuclear Industry Status Report 2012', pp. 21–28: [http://www.worldnuclearreport.org/IMG/pdf/2012MSC-World-NuclearReport-EN-V2-LQ.pdf].

11 'Nuclear Programmes in the Middle East: In the Shadow of Iran', IISS, May 2008: [http://www.telegraph.co.uk/comment/columnists/concoughlin/3558653/Its-nuclear-power-not-oil-that-worries-the-Middle-East.html].

12 'Kuwait scraps nuclear power in light of 3/11', *Japan Times*, 23 February 2012.

13 Bahrain scraps nuclear power plan', Modern Power Systems, 26 February 2012: [http://www.modernpowersystems.com/story.asp?sectionCode=131&storyCode=2061836].

14 General Yukiya Amano, IAEA Director, ' Opening Statement at IAEA Ministerial Conference on Nuclear Power in the 21st Century', 27 June 2013: [http://www.iaea.org/newscenter/statements/2013/amsp2013n13.html].

15 'Nuclear Power in the United Arab Emirates', May 2013: [http://world-nuclear.org/info/Country-Profiles/Countries-T-Z/United-Arab-Emirates/].

16 'Nuclear Power in Saudi Arabia', World Nuclear Association, June 2013: [http://world-nuclear.org/info/Country-Profiles/Countries-O-S/Saudi-Arabia/].

17 J. Burke, 'Riyadh will build nuclear weapons if Iran gets them, Saudi prince warns', The Guardian, 30 June 2013: [http://www.guardian.co.uk/world/2011/jun/29/saudi-build-nuclear-weapons-iran].

18 'Nuclear Power in Vietnam', World Nuclear Association, May 2013: [http://world-nuclear.org/info/Country-Profiles/Countries-T-Z/Vietnam/].

19 'Nuclear Power in Bangladesh', World Nuclear Association, June 2013: [http://world-nuclear.org/info/Country-Profiles/Countries-A-F/Bangladesh/].

20 'Nuclear Power in Turkey', World Nuclear Association, July 2013: [http://world-nuclear.org/info/Country-Profiles/Countries-T-Z/Turkey/].

21 'Nuclear Power in Belarus', World Nuclear Association, April 2013: [http://world-nuclear.org/info/Country-Profiles/Countries-A-F/Belarus/].

22 General Yukiya Amano, IAEA Director, 'Opening Statement at IAEA Ministerial Conference on Nuclear Power in the 21st Century', 27 June 2013: [http://www.iaea.org/newscenter/statements/2013/amsp2013n13.html].

CHAPTER THIRTEEN

A Vast Endless Experiment –
Military Radioactive Pollution

JOHN LAFORGE

John LaForge has worked on the staff of Nukewatch, a nuclear watchdog and
environmental justice group in Wisconsin, for 22 years and edits its quarterly
newsletter. He has published numerous articles and has been called as an expert
witness in courts on the outlaw status of armour-piercing uranium munitions
which have been used widely by the United States.

> To put workers in situations of risk without information on the effects
> constitutes an experiment.
> DANIELLE GORDON, *Bulletin of the Atomic Scientists*[1]

> The nuclear age has become the cancer age.
> PETRA KELLY, *Fighting for Hope*[2]

> The US military continues to rank among the world's largest generators of
> hazardous waste, producing nearly a ton of toxic pollution every minute.
> WILLIAM THOMAS, *Scorched Earth: The Military's Assault
> on the Environment*[3]

THE MILITARY IS the single largest generator of hazardous wastes in the
United States, adding some 500,000 tons of toxins annually.[4] In 2006, the
US military generated more than one third of the country's toxic waste.[5]

In 1978, the federal government acknowledged that 50 US nuclear sites
were a human health hazard. Leukaemia and other cancers in nearby
areas were statistically more prevalent that in normal towns.[6] By 1989,
the government had identified 3,200 sites at 100 nuclear weapons facilities that had contaminated soil, ground water or both. The total is actually
45,000 potentially radioactive sites, 20,000 of them government owned.[7]
Testifying to Congress in 1988, Dexter Peach, an assistant comptroller
general at the General Accounting Office, said, 'to clean up thousands of
sites owned by the federal Government at which uncontained radioactive

wastes are contaminating soil and ground water... may be the Government's biggest challenge.'[8] George Kritz, a former Energy Department official with the remedial action division in Germantown, Maryland, told the *New York Times*, 'We're going to be in this cleanup business 50, 100, 150 years from now'. [9]

Nuclear weapons and reactor fuel production have radioactively contaminated so much of the United States that official cost estimates of merely a partial clean-up – the National Academy of Sciences concluded in 2,000 that large areas cannot be cleaned to safe levels – are $365 billion and climbing.[10] Part of the reason for the daunting dilemma is that, as the government discovered in 2000, ten times more plutonium waste from weapons production were dumped 'into soil or buried in flimsy containers' than was earlier estimated.[11]

Radioactive contamination of the environment occurs all day, every day, as a result of the normal operation of commercial nuclear power reactors, military and civilian research reactors, shipboard propulsion reactors – the Russians are even building nuclear-powered ice breakers – as well as the transportation and use of radioactive isotopes in medicine, industry, science, war and war preparations. Nuclear reactors cannot even operate without ongoing releases of radioactive water and gases that are vented continuously in order to control the pressure, temperature and humidity inside their cores, and to keep workplace radiation levels from exceeding exposure limits for employees.

All the radioactive contamination in the world can be considered military pollution, because the whole of the nuclear power complex was born of the atom bomb. Waste fuel from civil nuclear power reactors was initially intended for use in bomb production. Only the failure of waste fuel reprocessing in the United States ended the civilian waste-to-weapons programme. Still, tritium gas for the nuclear arsenal has been produced at commercial reactors in Tennessee, putting the lie to official distinctions between civilian and military programmes and 'atoms for peace'. Nuclear power *is* the bomb.

The bio-accumulation of long-lived radioactive pollution from nuclear power and weapons presents a mostly unregulated and nearly unfathomable threat to human and environmental health, especially in conjunction with the cumulative effects of 85,000 other mostly unmonitored industrial chemicals[12] that are routinely poured, vented, leaked or dumped into the environment and the food chain.

In 1969, Ernest Sternglass of the University of Pittsburgh Medical School published 'Infant Mortality and Nuclear Tests' in the *Bulletin of the Atomic Scientists*. The article said that the advent of above-ground bomb testing in 1951 slowed the decline in infant mortality so much that the testing could be considered the cause of 375,000 infant deaths before their first birthdays.[13] The rate of decline returned to normal after open air tests ended in 1963.

The US National Cancer Institute reported in 2002 that 80,000 cancers – 15,000 of which would be fatal – in the US were attributable to just the iodine-131 in 90 of its above ground nuclear bomb tests.[14]

Interviewed by Eduardo Goncalves for 'The secret nuclear war'[15] in *The Ecologist*, the late Dr Rosalie Bertell estimated that as many 385 million cancers and 175 million cancer deaths could be attributed to industrial radiation from bomb building and testing, production reactor accidents and reactor leaks.

Colossal quantities, reckless disposal

As the country's worst polluter, it's possible that since World War Two, the Pentagon, the space programme, the Energy Department and its predecessors have done more to poison and endanger the US public than any enemy. In *Nuclear Wastelands*, Arjun Makhijani et al say nuclear weapons have 'profoundly damaged the very people and lands they were supposed to protect' in order to hide the Government's 'shocking readiness to harm people… [c]over-ups and fabrications targeted at the very citizens the weapons were supposed to protect have been a hallmark of nuclear weapons establishments.'[16]

Army records show that between 1945 and 1970, the military secretly dumped at least 500 tons of unidentified radioactive waste and 32,000 tons of chemical weapons into the Atlantic and Pacific off the coasts of 11 states. In June 1960 alone, about 317 tons of radioactive waste was thrown from ships off the Virginia-Maryland line.[17] The Government can't even find most of the 90,000 barrels of waste it dumped off the Californian coast before 1970.[18]

The fresh waters of the Great Lakes weren't even spared this trashing. During the same period, the Army Corps of Engineers dumped thousands of tons of toxic military wastes into Lake Superior. Over 350 tons of wastes from one production site alone, the Twin Cities Army Ammunition

Plant near Minneapolis, Minnesota, was secretly rolled off barges less than two miles from the drinking water intake for the cities of Duluth and Superior. The era of reckless endangerment of Great Lakes water resources started at least as far back as 1945, when 600 tons of World War Two machine gun ammunition was tossed into Lake Superior 1.5 miles from Duluth.[19]

More than five metric tons of plutonium was dispersed around the world by atmospheric bomb tests, satellite re-entries and burn-ups, effluents from uranium reprocessing, accidental radiation fires, explosions, spills and leaks.[20] The IPPNW and IEER have estimated that about six million curies of cesium-137 and about four million curies of strontium-90 were dispersed to the atmosphere by aboveground bomb tests.[21] The late Dr Rosalie Bertell said:

> It frightens me very much that there is a whole blanket of radioactive material in the upper atmosphere, and no matter what we do it's coming down. Not all of this radioactive material has impacted on the food chain yet, so it will be coming down from the atmosphere for a long time to time, getting into the ocean and the plankton, and the fish, then onto the dinner table.[22]

Altogether about 400 metric tons of plutonium have been produced for military and civilian uses worldwide and, in order to fuel the world's nuclear reactors and weapons, between 100 and 200 million metric tons of uranium mill tailings have been left out in the open at mine sites around the world.[23]

The military's mass environmental degradation is made obvious in wartime when toxins are employed without caution or concern for either targeted peoples or allied troops. In South Vietnam the United States between 1962 and 1969 sprayed at least 100 million pounds of various herbicides like Agent Orange over four million acres[24] — roughly 25 pounds per acre. This chemical warfare destroyed over 460,000 acres of crops[25] and the Vietnamese Red Cross counts 150,000 children whose birth abnormalities were caused by their parents' exposure to Agent Orange.[26]

In the US, areas the size of whole states have been contaminated with radioactive wastes that will threaten national security for thousands of years. The four most widely poisoned weapons sites in the US – the Hanford nuclear Reservation in Washington, the Idaho National Engineering Lab., the Nevada Test Site and South Carolina's Savannah River Site (SRS) –

encompass 3,090 square miles. (Rhode Island covers 1,046 square miles, and Delaware just 2,489).

The SRS is 300 square miles of the most humid radioactive territory in the world. Up to 30 million gallons of radioactive effluent were discharged every year – for decades – into so-called seepage basins, causing severe poisoning of shallow aquifers and groundwater that endangers the drinking water used by Atlanta's 432,000 people. Roughly 600,000 people live within a 50-mile radius.

The US Environmental Protection Agency says:

> Based on current scientific evidence, any exposure to radiation can be harmful (or can increase the risk of cancer)... In other words, it is assumed that no radiation exposure is completely risk free.[27]

Every federal agency that regulates industrial releases or the medical uses of radiation warns likewise.[28]

For many years the government's estimate of the public's average radiation exposure over a one-year period was 170 millirem (mR) of whole body exposure.[29] However, this estimate by the National Council on Radiation Protection and Measurements was doubled in 1987 (from 170 mR to 360 mR/yr).[30] This doubling occurred 18 months after the April 1986 Chernobyl catastrophe spread between one and nine billion curies of radioactive isotopes around the world.[31]

Then, on 20, March 2009, the National Council on Radiation Protection again nearly doubled its estimate, to 620 mR per year.[32] The NCRP reported at the time that the latest near doubling, and about half the 620 mR exposure was due mostly to rapid growth in the use of medical x-rays and radio-isotopes in medicine – things like tracer isotopes, whole-head dental scans, and high-dose medical CT and PET scans (in addition to whole body x-ray scans at airports).

It's true that the use of CT and PET scans has skyrocketed. In 1980, there were three million CT scans performed in the United States. The number rose to 62 million in 2006,[33] to about 70 million in 2007,[34] and according to NBC News to 72 million in 2009.[35] Some researchers now say that CT scans are the primary cause of breast cancer in women.[36] However inexact or experimental, the use of radiation in medicine at least has the prospect of the patient's informed consent regarding its risks. It is the government's secret, misreported, covered up or unreported use and dispersal of extremely dangerous radioactive materials that might be considered its most nefarious and consequential endangerment of the population.

Human radiation experiments

Over a period of 60 years the US conducted 2,000 radiation experiments on as many as 23,000 vulnerable US citizens.[37] US Rep. Edward Markey had earlier reported to Congress on the studies, but his 1986 subcommittee report[38] was not well publicized. The experiments' victims included civilians, prison inmates, federal workers, hospital patients, pregnant women, infants, developmentally disabled children and military personnel – most of them powerless, poor, sick, elderly or terminally ill. Eileen Welsome's 1999 exposé *The Plutonium Files: America's Secret Medical Experiments in the Cold War* details 'the unspeakable scientific trials that reduced thousands of men, women, and even children to nameless specimens'. [39]

The tests were kept secret for decades 'to avoid lawsuits and negative public reaction,'[40] because the culpable scientific community from government, industry and academia had known from the beginning of the 20th century that ionizing radiation can cause genetic damage, cell damage, cell death, radiation sickness and even death, depending on the dose. In the 1940s, Alice Stewart proved that x-rays were harming the foetuses of pregnant women.[41]

The tests ensnared hapless patients or wards of the state in order to note the short-term effects of radioactive exposure and contamination – with everything from plutonium to radioactive arsenic.[42] The human subjects were mostly endangered without their knowledge or consent. An April 17 1947 memo by Col. O.G. Haywood of the Army Corps of Engineers explained why the studies were classified:

> It is desired that no document be released which refers to experiments with humans and might have adverse effect on public opinion or result in legal suits.[43]

In one Vanderbilt University study, 829 pregnant women were unknowingly fed radioactive iron. In another, 188 children were given radioactive iron-laced lemonade. From 1963 to 1971, 67 inmates in Oregon and 64 prisoners in Washington had their testicles targeted with x-rays to see what doses made them sterile.[44] At the Fernald State School in Massachusetts, more than 100 boys 'inaccurately classified as mentally retarded' were fed radioactive iron and calcium but consent forms sent to their parents didn't mention radiation.[45] Elsewhere, psychiatric patients and infants were injected with radioactive iodine.[46]

The vast testing programme went ahead in spite of a warning to use chimpanzees instead of humans, because, as a top radiation biologist wrote at the time, using a reference to Nazi torture of concentration camp detainees, the experiments might have 'a little of the Buchenwald touch'. [47] A rare public condemnation came from Clinton Administration Energy Secretary Hazel O'Leary in 1994, who confessed to being similarly aghast at the conduct of the scientists. She told Newsweek, 'I said, "Who were these people and why did this happen?" The only thing I could think of was Nazi Germany.'[48] None of the victims were provided follow-on medical care.

A Presidential Advisory Committee on Human Radiation Experiments was established in 1993 to investigate allegations of criminal conduct by the experimenters. Its findings were published by Oxford University Press in 1996 as The Human Radiation Experiments.

Abusive x-radiation 'therapy' was also conducted throughout the '40s and '50s. Everything from ringworm to tonsillitis was 'treated' with x-radiation because the long-term risks were unknown or considered tolerable. Children were routinely exposed to alarmingly high doses of radiation from devices like 'fluoroscopes' to measure foot size in shoe stores.[49] Nasal radium capsules inserted in nostrils, used to attack hearing loss, are now thought to be the cause of cancers, thyroid and dental problems, immune dysfunction and more.[50]

As many as 2.3 million children in the US were part of nasal radium experiments or treatments for ear and adenoid infections between 1945 and 1965. The Radium Experiment Assessment Project found that 'between 2,368 and 10, 241 people would die of cancer from this exposure'.[51]

In large scale experiments as late as 1985, the Energy Department deliberately produced reactor meltdowns which spewed radiation across Idaho and beyond.[52] The Air Force conducted at least eight deliberate meltdowns in the Utah desert, dispersing 14 times the radiation released by the partial meltdown of Three Mile Island in Pennsylvania in 1979.[53]

The military also dumped radiation from planes, spreading it across wide areas around Oak Ridge, Tennessee, Los Alamos, New Mexico, and Dugway, Utah. A 'systematic radiation warfare programme' conducted between 1944 and 1961 was kept secret for 40 years.[54] 'Radiation bombs' thrown from USAF planes intentionally spread radiation 'unknown distances' endangering untold numbers of young and old alike. According to Senator John Glen, D-Ohio who released a report on the programme 20 years ago, one experiment doused Utah with 60 times more radiation than escaped the partial reactor meltdown at Three Mile Island in 1979.[55]

The Advisory Committee's 1996 report did not consider US uranium miners – mostly Native Americans – to be victims of official radiation experiments, even though the Atomic Energy Commission (AEC) collected data on their health. The AEC nefariously kept the dangers of radon and uranium dust inhalation secret from the miners and it never required mine operators to install ventilation systems to protect workers. Although it studied only 4,100 miners, the committee declared that there was five times the number of lung cancer deaths than could be expected among them.[56]

Permissible radiation doses established by polluters

There is no safe level of exposure to ionising radiation. Even the smallest exposures have cellular level effects. The US National Academy of Sciences' seventh book-length study on the biological effects of ionizing radiation exposure, BEIR-VII of 2005, declared that any exposure, regardless of how small, may cause the induction of cancer.[57] BEIR-VII also explicitly refuted the pop culture 'hormesus' theory – that a little radiation is good and acts like a vaccination – promoted by industry boosters in business and academia.

Today the nuclear military-industrial-medical complex is merely required to keep radioactive exposure 'as low as reasonably achievable (ALARA)'. This tragicomic standard is not a medical or scientific concept. It is not based on health physics or biology. It is merely the formal admission that the nuclearists cannot keep our worker or public exposures to a level that is safe – that is to zero.

Exposure standards have been established at the convenience of the military and the nuclear industry, not by medical doctors or health physicists.[58] Rosalie Bertell makes clear:

> [T]he people with the highest vested interest are the ones that are making the nuclear bombs. And it turns out they have complete control over setting the permissible [radiation exposure] levels. If you were to fix radiation limits at levels that were really protective of human health, you couldn't get anybody to make bombs.[59]

What's been declared an allowable dose of ionising radiation for nuclear industry workers and for the public has steadily decreased over the years as science has come to understand the toxic, carcinogenic, mutagenic and teratogenic properties of even the lowest exposures.[60]

In the 1920s, the government set the permissible workplace radiation dose for nuclear workers at 75 rem per year. In 1936 the limit was reduced to 50 rem per year, then 20 to 25 in 1948, 15 in 1954, and down to five rem per year in 1958.[61] This five rem/year annual legal dose limit for nuclear workers is still in effect. The general public is officially allowed to be exposed to one 50th of a nuclear workers' permitted radiation dose per year, or 0.1 rem (100 millirem) over a 70-year lifespan.[62]

According to research by the Nuclear Information and Resource Service, this allowable 100 millirem public dose set by the NRC is a 'one of 286' fatal risk standard. That is the number of fatal cancers – one out of every 286 people – considered 'acceptable,' 'permissible' or 'allowable' based on the 100 millirem per year exposure. A report by the National Academy of Sciences found that 'radiation at this level to women results in one fatal cancer in every 201 women'. [63]

Bomb test fallout

The US government's 235[64] open-air bomb tests conducted in the western desert and the Pacific Ocean were not included in its official list of 'radiation experiments'. As many as 500,000 US military personnel were contaminated and made ill during their compulsory participation in the bomb tests done at the Nevada Test Site, in the Pacific[65] and during the military occupation of post-war Japan.[66] Atomic veterans were also exposed by radiation experiments and by their proximity to submarine reactor accidents and tests.

A 1988 law provides some compensation to sick veterans or their survivors, but a critical catch 22 was written into the statute that nullifies most claims. Facing billions of dollars in compensation payments, the law says that veterans or their survivors must prove they were present at a given radiation site and that radiation exposure could have caused their illness or death.

Proof is found in veterans' service records, but hundreds of thousands of them were destroyed in an extremely convenient 1973 warehouse fire. In 2006, a class action lawsuit sought but failed to compel the Pentagon to release all relevant records related to veterans' radiation sicknesses. The US Court of Appeals for the DC Circuit ruled that the veterans could not force a comprehensive mass release of all the pertinent Pentagon records. The Appeals Court said individual veterans have to file individual claims. Even before this devastating decision, a study in the *Elder Law Journal* found that of 18,275 claims filed by 2004, only 1,875 claims had been granted.[67]

Documents uncovered by the Presidential Advisory Committee on Human Radiation Experiments found that the military knew there were serious health risks from the radioactive fallout from its Nevada Test Site explosions, but decided not to use more remote Alaskan sites or Florida from where fallout would have blown out to sea. 'The officials determined it was probably not safe, but went ahead anyway,' said Pat Fitzgerald, a scientist on the committee staff.[68] Dr Gioacchino Failla, a Columbia University scientist who worked for the AEC, said at the time, 'We should take some risk... we are faced with a war in which atomic weapons will undoubtedly be used, and we have to have some information about these things'.[69]

The National Cancer Institute disclosed in 1997 that 90 of the tests spewed 'more than 100 times' the radioactive iodine-131 that authorities claimed at the time, estimating now that those tests dispersed 'about 150 million curies of iodine-131 mainly in the years 1952, 1953, 1955, and 1957'.[70] The 14 year long NCI study found that all 160 million people in the country at the time were exposed to the iodine-131 (the only isotope studied out of over 300[71] that were dispersed by the bomb blasts).[72] The NCI study reported that between 25,000 and 75,000 thyroid cancers would result in the US from the aboveground bomb tests, and that 10 per cent of them would be fatal.[73] The Institute for Energy and Environmental Research noted then that the upper estimate of:

> 75,000 is more plausible, since the lower estimate assumes that internal radiation doses from iodine-131 are 'as little as one fifth as hazardous' as the same dose of external radiation. This assumption is very dubious, not based on human data, and not protective of public health.[74]

The 1997 NCI study found that 16,000 cases of thyroid cancer were diagnosed in the US every year, and that 1,230 would die from the disease.[75] This year, the NCI reports that there will be 60,220 new cases of thyroid cancer, 1,850 of which will be fatal.[76]

Left mostly unreported in the press, the study says the 'incidence rate for women is more than twice as high as that for men'.[77] Summarising the 100,000 page study, Dr. Arjun Makhajani, President of the IEER wrote, '... it estimates that the iodine-131 would cause about 50,000 cancers, about 2,500 of which would be fatal'.[78]

Radioactive fallout from the bomb tests exposed nearly all 160 million people living in the US at the time (especially children) to radiation.[79] Some children received especially large doses because of the 'milk pathway' in which radioactive iodine-131 quickly gets into the milk supply, and because of the large amount of milk that children consume. Later in 1997 the government admitted that while it kept the radioactive fallout's direction and intensities secret from the public, it all the while informed the giant photographic industry (Kodak, etc.) of the areas hit.[80] In 1951, Kodak had threatened to sue the Atomic Energy Commission over radiation damage to it photographic film. Kodak's film was being exposed and destroyed when it was packaged not with today's bubble wrap but in contaminated corn stalks used as stuffing.

The CIA's record of similar experiments was kept secret. Author John Marks has said the CIA's:

> experiments on unwitting subjects... clearly violated the Nuremberg standards – the standards under which, after World War II, we executed Nazi doctors for crimes against humanity.[81]

Not-so-depleted uranium

The name 'depleted uranium' (DU) refers to uranium-238, an alpha particle-emitting radioactive waste that loses just half its radioactivity in 4.5 billion years – the age of the solar system. The US government has between 505,000[82] and 740,000 tons of DU left from uranium enrichment for nuclear weapons and reactor fuel.[83] It is chemically toxic like other heavy metals, is 65 per cent more dense than lead, and is pyrophoric – it ignites when it smashes a hard target.[84] DU is given away free to military contractors to make armour-piercing ammunition.[85]

In 1991, between 315[86] and 800 tons of DU munitions were blasted into Iraq, Saudi Arabia and Kuwait during the 40-day, 1,000 bombing sortie per day assault by US forces.[87] William Arkin reported in *Bulletin of the Atomic Scientists* that 940,000 Air Force 30mm DU shells (23,500 a day) and 4,000 Army 120mm DU anti-tank shells were fired.[88] The US military has its own classified estimate, but the 4,000 tank shells alone contained more than 25 tons of DU. The Air Force fired such an astonishing number of shells because its A-10 warplane shoots 65 rounds per second, or 3,900 per minute.[89]

In his introduction to Gut and Vitale's *Depleted Uranium*, Peter Low put the use of DU this way:

> The people responsible for the spreading of 400 tonnes of DU there [Southern Iraq] in 1991 were conducting a very peculiar sort of experiment – one in which the 'guinea-pigs' were the soldiers and civilians present... and in which the 'experimenters' did not want to know the results.[90]

Indeed, 'uranium has been shown to cause mutations, cell transformation, and DNA strand breaks in both in vitro and in vivo studies.'[91]

The Pentagon says it fired about 10,800 DU rounds – close to three tons – into Bosnia in 1994 and 1995. More than 31,000 rounds, about ten tons, were shot into Kosovo by the US and NATO in 1999, according to the UN.[92] DU has also contaminated large parts of Okinawa, Panama, Puerto Rico/Vieques and other US bases where target practice is conducted.[93]

Thirty millimetre DU shells now litter Kosovo where the US used the weapons against all sorts of targets, not just the tank armour it was designed to penetrate. DU was used against a radio tower near Vranje where a Swiss-led international team found 'serious radioactivity' when it dug up DU rounds there.[94]

After the US/NATO bombardment of Kosovo, DU weapons were found to be *spiked with plutonium* and other fission products far more radioactive than uranium,[95] a revelation that created a political uproar in Europe. The disclosure that 'the entire US stock of depleted uranium was contaminated'[96] with plutonium, americium, neptunium and technetium was made by UN investigators in Kosovo, who found DU-targeted sites poisoned with all these exotic isotopes.[97] The Nation reported that about 150,000 of tons uranium was dirtied with plutonium-239 and neptunium-237 and that 'some apparently found its way to the Persian Gulf and Balkans battlefields'.[98]

> The tainted DU forced Pentagon and NATO officials to claim that its shells contain 'mere traces of plutonium, not enough to cause harm'.[99] NATO Secretary General Lord Robertson said, 'traces of highly radioactive elements such as plutonium... were not relevant

to soldiers' health because of their minute quantities'.[100] Yet plutonium is 200,000 times more radioactive than DU,[101] and less than
27 micrograms of pu-239 – about a millionth of an ounce – will
cause lung cancer.[102] Adding insult to injury, americium-243 decays
to plutonium-239, which is more toxic than the americium.[103]

In 1997, the Associated Press disclosed that the US Army had secretly
studied the use of radioactive poisons 'to contaminate swaths of enemy
land', etc. [104] The declassified response to the AP's 1995 Freedom of Information Act request was heavily censored in part because, '[u]sing radioactive poisons as a weapon is more than a historic footnote'. In 1945, the
government reported that, as the AP put it, 'radioactive fission products
from a uranium-fuelled reactor could be extracted and used 'like a particularly vicious form of poison gas'.

Without any public debate, an experimental low intensity nuclear war
was foisted upon the world by the United States in 1991 in a sort of back-
door Hiroshima. Much like its igniting of the atomic age over Japan 68
years ago, the human costs of testing radioactive weapons in Iraq, Bosnia,
Serbia (including Kosovo) and Afghanistan may prove to be as much
cancer in the US as in targeted countries. Arjun Makhijani has reported
that DU's small amounts of technetium-99, americium-241 and plutonium
'may cause a significant contribution to the total dose to workers during
processing of the DU into metal'.[105] And some 700,000 veterans served in
the 1991 Persian Gulf bombardment and invasion.[106]

NATO officials warned United Nations de-mining teams in Kosovo to
'exercise caution' and not to 'climb upon or into destroyed armoured
vehicles'. The British National Radiation Protection Board warned British
troops in July 1999, 'If the areas are contaminated by insoluble uranium
oxides (DU dust), then any hazard would arise from disturbing the
contamination and inhaling the dust'.[107] Still, Pentagon spokesman Lt.
Col. Victor Warzinski had the nerve to tell the *Christian Science Monitor*
that, 'Residual depleted uranium from battlefield engagements in Kosovo
does not pose a significant risk to human health'.[108]

The UN Environment Programme (for post conflict Balkans) disagrees.
After finishing a comprehensive study of the ecological impact of DU in
the Balkan war, it said the 'highest priority' should be given to forbidding
public access, collecting and removing pieces and decontaminating areas
where possible. UNEP said ground water should be monitored, because,
DU particles were 'still in the air two years after the conflict's end'.[109]

'Byproduct' experiments: 1, 2 and 3

The incalculable amounts of the Energy Department's radioactive waste and the unquantifiable cost of problems with its management have moved the agency to propose a 'Byproduct Utilization Programme' in the 1970s. The agency said then that plutonium production's byproducts 'have a wide range of applications in food technology, agriculture, energy, public health, medicine, and industrial technology,' and that it wished to 'ensure full realisation of the benefits of the peaceful atom'.[110]

One unstated benefit of the programme was to save the DOE billions of dollars while putting dump workers, neighbours and downriver residents at risk. This was accomplished when heavy isotopes called 'transuranics' were redefined in the 1980s. Such waste in concentrations less than 100 nanocuries – one billionth of a curie – per gram is now considered 'low-level' waste and disposable in unrestricted shallow land burial. 'Previously, the limit was ten nanocuries per gram,' and magically, the amount of soil designated as transuranic-contaminated far less. At the Hanford plutonium-production complex in Washington State for example, the new 'definition' of plutonium-contaminated soil meant the total to be cleaned up was only 1,000,000 cubic feet, instead of 400,000,000.[111]

1 Food Irradiation

A global 'irradiation industry' has developed which uses highly radioactive waste – cobalt-60 or cesium-137 – as gamma ray sources, or high energy electron beams, to kill pathogens in food and sterilise medical equipment, food containers, cosmetics, tampons, adhesive bandages and cleaning solutions for contact lenses.

The irradiation of food has been approved in spite of the fact that chemicals called 'radiolytic products' created by irradiation – including benzene and formaldehyde – can 'break apart molecular bonds and create mutagens' and cause cancer, kidney and liver disease, birth defects and other reproductive abnormalities.[112] Not a single study has ever been done to examine whether the effects of a long-term diet of irradiated food is safe.[113] The Food and Drug Administration reviewed 441 toxicity reports to determine the risks of irradiated foods. Dr Marcia van Gemert, the chair of the FDA study committee, later testified that all 441 were flawed.[114]

The consumption of irradiated food, by children especially, is a modern day and completely unmonitored human test. Dr George Tritsch, a cancer researcher at Roswell Park Cancer Institute in Buffalo, NY, is a steadfast opponent of exposing food to radiation. He told *Food and Water Journal*:

> If consumption of irradiated food were to become widespread, it would take four to five decades to show statistically significant increases in cancer incidence... This will therefore be an experiment of a century's duration![115]

Foods approved for irradiation in the United States includes frozen beef, pork, and lamb, as well as poultry, nuts, potatoes, wheat, wheat flour, fruits and vegetables, hamburger, eggs, hot dogs, luncheon meat, all tea and 60 dried herbs and spices. Irradiated poultry products can be used as ingredients in other processed foods like TV dinners and baby food, according to *Public Citizen*.[116]

The cesium and cobalt are radioactive wastes left in huge quantities from nuclear weapons production. Food and Drug Administration spokesman Jim Greene said in 1986 that the nuclear industry's use of cesium-137 'could substantially reduce the cost of disposing of nuclear waste'.[117] Energy Department spokesman, F.C. Gilbert, testified to the House Armed Services Subcommittee in 1983 that:

> The utilisation of these radioactive materials simply reduces our waste handling problem... We get some of these very hot elements like cesium and strontium out of the waste.[118]

Irradiation facilities have caused at least 54 accidents at 132 sites worldwide between 1974 and 1998 including five major incidents in the US.[119] In Decatur, Georgia, Radiation Sterilizers, Inc. (RSI) took 252 21 inch cesium-137 capsules (which were never designed for use at an irradiation facility) from the DOE. In 1988, RSI began using the cesium to irradiate spices. After only two years, a capsule began leaking, contaminating 25,000 gallons of water in the storage pool.[120] It took federal officials six months to find the leak's source, while an estimated 70,000 milk cartons, contact lens solution boxes and other containers were shipped out after being splashed with radioactive water.[121] Contaminated workers took the poison home with them. In 1992, the contaminated building was abandoned and RSI took the word 'radiation' out of its name. Now they're 'Sterigenics'.[122]

2 Radioactive scrap metals

During the 1980s, the Nuclear Regulatory Commission adopted a standard it called 'Below Regulatory Concern (BRC),' that could have seen 30 per cent of the US's 'low-level' radioactive waste treated as plain garbage and dumped in landfills, burned in incinerators, and recycled into consumer products. The thought was to convince the public that some radiation exposure is not worth mentioning. The motive was to give a major financial boost to the nuclear industry and military nuclear waste producers, which are required otherwise to spend billions to dispose of or manage contaminated metals as radioactive waste.

A coalition led by the Nuclear Information and Resource Service[123] eventually got Congress to rescind the BRC policy in 1992. But in April 1998, the NRC, DOE and Environmental Protection Agency announced another attempt to set radiation exposure standards that would allow the use of RSM in smelters along with regular scrap metal for the production of consumer goods.

A month later, a radiological accident at a smelter in Spain sent a plume of radiation across Europe, setting off radiation monitors in France, Switzerland, Italy, Germany, Bulgaria, the Czech Republic and Greece — alarms not heard on a mass scale since the 1986 Chernobyl catastrophe. The smelter at Acerinox in Algeciras, Spain, had accidentally recycled an unknown amount of cesium-137, contaminating the plant and requiring vast clean-up operations.[124]

Still, in 1999, the State of Tennessee officially approved the recycling of RSM, although critics charged that the Energy Department cynically used the state's lax environmental rules to avoid federal regulations that would never allow RSM in 'clean' smelters. The 54,000 acre Oak Ridge uranium weapons site in Tennessee is the source of hundreds of tons of this contaminated metal. Again, opposition succeeded in dumping the plan and even forcing a moratorium on RSM smelting begun in 2000 that is still law.

Another attempt to legalise the smelting of radioactive metals was renewed in 2012. The DOE proposed to deregulate and actually sell 14,000 tons of scrap from the nuclear weapons complex that is contaminated both volumetrically and topically, and move it into the commercial scrap metal 'stream'.[125] From there, according to NIRS, the waste 'could be turned into anything from your next pants zipper to baby toys'. Again, a broad coalition is raising a howling protest against the proposal.

3   Radioisotope thermoelectric generators (RTGS)

For over 30 years, the National Aeronautics and Space Administration (NASA) has been experimenting with on-board radioisotope thermoelectric generators (RTGS) made of plutonium-238. Unlike plutonium-239, the pu-238 is not a bomb-making material but it is ferociously radioactive – 280 times more radioactive than pu-239 – and it generates tremendous heat that is converted to electricity for running on-board instruments for deep space missions.

NASA's twin *Voyager* spacecraft both use RTGS, as do the Mars rover, *Curiosity*, and the *Cassini* probe which is now orbiting Jupiter.

The 1997 Cassini spacecraft carried 72.3 pounds of plutonium-238, and NASA launched it aboard a Titan-V rocket which has a failure rate of between one in ten and one in 20.[126] The chance that Cassini's plutonium would be scattered globally by an accident was officially accepted in NASA's environmental impact statement which boldly admitted, 'approximately five billion of the estimated seven to eight billion world population at the time of the 'swingby' [when the craft came flying around the Earth in a slingshot manoeuvre] could receive 99 per cent or more of the radiation exposure'.[127] The agency decided to take this risk with everyone else's lives again without receiving informed consent of the potential victims.

RTGS have been produced at the Los Alamos National Laboratory (LANL) in New Mexico, where workers have suffered hundreds of radiation accidents,[128] including 241 cases of contamination between 1993 and 1995, and that the official denials made by NASA and the DOE concerning workers doses at the time were cover-ups.[129] The workers' endangerment is still considered necessary by NASA in order to get nice photographs of planets and moons, like those being returned by Cassini.

Today, some scientists claim the US's plutonium-238 stock is 'alarmingly low', *Scientific American* reports a 'worry' that future NASA missions could be put on hold until more is available. In March this year, NASA said it was producing plutonium-238 at the Oak Ridge National Laboratory in Tennessee, where engineers successfully did so by bombarding neptunium-237 with neutrons. The process is still in an experiment, but NASA's Jim Green, head of NASA's planetary science division, says it will eventually 'revive our supply...'[130]

In spite of NASA's record of RTG accidents – the *Apollo 13* crash with 5.5 pounds of pu-238, the *Nimbus B-1* crash with 4.2 pounds, and the *Transit* re-entry that spread 2.1 pounds of the toxin worldwide[131] – the agency plans a dozen future plutonium-roulette shots. None of this risk taking is necessary since the European Space Agency has long advocated high efficiency solar cells for deep space missions. Even 26 years ago, Gerhard Stroble, a project leader for the European agency, said without reservation that 'we can do solar cells for deep space missions'.

Weakening radiation exposure standards

Today, as the nuclear industry struggles against economic collapse due to sky rocketing costs, the Government appears to have caved in to long standing pressure to de-regulate even further. 'Some people think that too much money is being... spent to achieve low levels of residual contamination,' said Roger Clarke, the president of the International Commission of Radiological Protection (ICRP) in 2002.[132] The ICRP sets radiation exposure standards for nuclear industry workers.

On 15 April this year, the Environmental Protection Agency issued new Protective Action Guides (PAGs) for dealing with large accidental radioactive releases. The new PAGs are much worse than the extremely weak PAGs former US President Bush tried to peddle and which the Obama White House retracted.

According to Daniel Hirsch, President of the Committee to Bridge the Gap, the new PAGs take effect immediately but can be amended – and EPA is taking comments. The National Council on Radiation Protection's plans for implementing the new PAGs 'would allow the public to be exposed to extraordinarily higher levels of radiation than previously permitted' during reactor accident emergencies. The new PAGs also allow extremely high contamination of food. 'In essence,' Hirsch reports, the PAGs say 'nuclear power accidents could be so widespread and produce such immense radiation levels that the government would abandon clean-up obligations,' forcing people to absorb and live with far more cancers.

Thoughts on the future

Independent scientists say radiation exposure standards should be getting stiffer, not more lax. The Institute for Energy and Environmental Research, in its monumental study *Nuclear Wasteland*, concludes that with 'chronic low-dose exposure, there is evidence for an increased risk of cancer...' [133] The most important radiation experiments tend to repeat the finding that extremely small doses harm human health and reproductive cells far more seriously than previously estimated. For example:

- In 1974, pioneering epidemiologist Samuel Milham found that among nuclear weapons production workers at the Hanford Reservation in Washington State cancer deaths were about 25 percent higher than for men the same age in other industries. [134]

- Since 1977, scientists have tripled their estimate of the damage caused by a given dose of radiation.[135] Some cellular studies hint that chronic exposure to low doses may pose an even greater cancer risk, proportionally, than single exposures to high doses.[136]

- In 1989, the US National Research Council found that the cancer risk from low level radiation doses was four times higher than was previously estimated.[137]

- In 1990, the International Commission of Radiological Protection, which sets radiation exposure standards for nuclear industry workers, urged drastic cuts in allowable doses. The current limit of five rem per year (5,000 millirem) should be cut to two rem per year, the ICRP said.[138] This 33 year old recommendation has not been adopted. *The Bulletin of the Atomic Scientists* reported in 2012 that regulations are 'decades out of date'. [139]

- In 1992, two independent research teams at Harvard and Oxford simultaneously found that cell damage from very low radiation exposures may not appear until many cell divisions after exposure. The findings suggest a ballooning of cancer cases could appear in the coming years, and be made worse if exposure limits are not drastically reduced.[140]

- In 2003, the European Committee on Radiation Risk concluded that for low dose exposures the health effects relative to radiation dose are proportionately higher at low doses.[141]

- Studies published separately in 2002, 2007 and 2008 indicate that allowable radiation exposures could be the cause of up to twice as much childhood leukaemia among kids living near operating nuclear reactors compared to children elsewhere and could also be the cause of elevated childhood mortality rates near reactors.[142]

Stricter radiation protection rules are obviously necessary to safeguard nuclear workers, the public and the most vulnerable: women, infants and children. Billions of dollars are at stake because tougher limits increase the cost of running uranium mines, fuel fabrication systems and reactors, and of containerising wastes, cleaning up after disasters and monitoring contaminated foods over extremely long time frames. Better regulations also threaten federal plans for radioactive scrap metal recycling, 'by-product utilization,' the licensing of new reactors and of course the building of new nuclear weapons. In 2002, DOE official Donald Alexander said, 'If our clean-up is required to go the... low levels that we're currently being driven to, it could cost the US a trillion dollars or more'.[143]

The industry's partners in the US Congress have chosen the opposite course and decided to experiment with dramatically higher exposures. The question is whether we're going to stand for it.

References and Select Bibliography

Bertell, Rosalie, *No Immediate Danger: Prognosis for a Radioactive Earth*, The Women's Press, London, 1985

Busby, Chris, Ed., *European Committee on Radiation Risk, 2003 Recommendations: Health Effects of Ionizing Radiation Exposure at Low Doses for Radiation Protection Purposes*, Brussels, Green Audit, 2003

Caldicott, Helen, *The New Nuclear Danger*, The New Press, New York, 2002

Caldicott, Helen, *Nuclear Madness*, Revised Edition, Norton & Co., New York, 1994

Caufield, Catherine, *Multiple Exposures: Chronicles of the Radiation Age*, Harper & Row, New York, 1989

Cooke, Stephanie, *In Mortal Hands: A Cautionary History of the Nuclear Age*, Bloomsbury, 2009

Coyle, Dana, et al, *Deadly Defense: Military Radioactive Landfills*, Radioactive Waste Campaign, New York, 1988

Del Tredici, Robert, *At Work in the Fields of the Bomb*, Harper and Row, New York, 1987

DU Education Project, Ed., *Metal of Dishonor: Depleted Uranium*, New York, 1997

US Dept. of Energy, *United States Nuclear Tests, July 1945 through September 1992*, by the Nevada Operations Office, DOE/NV-209-REV15, December 2000

Gladstone, Samuel and Dolan, Philip, *The Effects of Nuclear Weapons*, 3d Ed., US Dept. of Defense and Dept. of Energy, 1977

Greene, Gayle, *The Woman Who Knew Too Much: Alice Stewart and the Secrets of Radiation*, Univ. of Michigan Press, Ann Arbor, 1999

Gut, Anne & Vitale, Bruno, *Depleted Uranium: Deadly, Dangerous and Indiscriminate*, Spokesman, Nottingham UK, 2003

International Physicians for the Prevention of Nuclear War & Institute for Energy and Environmental Research, *Plutonium: Deadly Gold of the Nuclear Age*, International Physicians Press, Cambridge, Mass., 1992

IPPNW & Institute for Energy and Environmental Research, *Radioactive Heaven and Earth: The health and environmental effects of nuclear weapons testing in, on, and above the earth*, Apex press, 1991

Iversen, Kristen, *Full Body Burden*, Crown, New York, 2012

Kelly, Petra, *Fighting for Hope*, South End Press, Boston, 1983

Makhijani, Arjun, Hu, Howard, and Yih, Katherine, Editors, *Nuclear Wastelands: A Global Guide to Nuclear Weapons Production and Its Health and Environmental Effects*, MIT Press, Cambridge, 1995

Mangano, Joe, *Mad Science: The Nuclear Power Experiment*, OR Books, New York, 2012

McDonald, Avril, et al, editors, *Depleted Uranium Weapons & International Law: A Precautionary Approach*, TMC Asser Press, 2008

Moran, Barbara, *The Day We Lost the H-Bomb*, Ballantine Books, 2009

Moreno, Jonathan, *Undue Risk: Secret State Experiments on Humans*, W.H. Freeman & Company, 1999

Nader, Ralph & Abbotts, John, *The Menace of Atomic Energy*, Norton, 1979

National Research Council, *Review of the Toxicologic & Radiologic Risks to Military Personnel from Exposures to Depleted Uranium During & After Combat*, National Academies Press, 2008

Patterson, Walter, *Nuclear Power*, Penguin Books, 1976

Presidential Advisory Committee on Human Radiation Experiments, *The Human Radiation Experiments: Final Report*, Oxford University Press, 1996

Prins, Gwyn & Stamp, Robbie, *Top Guns & Toxic Whales: The Environment & Global Security*, Earthscan Publications, 1991

Thomas, William, *Scorched Earth: The Military's Assault on the Environment*, New Society Publishers, Philadelphia, 1995

Wasserman, Harvey & Solomon, Norman, *Killing Our Own: The Disaster of America's Experience with Atomic Radiation*, Dell Publishing, New York, 1982

Welsome, Eileen, *The Plutonium Files: America's Secret Medical Experiments in the Cold War*, Dell Publishing, New York, 1999

Whiteside, Thomas, *Defoliation*, Ballantine/Friends of the Earth, New York, 1970

Zimmerman, Paul, *A Primer in the Art of Deception: The Cult of Nuclearists, Uranium Weapons and Fraudulent Science*, self-published, Lyndonville, New York, 2009

Notes

1   Danielle Gordon, 'No Harm, No Foul,' *Bulletin of the Atomic Scientists*, January 1996, p. 39.

2   Petra Kelly, *Fighting for Hope*, (Boston: South End Press, 1983), p. 87.

3   *William Thomas, Scorched Earth: The Military's Assault on the Environment*, (Philadelphia: New Society Publishers, 1995), p. 5, citing Seth Shulman, 'Toxic Travels,' *Nuclear Times*, Autumn 1990.

4   Michael G. Renner, World Watch, May/June 1991; Center for Defense Information, 'Defending the Environment? The Record of the US Military,' Vol. 18, No. 6 in *Defense Monitor series*, Oct. 24, 1989; PBS Frontline, 'Poison and the Pentagon'; Mary Chandler, 'Frontline' takes aim at Pentagon toxic waste,' *Rocky Mountain News*, 5 April 1988.

5   Sunaura Taylor and Astra Taylor, 'Military Waste In Our Drinking Water,' *AlterNet*, 4 August 2006: [http://www.alternet.org/environmental/ 39723?page=entire#wp-comments].

6   Kelly, *Fighting for Hope*, p. 88.

7   Helen Caldicott, *Nuclear Madness*, (New York: W. W. Norton, 1994, Rev. Ed), p. 159 (citing John Cashman, 'Report Lists 45,000 Potential Radioactive Sites,' *New York Times*, 9 April 1992).

8   New York Times Service, 'Radioactive waste danger won't relent,' *Wisconsin State Journal*, 17 April 1988.

9   New York Times News Service, 'Radioactive waste danger won't relent,' *Wisconsin State Journal*, 17 April 1988.

10   Robert Alvarez, 'DU at Home,' *The Nation*, 9 April 2001, p. 24; 'Cleanup of nuclear waste to cost at least $230 billion,' Minneapolis *Star-Tribune*, 4 April 1995, p. 7A.

11   Matthew Wald, 'US Estimate of Spewed Plutonium Is Raised: Tenfold,' *New York Times*, 21 October 2000.

12   Ian Urbina, 'Think Those Chemicals Have Been Tested?' *New York Times*, 14 April 2013, p. SR12; Nicholas Kristof, ' New Alarm Bells About Chemicals and Cancer,' *New York Times*, 15 May 2010.

13   Paul Zimmerman, *A Primer in the Art of Deception: The Cult of Nuclearists, Uranium Weapons and Fraudulent Science*, self-published, (New York: Lyndonville, 2009), p. 192.

14   Institute for Energy and Environmental Research, press release, 28 February 2002.

15 Eduardo Goncalves, 'The secret nuclear war,' *The Ecologist*, Vol. 31, No. 3, April 2001, pp. 28–33.
16 Arjun Makhijani, et al (eds.), *Nuclear Wastelands: A Global Guide to Nuclear Weapons Production and Its Health and Environmental Effects*, (Cambridge: MIT Press, 1995), pp. 1, 4, 6.
17 John Bull, 'Army wants to know where all chemical weapons were dumped,' 11 December and 'Veteran recounts dumping toxins off us shore,' *Newport News Daily Press*, 27 November 2005.
18 Stuart Diamond, 'Navy considering plan to sink obsolete nuclear subs in Ocean,' Minneapolis *Star-Tribune*, 16 May 1983; 'Congress Bans Radioactive Dumping By Navy,' *St Louis Post-Dispatch*, 29 December 1982.
19 'Vast Pile of Cartridges Dumped Into Lake Here,' Duluth *News-Tribune*, 28 September 1945.
20 Caldicott, *Nuclear Madness*, p. 90.
21 Makhijani, et al, *Nuclear Wastelands*, p. 226.
22 Robert Del Tredici, *At Work in the Fields of the Bomb*, Harper and Row, New York, 1987, p. 183.
23 Makhijani, et al *Nuclear Wastelands*, 1995, p. 583.
24 Thomas Whiteside, *Defoliation*, Ballantine/Friends of the Earth, 1970, pp. 107–108.
25 Ibid. p. 85.
26 Sunaura Taylor and Astra Taylor, 'Military Waste In Our Drinking Water,' AlterNet, 4 August 2006.
27 us Environmental Protection Agency, 'A Fact Sheet on the Health Effects from Ionizing Radiation,' EPA 402-F-98-010, May 1998.
28 Nukewatch Fact Sheet, 'No Dose Too Low: Every Radiation Exposure Can Cause Cancer,' 2006.
29 us Environmental Protection Agency, 'A Fact Sheet on the Health Effects from Ionizing Radiation, EPA 402-F-98-010, May 1998.
30 Warren Leary, 'Radiation Estimate in us Almost Doubled in Report,' *New York Times*, 20 November 1987.
31 Michael D. Lemonick, 'Environment: The Chernobyl Cover-up,' *Time* magazine, 13 November 1989, p. 73 and Kennedy Maize, senior energy analyst, Union of Concerned Scientists, in *Not Man Apart*, Friends of the Earth, March 1987; Casey Bukro, 'Fallout from '60s A-tests worse than Chernobyl,' *Chicago Tribune*, 22 June 1986.
32 Radiological Society of North America, 'National Council on Radiation Protection and Measurements Report Shows Substantial Medical Exposure Increase,' *Radiology*: [http://radiology.rsna.org/content/253/2/293.full]
33 *The Bend Bulletin*, 29 October 2009: [http://www.bendbulletin.com/apps/pbcs.dll/article?AID=/20091029/NEWS0107/910290309/-1/RSS-NEWS

MAP]; 'Report Links Increased Cancer Risk to CT Scans,' New York Times, AP, 29 November 2007.

34 USA Today, 27 April 2010: [http://www.usatoday.com/news/health/2010-04-28-chestct28_ST_N.htm].

35 NBC News, '15,000 will die from CT scans done in 1 year,' 14 December 2009, [http://www.msnbc.msn.com/id/34420356/ns/health-cancer/#.Tufgm7KmTBE].

36 Denise Grady, 'Panel Finds Few Clear Environmental Links to Breast Cancer', The New York Times, 8 December 2011, p. A3.

37 'Radiation Test Involved At Least 23,000,' Seattle Times, 22 October 1994, p. A1, cited in Glenn Alcalay, 'Damage Control on Human Radiation Experiments,' Covert Action, Spring 1995, p. 46; and ' Secret Radioactive Experiments to Bring Compensation by US,' New York Times, 20 November 1996.

38 Subcommittee on Energy Conservation and Power, Committee on Energy and Commerce, US House of Representatives, 'American Nuclear Guinea Pigs: Three Decades of Radiation Experiments on US Citizens,' US Gov't Printing Office, November 1986, 65-019-O.

39 Eileen Welsome, The Plutonium Files: America's Secret Medical Experiments in the Cold War, (New York: Delta Books, 1999), dust jacket.

40 'Radiation tests kept deliberately secret,' Washington Post, 16 December 1993.

41 Gayle Green, The Woman Who Knew Too Much, University of Michigan Press, Ann Arbor, 1999, pp. 83–85.

42 Ibid., p. 9.

43 'Radiation tests kept deliberately secret,' Washington Post, 16 December 1994; Geoffrey Sea, 'The Radiation Story No One Would Touch,' Project Censored, March/April 1994.

44 Ibid. note 39, p. 2; Gina Kolata, New York Times service, 'Radiation's Effects on human subjects up for speculation,' St Paul Pioneer, 4 January 1994.

45 'Radioactive Oatmeal Suit Settled for $1.85 Million,' Washington Post, 1 January 1988.

46 '48 more human radiation experiments revealed,' Minneapolis Star-Tribune, 28 June 1994; and Milwaukee Journal, 29 June 1994.

47 Keith Schneider, '1950 Note Warns About Radiation Test,' New York Times, 28 December 1993.

48 Russell Watson, et al, 'America's Nuclear Secrets,' Newsweek, 27 December 1993, pp. 14–15.

49 Joseph Mangano, Mad Science: The Nuclear Power Experiment, OR Books, New York, 2012, p. 36.

50 'Nasal radium treatments of '50s linked to cancer,' *Milwaukee Journal*, 31 August 1994.
51 Danielle Gordon, 'No Harm, No Foul,' *Bulletin of the Atomic Scientists*, January/February 1996, p. 35.
52 'Reactor core is melted in experiment' Washington Post service, *Milwaukee Journal*, 10 July 1985.
53 'Tests spewed radiation, paper reports,' AP, *Milwaukee Journal*, 11 October 1994.
54 'Secret US experiments in '40s and '50s included dropping radiation from sky,' *St Paul Pioneer Press*, 16 December 1993.
55 Katherine Rizzo, Associated Press, 'A bombshell: US spread radiation,' Duluth *News Tribune*, 16 December 1993.
56 Danielle Gordon, 'No Harm, No Foul,' *Bulletin of the Atomic Scientists*, January/February 1996, p. 34.
57 National Academy of Sciences, 'Health Risks from Exposure to Low Levels of Ionizing Radiation: BEIR-VII, Phase 2,' Committee to Assess Health Risks from Exposure to Low Levels of Ionizing Radiation, National Research Council, 29 June 2005.
58 Rosalie Bertell, *No Immediate Danger: Prognosis for a Radioactive Earth*, (London: The Women's Press, 1985), p. 173.
59 Del Tredici, *At Work in the Fields of the Bomb*, p. 182.
60 Green, *The Woman Who Knew Too Much*, p. 143; Stephanie Cooke, *In Mortal Hands: A Cautionary History of the Nuclear Age*, Bloomsbury, 2009, p. 169; Caldicott, *Nuclear Madness*, p. 39–40; Bertell, *No Immediate Danger*, pp. 45, 62, 172.
61 Greene, *The Woman Who Knew Too Much*, p. 143; Bertell, *No Immediate Danger*, p. 51–52.
62 Health Physics Society, 'Radiation Basics,' August 2011, [http://www.hps.org/publicinformation/ate/faqs/radiation.html]; and Diane D'Arrigo, 'Radiation Measurements,' Nuclear Information and Resource Service, [http://www.nirs.org/radiation/radiationhome.htm].
63 (NIRS, 'Atomic Radiation is More Harmful to Women,' briefing paper, 22 October 2011, p. 4; [http://www.nirs.org/radiation/radhealth/radiation-women.pdf].
64 'Vets had more radiation exposure than Pentagon admits, study says,' Associated Press, *St Paul Pioneer Press and Dispatch*, 5 December 1985; and 'Panel Told of Exposure to Test Danger,' Associated Press, *Tulsa World*, 24 January 1995.
65 Catherine Caufield, *Multiple Exposures: Chronicles of the Radiation Age*, (New York: Harper & Row, 1989), p. 107; Greg Gordon in 'Wellstone: Compensate atomic vets,' Minneapolis *Star-Tribune*, 17 March 1995;

Associated Press, 'Panel Told of Exposure to Test Danger,' Tulsa World, 24 January 1995.

66 'Over 200,000,' according to The Human Radiation Experiments, Final Report of the President's Advisory Committee, p. 284; Dr. Benjamin Spock, in his introduction to Killing Our Own, by Wasserman and Solomon, p. x, says 300,000; Caufield says 'between 250,000 and 500,000' in Multiple Exposures, p. 107; Greg Gordon says '400,000' in 'Wellstone: Compensate atomic vets,' Minneapolis Star-Tribune, 17 March 1995; and according to the Associated Press, 200,000 were used in bomb tests and 200,000 in the occupation of Hiroshima and Nagasaki, in 'Panel Told of Exposure to Test Danger,' Tulsa World, 24 January 1995.

67 Michael Doyle, 'Court ruling deals a blow to nation's "atomic veterans",' McClatchy Newspapers, 27 August 2006.

68 Philip Hilts, 'Fallout Risk Near Atom Tests Was Known, Documents Show,' New York Times, 15 March 1995, p. A13; and Pat Ortmeyer, 'Let Them Drink Milk,' IEER, November 1997, pp. 3 and 11.

69 Philip Hilts, 'Fallout Risk Near Atom Tests Was Known, Documents Show,' New York Times, 15 March 1995.

70 National Cancer Institute, 'Estimated Exposures and Thyroid Doses Received by the American People from Iodine-131 in Fallout Following Nevada Atmospheric Nuclear Bomb Tests,' October 1997, Exec. Sum., p. ES.1.

71 Samuel Gladstone and Philip Dolan, The Effects of Nuclear Weapons, 3d Ed., us Dept. of Defense and Dept. of Energy, 1977, Sec. 1.60–1.66.

72 National Cancer Institute, 'Estimated Exposures and Thyroid Doses Received by the American People from Iodine-131 in Fallout Following Nevada Atmospheric Nuclear Bomb Tests,' October 1997, Executive Summary, p. ES. 2.

73 National Cancer Institute, ' Estimated Exposures and Thyroid Doses Received by the American People from Iodine-131 in Fallout Following Nevada Atmospheric Nuclear Bomb Tests,' October 1997.

74 IEER, Science for Democratic Action, November 1997, Vol. 6, No. 2, p. 3.

75 National Cancer Institute, Office of Cancer Communication, 'Backgrounder,' 1 August 1997, p. 1.

76 National Cancer Institute [http://www.cancer.gov/cancertopics/types/thyroid].

77 National Cancer Institute press release, Office of Cancer Communications, 'NCI Releases Results of Nationwide Study of Radioactive Fallout from Nuclear Tests,' 1 August 1997.

78 Arjun Makhajani, 'Radioactive Milk in America,' IEER, 17 February 2003 [http://ieer.org/resource/commentary/radioactive-milk-in-america/].

79 Matthew Wald, 'US Atomic Tests in '50s Exposed Millions to Risk, Study Says,' *New York Times*, 29 July 1997.

80 Matthew Wald, 'US Warned Film Plants, Not Public, About Nuclear Fallout,' *New York Times*, 30 September 1997, p. A16.

81 *New York Times*, 10 March 1999; John D. Marks, *The Search for the 'Manchurian Candidate,'* Times Books, 1979.

82 Dan Fahey, 'Collateral Damage,' in *Metal of Dishonor: Depleted Uranium*, 2nd Ed., 1997, p. 40, n. 3.

83 'Uranium Enrichment Plant is Proposed for New Mexico,' *New York Times*, 10 February 2005; Arjun Makhijani, IEER press release, 'New Research Indicates Health Risks from Uranium May Be More Varied Than Reflected in Current Federal Policy,' 23 February 2005.

84 McDonald, et al, *Depleted Uranium Weapons & International Law*, p. 4–5; Arjun Makhijani, *Science for Democratic Action*, 2 February 2003, p. 4.

85 Scott Peterson, 'The Trail of a Bullet: New evidence emerges of radioactive contamination in Kosovo,' *Christian Science Monitor*, 5 October 1999; and William Arkin, 'The desert glows – with propaganda,' *Bulletin of Atomic the Scientists*, May 1993, p. 12: [http://books.google.com/books?id= qQ w AAAAAMBAJ&printsec=frontcover&source=gbs_ge_summary_r& cad=o#v=onepage&q&f=false].

86 Anne Gut and Bruno Vitale, *Depleted Uranium: Deadly, Dangerous and Indiscriminate*, Spokesman, Nottingham UK, 2003, p. 93.

87 Bill Mesler, 'Pentagon Poison: The Great Radioactive Ammo Cover-up,' *The Nation*, 26 May 1997, pp. 17–18.

88 William Arkin, 'The Desert Glows with Propaganda,' *Bulletin of Atomic the Scientists*, May 1993, p. 12.

89 Gut & Vitale, *Depleted Uranium*, p. 50.

90 Gut & Vitale, *Depleted Uranium*, pp. 12 and 87.

91 National Research Council, 'Review of the Toxicologic & Radiologic Risks to Military Personnel from Exposures to Depleted Uranium During & After Combat,' (National Academies Press, 2008), p. 5.

92 Gut & Vitale, *Depleted Uranium*, pp. 93 and 97; Kathleen Sullivan, 'NATO confirms US jets fired radioactive bullets, *San Francisco Examiner*, 22 March 2000; Peter Capella, 'UN raises alarm on toxic risk in Kosovo,' *Guardian Weekly*, 30 March – 5 April 2000, p. 5.

93 Gut & Vitale, *Depleted Uranium*, pp. 103–106.

94 Scott Peterson, 'The Trail of a Bullet: New evidence emerges of radioactive contamination in Kosovo,' Christian Science Monitor, 5 October 1999.

95 McDonald, et al, *Depleted Uranium Weapons & International* Law, pp. 4 and 10–11; Gut and Vitale, *Depleted Uranium*, pp. 46–48; Douglas Hamilton, 'Plutonium Row Set to Rock Bush Debut with Europe,' Reuters,

21 January 2001; AP, 'Pentagon admits plutonium exposure,' *The Capital Times* (Madison, Wis.) 3 February 2001; David Michaels, Assistant Sec. for Environment, Safety and Health, US Department of Energy, open letter to Tara Thornton, *The Military Toxics Project*, 20 January 2000.

96 Paul Zimmerman, *A Primer in the Art of Deception*, p. 396, citing US Dept. of Energy study 'A Preliminary Review of the Flow and Characteristics of Recycled Uranium Throughout the DOE Complex: 1952–1999'.

97 *New York Times*, 17–18 January 2001; Douglas Hamilton, 'Plutonium Row Set to Rock Bush Debut with Europe,' Reuters, 21 January 2001.

98 Robert Alvarez, 'DU at Home,' *The Nation*, 9 April 2001, p. 24.

99 Associated Press, 'Pentagon admits plutonium exposure: NATO shells used radioactive metals,' *Capitol Times* (Madison, WI) 3 February 2001; Marlise Simons, 'Doctor's Gulf War Studies Link Cancer to Depleted Uranium,' *New York Times*, 29 January 2001.

100 *New York Times*, 18 January 2001.

101 Steve Fetter and Frank von Hippel, 'After the Dust Settles,' *Bulletin of the Atomic Scientists*, November 1999, p. 43

102 Hu, Makhijani and Yih, *Plutonium*, p. 14.

103 Ralph Nader and John Abbotts, *The Menace of Atomic Energy*, p. 149.

104 Robert Burns, AP, 'During Cold War, US studied radiological weapons to kill leaders,' *Milwaukee Journal Sentinel*, 14 October 2007.

105 Arjun Makhijani, *Science for Democratic Action*, IEER, 2 February 2003, p. 4.

106 Robert Parsons, 'The Balkan DU Cover-Up,' *The Nation*, 9 April 2001, p. 22.

107 Kathleen Sullivan, 'Radioactive ammo used "throughout Kosovo",' *San Francisco Examiner*/Scripps Howard News Service, *Augusta Chronicle*, 25 March 2000.

108 Scott Peterson, 'The Trail of a Bullet: New evidence emerges of radioactive contamination in Kosovo,' *Christian Science Monitor*, 5 October 1999.

109 Marlise Simons, 'On a Balkan War's Last Day, Poison From the Sky,' *New York Times*, 2 September 2002.

110 Food and Water, Inc., 'Food Irradiation: An Activist Primer,' 2d ed., 2000, pp. 9–10.

111 Dana Coyle, et al, Deadly Defense: Military Radioactive Landfills, Radio-active Waste Campaign, New York, p. 22.

112 Teresa Barker, 'Safety debate heats up as irradiated food heads to stores,' *Chicago Sun Times*, 24 September 1986.

113 Food and Water, Inc., 'Food Irradiation: An Activist Primer,' 2d ed., 2000, p. 3.

114 Susan Meeker-Lowry and Jennifer Ferrara, 'Meat Monopolies: Dirty Meat and the False Promises of Irradiation,' 2d Ed., Food & Water, Inc., 1998, p. 24.

115 'Cancer Researcher Speaks Out Against Irradiation,' *Food & Water Journal*, fall 2000, p. 39.

116 Public Citizen, 'A Citizen's Guide to Fighting Food Irradiation, July 2000, p. 3.

117 *Grand Forks Herald*, 28 April 1986.

118 Susan Meeker-Lowry & Jennifer Ferrara, 'Meat Monopolies: Dirty Meat and the False Promises of Irradiation,' 2d Ed., Food & Water, Inc., 1998, p. 27.

119 Michael Colby 'Food Irradiation's Nuclear Nightmares,' *Food & Water Journal*, Spring 1998, pp. 25–26.

120 Ibid. pp. 26–27; and Susan Meeker-Lowry and Jennifer Ferrara, 'Meat Monopolies: Dirty Meat and the False Promises of Irradiation,' 2d Ed., Food & Water, Inc., 1998, p. 25.

121 Public Citizen, Critical Mass Energy and Environment Programme, 'The Dangers of Irradiation Facilities,' undated fact sheet, p. 1.

122 *Food & Water Journal*, Spring 1998, p. 26.

123 Nuclear Information & Resource Service, 'Radioactive Zippers & Silverware? Tell DOE No Way,' 21 December 2012: [http://org2.democracyinaction.org/o/5502/t/o/blastContent.jsp?email_blast_KEY=1231167].

124 John LaForge, 'Radioactive Cesium Spill Cooks Europe,' *Earth Island Journal*, Winter/Spring 1999, p. 26.

125 Write to: Jane Summerson, DOE NNSA, PO Box 5400, Bldg. 401K, AFB East, Albuquerque, New Mexico 87185 <scrap_PEAcomments@hq.doe.gov>

126 Global Response (Boulder, Colo.), 'Stop Using Plutonium in Space,' G.R. No. 3, 1997.

127 NASA, Final Environmental Impact Statement for the Cassini Mission, June 1995.

128 'Lab contamination rises: Alamos cites NASA project,' *Denver Post*, 30 July 1996.

129 Ibid.

130 Mike Wall, 'US Makes First Plutonium in 25 Years, for Spacecraft,' *Scientific American*, 19 March 2013.

131 Nukewatch Special Report, 'Cassini: Interplanetary Trajectory,' 1997, p. 2.

132 LeRoy Moore, 'Lowering the Bar,' *Bulletin of the Atomic Scientists*, May/June 2002, p. 36.

133 Makhijani, Arjun, et al, Editors, *Nuclear Wastelands: A Global Guide to Nuclear Weapons Production and Its Health and Environmental Effects*, MIT Press, 1995, p. 579.

134 Gayle Greene, *The Woman Who Knew Too Much*, University of Michigan Press, Ann Arbor, 1999, p. 117.

135 Matthew Wald, 'International Panel Urges Cut In Allowable Radiation Dose,' *New York Times*, 23 June 1990.

136 *Science*, 9 July 1999, p. 177.

137 Philip Hilts, 'Higher Cancer Risk Found in Low-Level Radiation,' Hi*New York Times*, 20 December 1989.

138 Matthew Wald, 'International Panel Urges Cut In Allowable Radiation Dose,' *New York Times*, 23 June 1990.

139 Jan Beyea, 'The scientific jigsaw puzzle: Fitting the pieces of the low-level radiation debate,' *Bulletin of the Atomic Scientists*, 1 May 2012.

140 Warren Leary, 'British and US Researchers Find a New Form of Radiation Injury,' *New York Times*, 20 February 1992, p. A12.

141 European Committee on Radiation Risk, 'Health Effects of Ionising Radiation Exposure at Low Doses for Radiation Protection Purposes,' Brussels, 2003, p. 181.

142 Peter Baker, 'Meta-analysis of standardized incidence and mortality rates of childhood leukemia in proximity to nuclear facilities,' *European Journal of Cancer Care*, Vol. 16 Issue 4, July 2007, 335–363; Mangano, Gould, Sternglass, Sherman, Brown, McDonnell, 'Infant Death and Childhood Cancer Reductions afer Nuclear Plant Closing in the United States,' Archives of Environmental Health, Vol. 57, No. 1, January 2002; Spix, Schmiedel, Kaatsch, Schulze-Rath, Blettner, 'Case–control study on childhood cancer in the vicinity of nuclear power reactors in Germany 1980–2003,' *European Journal of Cancer*, January 2008, Vol. 44, Issue 2, pp. 275–284.

143 LeRoy Moore, 'Lowering the Bar,' *Bulletin of the Atomic Scientists*, May 2002, p. 36.

CHAPTER FOURTEEN

Of Sledgehammers and Nuts: Counter-Terrorism and Anti-Nuclear Protest

SIÂN JONES

Siân Jones has been engaged in anti-nuclear and anti-war activism for several decades, including as a legal observer. She has provided legal support for non-violent direct action at nuclear and military sites, and training for legal observers. She is a member of NetPol (the network for police monitoring), Women in Black and a former member of the Aldermaston Women's Peace Camp(aign).

> Domestic legislation designed to counter terrorism or 'extremism' should narrowly define these terms so as not to include forms of civil disobedience and protest; the pursuit of certain political, religious, or ideological ends; or attempts to exert influence on other sections of society, the government, or international opinion.[1]

WHEN A STATE IS in possession of nuclear weapons, the rights of its citizens are curtailed. Such states will generally adopt measures, in the name of national security, to protect those weapons from the threat of serious harm. This includes curtailing the right to protest at the military-industrial sites where nuclear weapons are manufactured, stored and deployed.

Since 2000, legislation introduced in the UK in the context of counter-terrorism and national security has, both intentionally and through over-broad drafting, restricted and criminalised protest, including anti-nuclear protest. Consequently, non-violent protest against nuclear weapons (and nuclear power installations) has been perceived through the lens of serious crime and terrorism, and anti-nuclear protesters may be considered 'domestic extremists'.

This essay examines legislative and other measures – including intelligence gathering – used to limit anti-nuclear protest over the last decade; notes that where such legislation has been imposed, it has been repeatedly challenged, including in the courts; and finally examines whether it has physically, psychologically or culturally reduced the landscape of anti-nuclear protest.

The context

The UK has been a nuclear weapons state since the 1950s, and was a founding signatory to the Nuclear Non-Proliferation Treaty in 1968. Under the 1958 Mutual Defence Agreement with the USA (renewed in 2004), the UK currently deploys a nuclear weapons system, based on the US W76 warhead design: the D5 missiles are leased from a US pool.

Warhead design, test, manufacturing and assembly facilities are located at the Atomic Weapons Establishments (AWE) Aldermaston and Burghfield in Berkshire, run as a joint venture by Lockheed Martin, Jacob's Engineering and Serco, on behalf of the UK government. Vanguard class submarines are based in Scotland at Her Majesty's Naval Base (HMNB) Clyde at Faslane, and warheads are stored at the Royal Navy Armaments Depot (RNAD) Coulport. The Ministry of Defence polices each site.

The right to protest vs. national security

The right to 'peaceful assembly' (the right to protest) is based in Articles 10 (Freedom of Expression) and 11 (Freedom of Assembly and Association) of the European Convention on Human Rights and Fundamental Freedoms (ECHR). The implementation of these rights is supported by the jurisprudence of the European Court of Human Rights (ECtHR).[2] In England and Wales, the ECHR is given effect in domestic law by the Human Rights Act (HRA); in Scotland, through the Scotland Act.[3]

Articles 10 and 11 HRA state that no restriction shall be placed on those rights except 'in the interests of national security or public safety, for the prevention of disorder or crime'.[4] In most public order policing contexts, the notion of security is almost always associated with the potential for protest to descend/ascend into 'disorder'. Yet anti-nuclear protest in the UK is often explicitly and almost invariably non-violent, and seldom likely to amount to anything resembling disorder.[5]

Thus in the context of protest against nuclear weapons, security means national security. Aldermaston Women's Peace Camp (AWPC), in a submission to a parliamentary Human Rights Committee observed:

'Nothing can be weighed against security concerns (because they are subjective), and because the police and government see protest itself as a security concern'.[6] So, while Cold War anti-nuclear protesters were viewed as subversives and spies,[7] over the past decade, measures taken against anti-nuclear protest have been in the context of anti-terrorism, and 'domestic extremism'.

The measures described below were introduced, despite legislation already providing the police with a myriad of public order powers to curtail the right to protest. The police are empowered to limit protesters' right to freedom of movement through the imposition of conditions on processions or assemblies, including by restricting routes or specifying locations for protest, and often imposing these conditions through arbitrary detention ('kettling') of protesters.[8] Stop and search powers also prevent or delay access to a protest location.[9]

Powers of detention, including for breach of the peace, enable police to remove protesters, even before an action takes place, or any violence is offered.[10] In practice this can result in arbitrary arrests, where there is no intention of taking detainees before a court, but merely releasing them only after the action is over.[11]

Definitions of Terrorism

The purpose qualifying such an action or threat as terrorist, i.e. advancing a 'political, religious or ideological cause', is also very wide and open to subjective interpretation. The definition is vaguely worded and could be extended to include supporters of, for example, animal liberation or anti-nuclear campaigns and others. The lack of a clear definition gives cause for concern because the decision to bring a prosecution for such offences could be seen to be political.[12]

The definition of terrorism in the Terrorism Act 2000 was sufficiently widely drawn to include anti-nuclear protest. Yet, although many activists feared that their protest would be rapidly curtailed, the Terrorism Act 2000 has been used infrequently against anti-nuclear protesters. However, in defining terrorism as serious damage to property for the purpose of influencing the government or for a 'political, religious or ideological cause,'[13] the Terrorism Act expanded the meaning of 'terror'.

Many explicitly non-violent anti-nuclear disarmament actions taken prior to 2000 would have fallen clearly under this definition, including the 'Maytime' action against a Trident-related research barge and the destruction of testing equipment on a Trident submarine by Trident Ploughshares activists.[14]

The Terrorism Act 2000 could in theory have restricted the monitoring of activities at nuclear bases or tracking the movements of nuclear convoys, which carry warheads between the AWES and Coulport. S. 58 (a) Terrorism Act introduced the offence of collecting or possessing ' information of a kind likely to be useful to a person committing or preparing an act of terrorism'.[15] While s.58 has not been used in an anti-nuclear context, an anti-war activist was arrested under s.58 in 2003 at a peace camp outside USAF Welford, in Berkshire, for possessing a map of the bomb-store, from where weapons convoys delivered ordnance to US aircraft operating out of Fairford during 'Operation Iraqi Freedom'.[16]

Section 44 of the Act authorised police to stop and search 'for articles of a kind which could be used in connection with terrorism' (s.45.1 [a]) without the necessity of reasonable suspicion (s.45.1 [b]). While these powers were most often used in discriminatory and disproportionate searches of black and Asian people, an estimated 2,132 searches under s.44 were conducted at USAF Fairford between March and April 2003 in an attempt to shut down protest against the bombing of Iraq[17] S.44 was also used extensively against protesters around the 2003 DSEI Arms Fair.[18]

Schedule 7 of the Terrorism Act 2000[19] has been widely criticised as a draconian stop and search power, based on ethnic profiling and primarily targeting migrant communities. Schedule 7 has also been used to target political activists, including anti-nuclear protesters, and journalists.[20] In 2008, an anti-nuclear peace activist was stopped at the UK border when returning from holiday in Germany just weeks before a major anti-NATO demonstration. He was stopped again in 2011, returning from an anti-NATO meeting in Dublin. He was detained on both occasions, for 45 minutes and 20 minutes respectively, and questioned on anti-nuclear and anti-militarist campaigns in which he was involved.[21]

While anti-nuclear protesters certainly seek to influence the government, and some commit serious criminal damage in attempting to disarm weapons systems or associated infrastructure, is this 'terrorism'? Or is the Terrorism Act 2000 an example of what the human rights NGO Peacerights has characterised as 'overbroad legislation'? [22]

... protesters are becoming the 'unforeseen' targets of legislation ostensibly enacted with the aim of dealing with a narrow problem such as hunt saboteurs or stalking [or 'terrorism'], which in practice are extended far beyond their originally stated intended targets. This can happen because legislation of this kind tends to be characterised by provisions which are broadly worded, ambiguous and open to a multitude of interpretations.[23]

Legislation at nuclear sites

In 2005 the Serious Organised Crime and Police Act (SOCPA) introduced the offence of criminal trespass on designated sites, including royal palaces, government buildings and military sites.[24] Under the widely criticized s.132-s.138 SOCPA 'unauthorised protests' in a wide area around the Houses of Parliament were criminalised. In addition, under powers granted in s.128 (3)(c), to the Secretary of State to 'designate [the] site in the interests of national security', trespass was criminalised at several Ministry of Defence (MOD) sites, including Faslane and Coulport.

According to Vernon Coaker, former Secretary of State in the Home Office, the legislation was introduced after the House of Commons Defence Select Committee noted the 'absence of effective legal sanctions against persistent protesters', following their inquiry into the MOD security response to the 'terrorist' attacks of 11 September 2001:

> After careful consideration it was decided to implement such an offence both as a deterrent to such intrusions and to provide the police with a specific power of arrest in such situations.[25]

The relevant 2002 Defence Select Committee minutes reveal that while the Ministry of Defence Police (MDP) were frustrated by their inability to prosecute trespassers at AWE Aldermaston under the Military Lands Byelaws, the then MDP Chief Constable, Lloyd Clarke, was concerned about the appropriateness of 'terrorist legislation':

> ... what you are asking is if they do not commit criminal damage, if they are not a terrorist threat what do we do with these individuals. I do not believe that MDP need any other legislation. I think it was certainly right we were not seeking anything under the terrorist legislation?

However, a member of the committee, Mr Howarth, countered:

> That is not the view of your men, they were very unhappy. It is absurd to have a situation where the only remedy is an injunction. If you then have

lots ∗∗∗[26] who have not done it before and they are caught in the middle of a facility and there is then no power to reprimand and prosecute those people then this is a licence to these people to come in and muck up the system. Secondly, of course, it makes it very difficult for your men to distinguish between these nuisances and the terrorists?[27]

Under s.12 of the Terrorism Act 2006, the provisions of s.128 were extended to Nuclear Licensed Sites (NLS) – including civil nuclear sites, nuclear power stations and 'defence sites', including AWE Aldermaston and Burghfield.[28]

The act introduced criminal trespass to 'Protected' areas of these sites, many of them previously covered by Military Lands Act byelaws. It became an offence to 'enter or be on... protected areas... as a trespasser'; the offence carried a maximum penalty of 51 weeks imprisonment and/or a £5,000 fine. Prosecution was to be authorised by the Attorney General, whose consent is required in cases related to national security.

While protesters were not defined as 'terrorists', the context in which the legislation was conceived, the enabling legislation and the extent of its provisions, clearly blurred the lines between terrorism and protest.[29] According to Vernon Coaker:

> Designation ensures that protests are conducted outside of the sites, thus reducing the risk to both protesters and police forces and preventing the activities of protesters being exploited by terrorists.[30]

Following the designation of sites under the Terrorism Act 2006, the MOD started to roll out a series of new byelaws, beginning at Aldermaston, covering 'controlled areas' inside and MOD land outside the perimeter fence. In April 2006, draft byelaws were quietly put out to consultation. Although the MOD claimed that the proposed byelaws were designed to facilitate protest, they included clauses prohibiting almost all forms of non-violent protest, including meetings, assemblies and processions, the distribution of leaflets and display of placards.

This attack on the right to peaceful protest was challenged by Aldermaston Women's Peace Camp(aign) (AWPC), who succeeded in removing those clauses from the byelaws.[31] However, further clauses remained, which prohibited camping and 'attaching anything to any surface' (which effectively prohibited hanging banners on a perimeter fence).

In June 2007, following introduction of the byelaws on 31 May,[32] ten AWPC women were arrested outside the perimeter fence for allegedly breaking two byelaws (camping and lighting a fire). Bail conditions prohibited the women from being within a five-mile radius of AWE Aldermaston, but on 9 August, the case was dropped.[33] In February 2009, after a judicial review brought by a member of AWPC, and following an appeal at the High Court, the prohibition on camping and attaching things to surfaces were both revoked.[34]

The SOCPA challenge

Between July 2003 and June 2004 the MDP and local constabularies arrested 147 individuals for breaching the security perimeter at 23 separate establishments. The resources expended dealing with this problem were significant, and reduced the ability of the security forces concerned to deter and remain responsive to terrorist threats.

> Since April 2005 when the MOD sites were designated, there have been very few incidents of criminal trespass, with only three prosecutions, two of which resulted in convictions. The resulting reduction in risk to both protestors and armed guards is considered to be a proportionate response to what was an escalating security problem.[35]

The act of entering a military base or nuclear establishment is perhaps one of the most symbolic acts in the lexicon of anti-nuclear and anti-militarist protest. It may, or may not, involve criminal damage but, irrespective of any other intent, it is a direct challenge to the power of the state, an act – however temporary – of non-violent occupation of land used for war. Breaking into nuclear establishments was pioneered in the 1950s by Spies for Peace: by the 1980s, as exemplified by women opposing US cruise missiles based at Greenham Common, it become not only routine, but a transformative and creative act. Bringing in a law that sought to prevent trespass was therefore bound, from its inception, to be challenged.

On 1 April 2006, the first day s.128 SOCPA came into force, Helen John and Sylvia Boyes walked into RAF/USAF Menwith Hill in North Yorkshire, with the explicit intention of challenging the law, and in particular its application to a US establishment. After several hearings, in which they continued to question the use of SOCPA, Helen and Sylvia were convicted in October 2007, but received only suspended sentences and £50 court costs.[36]

In September 2007, six Trident Ploughshares (TP) activists were arrested under SOCPA at Faslane in September 2007, three for climbing the fence and three others for cycling through the oil depot gate next to Faslane in another explicit challenge to the legislation. At Dumbarton Sheriff Court on 19 March 2008, after evidence was presented, SOCPA charges against one of the first trio were dropped. She was then prosecuted for breach of the peace, and acquitted. The two others were convicted for SOCPA, but only admonished.[37] SOCPA charges against the three others were dropped, and they were prosecuted for 'Breach of the Peace' at Helensburgh District Court in March 2008, and acquitted after the court found no case to answer. According to Janet Fenton, one of the cyclists, 'It seemed to me that the police were expecting that there would be unspecified but more serious consequences of our actions because it was SOCPA'.[38]

It rapidly became clear, in Scotland at least, that while the MDP would arrest under SOCPA, the courts were disinclined to prosecute. On 17 August 2009, Sylvia Boyes and four other TP activists were charged with entering a SOCPA area after they walked past security guards at the north gate at Faslane, reaching the perimeter of the high security area before they were stopped by MDP. SOCPA charges were dropped, and eventually only Sylvia was prosecuted and convicted under the byelaws. Sylvia Boyes noted: 'Neither Trident nor SOCPA were to be mentioned as they were not relevant to the events of that day in August'.

Similarly, two activists from Faslane Peace Camp arrested near the High Explosives Jetty at RNAD Coulport on 14 June 2012, were originally charged with SOCPA – but subsequently prosecuted under the byelaws.[39] On 7 July 2012, Brian Larkin and eight others were arrested under both SOCPA and the byelaws at Faslane. Four were held overnight for court, the others 'released on an undertaking': charges against all but Brian Larkin were dropped before they appeared in court the next day; his were dropped later.[40]

In England, at RAF/USAF Lakenheath, where US nuclear weapons were then located under NATO's nuclear sharing agreement, eight activists entered the site in October 2006 and locked themselves to the gates of the Special Munitions Store to prevent the deployment of cluster bombs, used in raids on Afghanistan. They were arrested under SOCPA, but on conviction in December 2008 the 'Lakenheath 8' received only a suspended sentence and were ordered to pay £250 court costs.[41]

At most sites, the 'Protected' area under s.128 SOCPA is contiguous with the external perimeter: at Aldermaston the 'Protected' area (the Nuclear Licensed Site) includes only the land within an inner fence line.

Outside the NLS, but within the external perimeter, there are playing fields, bars and a theatre to which there is public access.[42] These areas are subject to byelaws, discussed below.

Juliet McBride of AWPC was arrested under s.128 in March 2007 while sitting on top of the inner fence at Aldermaston. In her defence, she demonstrated that the MOD police had failed to correctly identify the boundary of the NLS, which was clearly shown on the map issued with the license by the regulating authority, as well as multiple signs attached to the inner fence.[43] In August 2008, the court agreed that s.128 SOCPA applied only to the NLS, and the case against her was dismissed.

A similar failure to correctly identify the boundary of an NLS led to the acquittal in October 2008 of eight activists arrested under s. 128 SOCPA the previous April at Rolls Royce Derby, which manufactures reactor cores for Trident submarines. The eight were instead charged with aggravated trespass, when it was established that the Derby police had failed to accurately identify the perimeter of the protected area. According to Emma Bateman:

> The police were adamant that the red line painted on the road was the SOCPA boundary. The police did not know the legislation. When it was clear we were going to win, the Crown Prosecution Service tried to suggest we were somehow guilty under SOCPA even though we were not charged with it. They were eventually acquitted on the basis that the offence of aggravated trespass does not apply to land which is part of the public highway.[44]

At Devonport in November 2010, blockaders were threatened with arrest under s.128 SOCPA, until a legal observer was able to show the senior officer present that the blockade was outside the SOCPA designated area.

Again at Aldermaston, on 15 February 2010, five Trident Ploughshares activists taking part in a blockade of the site were arrested under SOCPA, after walking a few paces through Boilerhouse Gate, and briefly entering the NLS. Three were later convicted, but given only a three month conditional discharge and minimal court costs by Judge Crabtree, who stated that he 'had no idea what possible public benefit there was' in bringing the prosecution.[45]

The cases described above provide an illustrative, though not exhaustive, summary of arrests of anti-nuclear activists under SOCPA. They reveal how few arrests have resulted in prosecutions under the act, as a result of the incorrect application of the law or misinterpretation of its provisions, and how the courts have found the charge to be inappropriate, incorrect, or inconsistent with the reported intent of the law – to address 'substantial trespass'.[46] Where there have been convictions, penalties imposed have been low.

In 2009, the Human Rights Joint Committee concluded:

> ... we do not have confidence that section 128 has been implemented in a manner compatible with Convention rights, or that appropriate safeguards are in place to secure compatibility. We recommend that section 128(3)(c) be amended to permit the Home Secretary to designate sites on the grounds of national security only where it is necessary to do so.[47]

In April 2012, s.132-8 SOCPA covering 'unauthorised' protests in the vicinity of parliament were repealed.[48] S.128 remains in force.

Nukewatch

Nukewatch is a citizen verification organisation, which monitors the movement of the UK's nuclear warhead convoys and other Special Nuclear Materials (SNM) convoys.[49]

Convoys travel along UK roads and motorways carrying warheads between the assembly and disassembly facilities at AWE Burghfield, where the warheads are periodically refurbished, and warhead storage facilities at RNAD Coulport in Scotland. The warheads are then loaded onto the UK's Vanguard class nuclear submarines, based at nearby Faslane. SNM convoys carry nuclear materials back and forth between Aldermaston and other sites associated with the UK and US nuclear weapons and submarine programme.

Despite the potential risks to other road users and communities through which the vehicles travel, MOD policy is neither to confirm nor deny nuclear convoy movements, including to emergency services, in the interests of 'national security'.[50]

Nukewatch has taken the pragmatic decision not to publicly announce the whereabouts of convoys while they are travelling, but only to report convoy movements after the journey is over.

Nukewatch says: 'We recognise there are risks in collecting information about warhead convoys – and that the MOD and police would rather we didn't. Our aims are to promote disarmament /and act responsibly. We're sceptical of government rhetoric about terrorism, but we're also aware that they could accuse us of "helping terrorists" if we make it public when the convoy is on the road.'

Domestic Extremists?

I am... troubled by the definition of 'domestic extremism' as it is pres-
ently too broad, and heard real fears from peaceful protesters that they
could easily be grouped in this category, along with real extremists.
Indeed, some police officials, while ostensibly differentiating between
extremist groups and others that use direct action, often conflate them,
especially when the protest groups are horizontal – UN Special Rapporteur on the rights to freedom of peaceful assembly and association,
January 2013.[51]

In January 2011, in the context of an ongoing complaint, a MDP Chief
Inspector wrote to Juliet McBride, a member of AWPC, regarding her arrest
under SOCPA (above):

As the action was politically motivated to draw attention to Trident etc,
then an inference could be drawn that you were a 'domestic extremist' at
that time. Whether you remain one is a matter for you to decide.[52]

AWPC responded in February with a video, *Domestic extremists or domestic
goddesses*, which aimed to 'put the domestic back into extremism'.[53]

Since 2003, anti-nuclear groups protesting at Aldermaston, including
AWPC, Block the Builders and TP, have been under surveillance by the
National Public Order Intelligence Unit (NPOIU).[54] The same is true at
other nuclear weapons sites, including Faslane.[55] One officer, Ian Caswell,
has been recorded at demonstrations at Burghfield and Aldermaston since
at least 2004. He is probably seconded to the NPOIU, and associated with
the National Domestic Extremism Team, which assists police forces
around the country. In 2007, he was seen at Faslane365 blockades, and
in November 2010 at a blockade at Devonport dockyard, where Trident
submarines are refitted.

The National Public Order Intelligence Unit (NPOIU), established in
March 1999, is responsible for gathering and collating intelligence in
relation to 'politically motivated disorder (not legitimate protests)' in
England, Wales and Scotland.[56] In 2011, it came under the control of the
Metropolitan Police-led, National Domestic Extremism Unit.[57]

There is no legal definition of domestic extremism, but according to
the Association of Chief Police Officers (ACPO): Domestic extremism and
extremists are the terms used for activity, individuals or campaign groups
that carry out criminal acts of direct action in furtherance of what is typi-

cally a single issue campaign. They usually seek to prevent something from happening or to change legislation or domestic policy, but attempt to do so outside of the normal democratic process.[58]

The ACPO definition of domestic extremism fits anti-nuclear non-violent direct action like a glove.

Police spies

Just as the Cold War anti-nuclear movement was infiltrated by MI5, so post-2000 protest has been subject to police infiltration.

In January 2011, Mark Stone/Kennedy was exposed as an undercover police officer, based in the environmental movement. The revelation led to further revelations of undercover police in other protest movements, and later in January, 'Lynn Watson' was exposed as an undercover police officer, who had for several years infiltrated the anti-nuclear movement.[59] She first visited the women's camp at Aldermaston in 2003-4, at a time of growing opposition to the development of a new generation of nuclear weapons. From there she joined Block the Builders, a new non-violent direct action group which aimed to block the construction programme at Aldermaston, joining a TP affinity group in blockades at Aldermaston, and later at Faslane. She was also active in Leeds, joining the Clown Army and targeting environmental activists, including Climate Camp.[60] As far as her activities at Aldermaston are concerned, information gathered by Lynn Watson was never used to prevent any criminal offence or security threat; her role was to gather 'intelligence' on activists involved in non-violent direct action.[61]

In January 2013, the UN Special Rapporteur on the rights to freedom of peaceful assembly and association stated:

> I must emphasise that my mandate covers only those assemblies that are non-violent. In this connection, I am deeply concerned with the use of embedded undercover police officers in groups that are non-violent and which exercise their democratic rights to protest and take peaceful direct action.[62]

Under surveillance

John Catt, an 89-year-old activist, has been involved for many decades in peaceful protest, including at the EDO arms factory in Brighton, but has never been arrested. In 2012, he requested a judicial review of the police's actions in holding information on him on the National Domestic Extremist Database, which he believed had violated his right to privacy. His presence at 55 demonstrations was recorded over a four year period, and included observations that he 'took out his sketchpad and made drawings of the demonstration', and noted his presence at an exhibition where his drawings were displayed. In March 2013, a police appeal against the decision was pending at the Supreme Court at the time of writing.[63]

John Catt's case illustrates the breadth of the police's definition of domestic extremism, the degree of routine surveillance and the nature of 'intelligence' gathered. Similar routine surveillance takes place at nuclear-military sites, and it should be assumed that this is exchanged with the NPOIU. At AWE Aldermaston MDP 'intelligence gathering' has included: photography and video surveillance; police 'liaison'; 'health and safety' visits; stop and search; the recording of vehicle registration numbers, vehicle tracking and surveillance. Thames Valley Police (TVP) are also involved in surveillance, including in the local community.

In June 2011, for example, members of the public attending a viewing of the anti-nuclear film *Countdown to Zero*, hosted by the Nuclear Information Service in Reading, were videoed and their number plates recorded by two TVP officers who admitted they had been instructed to 'watch out for certain people'.[64]

At large scale actions intelligence gathering may also include 'informal interviews' by the MDP CID Force Intelligence Bureau (FIB),[65] which are conducted outside of the formal interview process, and with the complicity of the custody officer. In one such interview, a Block the Builders activist was asked if she would be willing to provide the police with details of how blockades were organised and information about other protesters: especially, 'Anyone we had concerns about'.[66] Evidence gathering teams and Forward Intelligence Teams (FIT), deployed by the MDP, local police forces, and occasionally the Metropolitan Police are also present at larger actions.

Intelligence gathering also takes place in advance of pre-planned actions through the use of 'police liaison officers'. Unlike many other protest groups, some anti-nuclear activists, particularly TP, Faslane365 and currently Action AWE, have – 'as part of our non-violent and peaceful process'[67] – initiated pre-action dialogue and negotiations with the police, often at a senior level, or with a dedicated Protest Liaison Officer (PLO).[68] The same PLOs now routinely gather intelligence, in advance of and during protests.[69]

The UN Special Rapporteur on the rights to freedom of peaceful assembly and association has expressed concern about the dual role of PLOs:

> ... for this [liaison] to function effectively, it is necessary to separate the liaison function from intelligence gathering, which negates the goodwill and good relations that police liaison officers can foster by fuelling mistrust among protesters.[70]

Nuclear new build [71]

The authorities continue to employ similar tactics, including in response to a new wave of protest, this time against the proposed new generation of nuclear power stations.

Following freedom of information requests, Spinwatch and the journalist Rob Edwards obtained from the Department of Energy and Climate Change (DECC), documentation of an 'Activism and Nuclear New Build: Stakeholder Roundtable' held in June 2011 which revealed that the NPOIU had been gathering intelligence on activists to 'manage the risk' that they posed to plans by the Government and private industry to build new nuclear power stations.[72]

According to the meeting's agenda, NPOIU presented an 'overview of the current situation and nature of the threat to DECC officials; members of the Civil Nuclear Constabulary, the three police forces in areas where new build is planned – Avon and Somerset (Hinkley Point), Suffolk (Sizewell) and North Wales (Wylfa); and representatives of three companies' then involved in nuclear new build, including EDF Energy. The meeting aimed:

> to obtain an agreed understanding of the available intelligence on the risk to the new build programme from environmental activism... and to identify any potential gaps in arrangements for managing the risk of direct action or protests at new build sites.[73]

By October 2011, Somerset and Avon police had deployed PLOs, and in March 2012, Ian Caswell of the NPOIU was running surveillance operations at a 24-hour blockade at Hinkley.

In March 2013 activists opposed to the building of Hinkley C nuclear power station, were informed by 'their' PLO that the site had been granted a NLS in October 2012, and was covered under SOCPA, amended by the Terrorism Act 2006:

I thought you should be aware so that your supporters appreciate that any future action involving trespass on to the C Site would mean a criminal trespass and could result in a criminal conviction.[74]

Reflections

Have anti-terrorist legislation and the surveillance of 'domestic extremists' restricted anti-nuclear protest? Certainly the UN Special rapporteur has observed that the changed norms of public order policing have curtailed the right to peaceful protest. But amongst those activists who have contributed to this essay, opinions differ.

Some have challenged the legislation, highlighting the irony of arresting non-violent protesters under anti-terrorist legislation, while the UK government continues to violate the Nuclear Non-Proliferation Treaty, by the possession, deployment and manufacture of nuclear weapons.[75] Yet, for some, like Juliet McBride, the physical, psychological and legal space for protest has been curtailed:

> Personally, SOCPA has totally stopped my personal form of protest! A physical fence is part of the physical protection of the weapons and their makers: the law is made into a legal fence protecting the weapons and their makers. I have always sought to overcome the physical fence by climbing it. Likewise I have sought to overcome the physical protection of the players within the system by meeting them inside the actual fence they have erected around themselves. By this action I hope to confront the mental barriers they erect between themselves and what they do through my physical presence within the space they have marked out for themselves, and in which they practice their criminal activities. To this end I have climbed every single fence inside AWE Aldermaston and Burghfield at some time, many of them often. I did this from about 1990–2005 when S.128 of SOCPA became law. It was then that the legal barrier finally coincided with the physical barrier… How ironic that moral force is totally disregarded by the law, and physical & legal force are left triumphant.

Another activist said she would think twice about entering a SOCPA site: indeed, amongst those happy to take non-violent direct action outside nuclear installations, relatively few now trespass on military-nuclear sites. Sylvia Boyes, convicted under SOCPA observed, 'I think the SOCPA legislation has worked, in as much it has made people hesitate about trying to enter the areas covered,' and others have suggested that it deters those new to direct action.

However, others – like Jane Tallents of TP, active at Faslane – have been encouraged by the ineffectiveness of the legislation in practice:

> It seems like SOCPA was designed to frighten protesters from entering military bases. However after the first prosecution in Scotland when the head Procurator Fiscal himself took the case and Emma defended herself so brilliantly the police may continue to charge people with SOCPA, but the courts don't prosecute it. The Sheriff in that first case said that they were not entitled to enter a designated area but that they had caused no danger and only inconvenienced police who were on patrol anyway so the great threat of a year in prison melted away as they were admonished.

Emma Bateman, arrested three times under SOCPA concurs:

> Although I was initially worried when I was arrested under SOCPA the first time because we didn't know how harsh the penalties would be, I am not especially concerned about SOCPA. It would not put me off taking action because fines and costs in magistrates courts are quite arbitrary (seems to be down to whether the judge is having a bad day at the office or not) and I have been fined more for other offences than I have for SOCPA.

For some, SOCPA – unlike Trident – is a deterrent: for others it's business as usual. While considerably fewer people now trespass on nuclear and military sites than the 147 cited by the MOD in 2003–4,[76] the culture of protest has changed. Rather than SOCPA or surveillance, other factors including new social movements and campaigns, digital activism and a less vibrant anti-nuclear movement have reduced the landscape of anti-nuclear protest. But while they may be fewer in number, some 'nuts' remain impervious to the sledgehammer, and it will take more than anti-terrorist legislation to curtail their right to protest.

Notes

1 OSCE/ODIHR, *Guidelines on Freedom of Peaceful Assembly*, para. 77: [http://www.osce.org/odihr/24523].

2 *Demonstrating respect for rights?* Memorandum submitted by JUSTICE: [http://www.publications.parliament.uk/pa/jt200809/jtselect/jtrights/47/47we38.htm], esp. para. 3.

3 [http://www.legislation.gov.uk/ukpga/1998/42/contents], entered into force, October 2000, 1988 Scotland Act, [http://www.legislation.gov.uk/ukpga/1998/46/contents].

4 Article 11.2: 'No restrictions shall be placed on the exercise of these rights other than such as are prescribed by law and are necessary in a democratic society in the interests of national security or public safety, for the prevention of disorder or crime, for the protection of health or morals or for the protection of the rights and freedoms of others.' Article 10.2 is slightly differently expressed, and adds 'territorial integrity'.

5 See *Demonstrating respect for rights?* Memorandum submitted by Aldermaston Women's Peace Campaign, (AWPC Memorandum), [http://www.publications.parliament.uk/pa/jt200809/jtselect/jtrights/47/47we11.htm]

6 AWPC Memorandum, para. 3.

7 See for example: [http://www.met.police.uk/foi/pdfs/other_information/borough/so12_introduction.pdf].

8 Respectively, s. 12 and s.14, Public Order Act, 1986: [http://www.legislation.gov.uk/ukpga/1986/64/section/12, http://www.legislation.gov.uk/ukpga/1986/64/section/14].

9 Including s. 60, Criminal Justice and Public Order Act 1994, which provides 'powers to stop and search in anticipation of violence': [http://www.legislation.gov.uk/ukpga/1994/33/section/60].

10 Despite the 1998 ruling of the ECtHR, in Steel and others v. The United Kingdom (67/1997/851/1058), 1998, para. 55: [http://hudoc.echr.coe.int/sites/eng/pages/search.aspx?i=001-58240#{'itemid' :[' 001-58240'].

11 In 2006–7 during the year-long Faslane 365 protest, Strathclyde Police detained hundreds of non violent blockaders overnight without any intention of investigation or prosecution, see Conway, A., 2008, 'We Fought the Law... and the Law Ran and hid', Chapter 6 in Zelter, A., (ed.) 2008, *Faslane 365 a year of anti-nuclear blockades*, Edinburgh, Luath Press. See also, http://policegeek.files.wordpress.com/2012/08/faslane-365-a-critical-analysis-of-the-policing.pdf.

12 Amnesty International, *Media briefing – UK Terrorism Act 2000*, 20 February 2001: [http://www.amnesty.org/ar/library/asset/EUR45/007/ 2001/ar/878ec96a-891f-4977-ba71-010f699ab134/eur450072001en.pdf].

13 Section 1, Terrorism Act 2000: [http://www.legislation.gov.uk/ukpga/2000/11/section/1], entered into force on 19 February 2001.

14 See for example, 'Maytime': [http://tridentploughshares.org/maytime-disarmer-challenges-high-court-to-declare-trident-illegal/]; AWTT, [http://www.guardian.co.uk/uk/2000/sep/21/angeliquechrisafis?INTCMP=SRCH]; a third trial also resulted in a hung jury.

15 Now s. 76 of the 2008 Terrorism Act.

16 Anti-Terrorism Laws used against Peaceful Protesters, 18 March 2003, [http://mob.indymedia.org.uk/en/2003/03/57670.html]; the author was also threatened with arrest under s. 58 and searched under s. 44 (below)

when noting down details of an ammunition convoy entering USAF Fairford on 11 April 2003.

17 Liberty, Gloucestershire Weapons Inspectors and Berkshire CIA, *Casualty of War: 8 weeks of Counter-Terrorism in Rural England,* July 2003: [http://www.liberty-human-rights.org.uk/policy/reports/casualty-of-war-counter-terror-legislation-in-rural-england-2003.pdf].

18 In January 2010, following a case brought by protesters searched under s.44 around the DSEI arms fair in 2003 the ECtHR ruled that s.44 powers were unlawful. S. 44 searches were subsequently suspended.

19 *Review of the operation of Schedule 7: A Public Consultation*: [http://www.homeoffice.gov.uk/publications/about-us/consultations/schedule-7-review/consultation-document?view=Binary].

20 Schedule 7 empowers border and port authorities to stop, detain and question a person who 'appears to be', or has been, 'concerned in the commission, preparation or instigation of acts of terrorism': [http://www.legislation.gov.uk/ukpga/2000/11/schedule/7], for journalists, see http://www.theguardian.com/world/david-miranda.

21 [http://netpol.files.wordpress.com/2012/12/netpol-submission-to-home-of-fice-consultation-on-schedule-7.pdf].

22 See also, *Demonstrating respect for rights?*: [http://www.publications.parliament.uk/pa/jt200809/jtselect/jtrights/47/4707.htm#n19], esp. para. 76.

23 *The Right to Protest Under UK Law: A Civil Liberty in Decline?* Peacerights, 2007.

24 [http://www.legislation.gov.uk/ukpga/2005/15/section/128].

25 Letter to the Chairman from Vernon Coaker MP, Minister of State, Home Office: [http://www.publications.parliament.uk/pa/jt200809/jtselect/jtrights/47/47we05.htm].

26 Some committee members visiting AWE Aldermaston had witnessed *** climbing in. They were unable to believe that she had not committed a criminal act.

27 *Select Committee on Defence Minutes of Evidence, Examination of Witnesses* (Questions 300 - 313), 30 January 2002: [http://www.publications.parliament.uk/pa/cm200102/cmselect/cmdfence/518-ii/2013018.htm]; thanks to Juliet McBride.

28 [http://www.legislation.gov.uk/ukpga/2006/11/pdfs/ukpga_20060011_en.pdf], esp. Appendix A and B; see also [http://www.hse.gov.uk/nuclear/licensees/pubregister.pdf]; Statutory Instrument 2005 No. 3447, [http://www.opsi.gov.uk/si/si2005/20053447.htm], Statutory Instrument 2007 No. 930, [http://www.opsi.gov.uk/si/si2007/uksi_20070930_en_1].

29 [http://www.publications.parliament.uk/pa/cm200506/cmhansrd/vo051103/debtext/51103-23.htm#51103 23_spnew20].

30 See also: [http://webarchive.nationalarchives.gov.uk/20121110140652/ http://www.mod.uk/DefenceInternet/MicroSite/DIO/OurPublications/ Byelaws/ByelawsSeriousOrganisedCrimeAndPoliceActsocap.htm].

31 [http://webarchive.nationalarchives.gov.uk/20121110140652/http://www. mod.uk/NR/rdonlyres/FoF515EC-3D07-48AB-8D6B-0AE0A853D9F6/0/ public_consultation_record_aldermaston.pdf].

32 The Atomic Weapons Establishment (AWE) Aldermaston Byelaws 2007: [http://www.legislation.gov.uk/uksi/2007/1066/contents/made].

33 Carry on camping: [http://peacenews.info/node/3733/carry-camping].

34 MOD defeated in freedom to protest case: [http://aldermaston.net/media/58]. For the decision, see: [http://aldermaston.net/sites/default/files/background-byelaws.pdf].

35 Letter to the Chairman from Vernon Coaker MP, Minister of State, Home Office, 24 February 2009: [http://www.publications.parliament.uk/pa/ jt200809/jtselect/jtrights/47/47we05.htm].

36 [http://www.thetelegraphandargus.co.uk/news/1750994.women_guilty_ in_spy_base_case/]; [http://www.cnduk.org/cnd-media/item/174-cnd-sup-ports-activists-challenge-to-socpa]; [http://www.yorkshiretoday.co.uk/ ViewArticle.aspx?ArticleID=2122948&SectionID=55]; [http://www. independent.co.uk/news/uk/crime/helen-and-sylvia-the-new-face-of-ter-rorism-472993.html].

37 In the Scottish legal system, 'not proven'. Admonishments are recorded as a conviction but there is no penalty.

38 'SOCRAP Weapons Inspectors group arrested in two waves', 2 September 2007: [http://www.faslane365.org/en/socrap_weapons_inspectors]; thanks to Jane Tallents and Helen Fenton for comments.

39 [http://faslanepeacecamp.wordpress.com/2012/06/14/trespass-at-coulport-nuclear-weapon-depot/].

40 [http://www.indymedia.org.uk/en/2012/07/497611.html]; all but one received letters from the Procurator Fiscal stating they although there was sufficient evidence they would not be prosecuted on this occasion, but would be if they repeated their actions.

41 [http://www.schnews.org.uk/archive/news6552.php]; sometime before 2006, the US nuclear weapons – up to 110 B-61 free fall nuclear bombs-were withdrawn: [http://www.fas.org/blog/ssp/2008/06/us-nuclear-weap-ons-withdrawn-from-the-united-kingdom.php].

42 The Atomic Weapons Establishment (AWE) Aldermaston Byelaws 2007, see 'Explanatory Note' for plans of protected and controlled areas: [http:// www.legislation.gov.uk/uksi/2007/1066/contents/made].

43 See: [http://www.aldermaston.net/action/266].

44 Eight Acquitted After Rolls Royce Blockade, 24 October 2008: [http://

tridentploughshares.org/wp-content/uploads/2013/02/News-Index-2008.
pdf]; s. 68, Criminal Justice and Public Order Act 1994, [http://www.legis-
lation.gov.uk/ukpga/1994/33/section/68].

45 *Three Scots in Newbury Court for* SOCPA *crime,* TP press release, June 2011.

46 [http://www.publications.parliament.uk/pa/cm200506/cmhansrd/
vo051103/debtext/51103-23.htm#51103-23_spnew20].

47 *Demonstrating respect for rights?* para. 108.

48 [http://www.legislation.gov.uk/ukpga/2011/13/part/3/crossheading/repeal-
of-socpa-2005-provisions/enacted].

49 [http://www.nukewatch.org.uk/index.php].

50 [http://www.robedwards.com/2009/06/silly-secrecy-over-nuclear-
bomb-convoys.html]; see, for example, Freedom of Information Request,
[http://www.ico.org.uk/upload/documents/decisionnotices/2010/
fs_50192677.pdf].

51 'Statement by the United Nations Special Rapporteur on the rights to
freedom of peaceful assembly and of association at the conclusion of his
visit to the United Kingdom', 23 January 2013: [http://www.ohchr.org/en/
NewsEvents/Pages/DisplayNews.aspx?NewsID=12945&LangID=E]. For
the full report, published in May 2013, see: [http://www.ohchr.org/
Documents/HRBodies/HRCouncil/RegularSession/Session23/A.
HRC.23.39.Add.1_AUV.pdf].

52 Email from MDP Chief Inspector Richard Willcocks to Juliet McBride, 25
January 2011.

53 [http://aldermaston.net/camp/415; http://aldermaston.net/video/417].

54 NPOIU was one of three units making up the National Coordinator Domestic
Extremism (NCDE).

55 'Anger over data use', *Evening Times* (Glasgow), 22 November 2002.

56 [http://www.acpo.police.uk/NationalPolicing/NCDENationalCoordinator-
DomesticExtremism/TheNationalPublicOrderIntelligenceUnitNPOIU.
aspx]. During the cold war, anti-nuclear activists were under the surveillance
of Special Branch, who passed information on to MI5: [http://www.guardian.
co.uk/politics/2006/aug/28/uk.freedomofinformation]; from 1994, Special
Branch increasingly monitored protest, particularly animal rights protesters,
and demonstrations: [http://www.independent.co.uk/news/special-branch-
to-target-protesters-1439755.html]; see also: [http://www.met.police.uk/
foi/pdfs/other_information/borough/so12_introduction.pdf], p. 6.

57 The National Domestic Extremist Unit merged the National Public Order
Intelligence Unit (NPOIU), the National Domestic Extremism Team (NDET)
and the National Extremism Tactical Coordination Unit (NETCU): [http://
www.acpo.police.uk/NationalPolicing/NCDENationalCoordinatorDomes-
ticExtremism/Default.aspx].

58 ACPO, 2006; ACPO is a private company; [http://www.guardian.co.uk/uk/2009/oct/25/police-surveillance-protest-domestic-extremism].

59 [http://www.guardian.co.uk/uk/2011/jan/19/undercover-police-officer-lynn-watson]; it is alleged she was deployed by the Special Demonstrations Squad, disbanded in 2008.

60 [http://climatecamp.org.uk/blog/2011/05/20/climate-camps-legal-team-refuse-to-participate-in-undercover-review/].

61 For continuing revelations about police spies, see coverage by Rob Evans and Paul Lewis in www.theguardian.com.

62 'Statement by the United Nations Special Rapporteur on the rights to freedom of peaceful assembly and of association at the conclusion of his visit to the United Kingdom', 23 January 2013, op.cit.

63 [http://www.bailii.org/ew/cases/EWCA/Civ/2013/192.html].

64 [http://www.nuclearinfo.org/article/civil-liberties/nis-complains-about-police-surveillance-countdown-zero-screening].

65 Ministry of Defence Police and Guarding Agency, Annual Report and Accounts, 2005-6: [http://www.official-documents.gov.uk/document/hc0506/hc12/1206/1206.pdf].

66 [http://aldermaston.net/blog/jk/171].

67 [http://actionawe.org/1st-letter-from-action-awe-to-police-commanders-prior-to-campaign-launch/]; for the nature of such dialogue, see: [http://actionawe.org/log-of-emailed-correspondence-between-action-awe-the-police/].

68 'The PLO role has been developed by TVP to negotiate with protest groups, in order to understand their intentions and the nature of their protest', see 'Thames Valley Police: 'The Big Blockade', Aldermaston', in *Policing Public Order. An overview and review of progress against the recommendations of Adapting to Protest and Nurturing the British Model of Policing*, HMIC, September 2011, see pp. 26-27: [http://www.hmic.gov.uk/media/policing-public-order-20110208.pdf].

69 See: [http://netpol.org/2012/09/07/the-intelligence-role-of-police-liaison-officers/].

70 *Statement by the United Nations Special Rapporteur*, January 2013.

71 'SECTION 6 – NUCLEAR NEW BUILD PROGRAMMEME: 6.1 The potential for anti-nuclear and environmental demonstrations at or near locations identified for new-builds is recognised. The Chief Constable of the Civil Nuclear Constabulary will ensure that Chief Constables/Commissioners are kept as fully informed as possible as to development proposals and that, where required, bespoke information/intelligence sharing arrange-

ments are put in place as part of a specific Memorandum of Understanding covering the proposed development': [http://www.acpo.police.uk/documents/uniformed/2011/201108UOCNCProt.pdf].

72 [http://www.robedwards.com/2012/10/police-trying-to-neuter-anti-nuclear-protest.html].

73 [http://www.scribd.com/doc/108974932/activism-and-nuclear-new-build-decc-document-released-under-foi]; it is reasonable to assume that similar meetings take place between the MDP, NPOIU and the private companies running Aldermaston.

74 Email to Stop New Nuclear police liaison team from Craig Kirk, Avon and Somerset Police, 11 March 2013.

75 On release after arrest under SOCPA 128 in 2012, TP activist Brian Larkin stated, 'The serious organised crime happens inside the base and not in these actions for peace and disarmament. It is the ongoing deployment of Trident submarines – each carrying 48 warheads, eight times more destructive than the bomb dropped on Hiroshima which killed 200,000 people – that constitutes serious organised crime and violates every principle of humanity in international law'.

76 During the first years of the war on Iraq.

CHAPTER FIFTEEN

Women, Men and Nuclear Weapons

PROFESSOR CYNTHIA COCKBURN

Cynthia Cockburn is a feminist researcher and writer on gender, war and peace. She is active in Women in Black against War and the Women's International League for Peace and Freedom, and is an Honorary Professor in the Centre for the Study of Women and Gender at Warwick University. For publications see www.cynthiacockburn.org.

THERE IS A LONG tradition of women organising against the Bomb. On the 1 March 1954 the United States tested a nuclear weapon on Bikini Atoll in the Pacific Ocean. Japanese fishermen in their boat *The Lucky Dragon* were caught in the radioactive fallout. The incident caused a wave of anti-nuclear activism in Japan beginning in Suginami, Tokyo. And it was mainly the women of Suginami who organised a petition to ban nuclear weapons that raised just short of 30 million signatures in two months. French and US atmospheric nuclear tests also sparked off another response, at the opposite end of the Pacific Ocean, an important part of which was 'Women for a Nuclear Free and Independent Pacific'. One reason women organised was because so many of the children to which they gave birth after they were irradiated by the nuclear tests had terrible birth defects.

Later, in the 1980s, there was a huge movement of women in the UK against the introduction here of US Cruise nuclear missiles that centred on the RAF base at Greenham Common, where a substantial arsenal of nuclear missiles was to be stationed. A group of women set out from Cardiff in Wales and walked 100 miles to Greenham. When they arrived, on 5 September 1981, four of them chained themselves to the fence, demanding a televised debate with the Secretary of State for Defence. This was the start of a spontaneous women's peace camp that soon had more than 100 women living under plastic and canvas, and thousands more coming at weekends from support groups that sprang up around the country. On 12 December 1982 an estimated 30,000 women completely 'embraced the base' around its 14 km fence. The camp persisted till after the last missile had been returned to the USA in 1991. Women who camped at Greenham went on to contribute hugely to anti-nuclear work elsewhere, setting up camps at the missile warning station at Menwith Hill, at the nuclear weapons research and manufacturing facilities at Aldermaston and Burghfield, organising the Nukewatch Network, and continuing worldwide links with other women protesting against nuclear weapons in their countries. Women still form the backbone of the anti-nuclear movement today.

What is it that brings women out *as women* against nuclear weapons, or against war, or against militarism itself? For 12 years now I have been researching feminist anti-war organising. In the course of fact-finding in a score of countries, I have found that women usually have three reasons for organising separately as women. The first is that women have an experience of militarism and war that is specific to their gender. Birthing babies with terrible birth defects *due to radiation* is just one of these experiences. Rape of women on an epidemic scale, as in the Bosnian war and in the Congo and Sudan now – that is another. Then again, women often feel special anger about military expenditure because it reduces the budget available for the public and social services on which so many women, who do the majority of domestic, health and care work, paid and unpaid, specially depend. Women organise as women to make women's particular experience in peace and war visible and understood.

The second reason behind 'women only' anti-war activism is simply for effectiveness, for women to be able to exercise choice. Often in mixed groups it is men who take the lead. They may not mean to dominate, but somehow their voices carry more weight. It is not the case in all groups. There are some in the peace movement that are very careful in the way they conduct gender relations. But some women in the not-so-wonderful groups sometimes get to think, they have told me, 'I can't waste my time with this 'double militancy' – having to struggle *in* the group in order to struggle *out there* in the world. Let's do it on our own'. That going 'WOMEN ONLY' makes women's voices more audible, and women can make choices, choose styles and strategies of organisation and action, that feel comfortable to them as women, and are different from those of some mixed groups.

So – first, getting women's experience visible; second, doing things in a particular way. But there is a third reason some women choose to organise as women, and it may be more significant than the other two. It is because there is a feminist analysis of militarism and war that is lacking in the thinking of the mainstream movement. Militarism and war are products of systems of power. The main two war-sustaining systems are:

(1) capitalism – the class power of money and property (2) national-ism – the racist power of the state, white rule, ethnic hatred. Both are systems of oppression and exploitation and are thus essentially, necessar-ily, violent.

The anti-war movement mobilises against both those systems of power. Feminists say: Hold on... there's another system of power intertwined with those two. It too is oppressive, exploitative and violent. It too predis-poses society to militarism and war. It's called patriarchy.

What feminists mean by patriarchy is the millennia-old, worldwide, almost universal form of gender order in which men exercise power over women, and which fosters a kind of masculinity that thrives on domina-tion and force.

So, some women say, the anti-war movement needs to address, yes, capitalist exploitation, and, yes, racist, nationalist impulses, but *also* systemic male power. All three, nothing less. Struggle for a transformation of gender relations has to be recognised as peace work. In our very own anti-war, antimilitarist and peace movements, just as we try not to behave like little capitalists, and just as we do not tolerate racism, so we should not tolerate sexism. Our activism has to reflect the world we want to create. Totally. Prefigurative struggle, it's called.

I want to end by stressing that we are not talking here about men and women as such, let alone about individual men and women. We are talking about cultures – cultures that thrive and multiply everywhere from bank boardrooms, to the pub on a Saturday night, from TV commercials to computer games, cultures that set up masculinity and femininity as cari-catures of human 'being', that create a whole symbolic system in which particular qualities are ascribed to masculinity, and given supremacy. What is a 'real man'? Being authoritative, combative, defended, controlling, hard, always ready to use violence to defend honour. It is clear that these qualities are deeply implicated in militarism and war. And women make a connection here: actual men either find the courage to refuse this model or they act it out. And when they act it out, they do so not only in the military, but also in everyday life, in ways that are very costly to women. So women can hardly avoid seeing violence as a continuum, one that stretches from the school playground, bedroom and back street to the battlefield, from their own bodies to the body politic. It may be that our movement is something more than an anti-war movement, more even than a peace movement. It may be a movement for a nonviolent world.

To come back to nuclear weapons... One day in the summer of 2005, two women went to Stockholm to address a meeting of the prestigious Weapons of Mass Destruction Commission, chaired by Hans Blix. He had invited them to speak on 'the relevance of gender for eliminating weapons of mass destruction'. They received a careful hearing. And they spoke about how ideas about gender – what is deemed masculine or feminine, powerful or impotent, affect our efforts towards halting the proliferation of WMD. They drew on detailed research that revealed the laddish, boys' own, culture of a certain nuclear policy institute. Research that had analysed and revealed how the fear of being seen as 'soft' or 'wimpish' had influenced actual political decisions to go to war in recent times. They also cited research that shows the tight link between masculine identity, men's sense of self, and the ownership of a gun (or a knife or a pit-bull terrier). The man-gun affinity is something that has been found in many countries to hinder demobilization after war. The two women told the Commissioners:

> There's now general recognition that there are significant gender dimensions to the possession of small arms and light weapons. It would be naïve to assume that this association suddenly becomes meaningless when we're talking about larger, more massively destructive weapons. And it's more naïve still to think it doesn't matter.

So, do not be surprised to find women taking an active part in the anti-nuclear movement, often with banners and placards with messages that might have been written by women in countries as far apart as Colombia and Spain, India and the Philippines, saying things like: 'Spend money on services not nuclear weapons', 'Security for women? Disarm masculinity. Disarm militaries', and 'No fists, no knives, no guns, no bombs – no to all violence'.

References and Selected Reading

Cockburn, Cynthia (2007) 'From Where We Stand: War, Women's Activism and Feminist Analysis.' London and New York: Zed Books.

Cohn, Carol with Felicity Hill and Sara Ruddick (2005) 'The relevance of gender for eliminating weapons of mass destruction'. Adaptation of a presentation to the Commission on 12 June 2005. Paper No.38. Stockholm: Commission on Weapons of Mass Destruction.

Website www.womeninblack.org

CHAPTER SIXTEEN

Linking US Military Empire and UK Nuclear Weapons

BRUCE GAGNON

Bruce Gagnon is Coordinator of the Global Network Against Weapons and Nuclear Power in Space and lives in Bath, Maine. He grew up in a military family and joined the Air Force during the Vietnam War where he became a peace activist. In 1959–1962 Bruce lived in Leicester where he learned to love peas, tea, and a good laugh.

IT IS TRUE THAT the US and UK have a 'special relationship' – it's called militarism and collaboration in controlling the resources, markets, and people of the planet.

The US took over primary imperial responsibilities after the sun set on the British Empire. Britain's oligarchy was shrewd enough to protect its investments by entering into a pact to serve as 'moral cheerleader' for the expansion of US militarism around the world. Now with more than 800 bases across the planet, and increasingly using space technology to coordinate all warfare, the Pentagon has become the primary resource extraction service for corporate globalisation.

As we saw with Tony Blair's theatrics in support of George W. Bush's 'shock and awe' attack on Iraq and the NATO occupation of Afghanistan, our countries continue to act as the 'two gangsters' behind today's imperial wars.

Obama's recent announcement of a 'pivot' of US foreign and military policy into the Asia-Pacific is nothing more than a deceptive way of saying the US will now divert 60 per cent of its military forces to surround China. But why? What is really happening here?

The US understands that it cannot compete with China economically. However, if the US could control China's access to vital resources (like oil) then it would hold the keys to China's economic engine. The same thing is happening today as the US and NATO move to surround Russia with so-called 'missile defence' systems that in fact are key elements in creating a 'successful' first-strike attack. Again one should ask why the US would want to restart a Cold War with Russia? Could it be because Russia has the world's largest supply of natural gas and significant supplies of oil?

Professor Noam Chomsky says US foreign policy is now all about controlling most of the world's declining resource supply as a 'lever of world domination'. One way to keep Europe, China, India and other emerging markets dependent on Washington, and in sync with its policies, is to maintain control of the keys to the world's economic engine.

Obama appointed former NATO commander Gen. James Jones as his first National Security Adviser. In March 2006 Gen. Jones told the Stars and Stripes newspaper that 'Our strategic goal is to expand... to Eastern Europe and Africa'. Months later he told the media that NATO was developing a 'special plan' to safeguard oil and gas fields in Africa and was 'ready to ensure the security of oil-producing and transporting regions'.

Who is the competitor of the US in Africa? The Pentagon maintains that it is China.

The entire US military empire is now tied together using space technology. With military satellites in space the US can see virtually everything on the Earth, can intercept all communications on the planet, and can target virtually any place on the Earth. The US currently has more than 100 active military satellites. Ground stations around the globe, including at the North and South poles, download images from the satellites that are used by the military for spying and offensive operations.

Space warfare ground stations like Fylingdales and Menwith Hill in Yorkshire help relay signals between military satellites and the 'war fighters'. Peace groups like CND and CAAB have organised for years in this part of the country and helped shine a light on the offensive nature of these military installations.

War today on this planet is directed using space technology. The Persian Gulf War in 1991 was called the 'first space war' because at that time the Space Command field tested all of their new space technology.

Before the Gulf War began, the Space Command pre-identified all of Iraq's military targets using military satellites. In the first two to three days of the war 95 per cent of those targets were hit. The war was essentially over at that point, but dragged on for weeks. During those remaining days the Pentagon launched 100 cruise missiles, costing $1 million each, and used up lots more military hardware that kept production lines humming round the clock back at home. But most importantly, the Space Command was learning how to tie all warfare – whether ground-based, sea-based, or air-based into the Space Command system.

It was out of this field test of the programme that the tag 'Full Spectrum Dominance' would come. The idea was that space technology would direct all warfare on the planet, at every level of conflict, and that the US would not allow anyone else to achieve that capability.

Today drones buzzing over Afghanistan, Pakistan, or Mali are 'flown' by pilots back in the US at places like Creech AFB, Nevada or Hancock Air Field, New York. This is possible because the military satellites in orbit link the pilot to the drone in 'real time' – split-second time. Space Command downlink ground stations spread around the globe help relay those signals. The Pentagon brags that this high-tech warfare increases 'the kill chain'.

In a way you could call the military satellites the 'triggers' that make the drone kills possible. These satellites allow the military to see everything, hear everything, and to target every place on the planet.

It is essentially these same military satellites and ground stations that would direct one of Britain's Trident nuclear missiles to its target after launch from a submarine.

The Space Command appears to have three primary missions. To provide global surveillance (the eyes and ears of corporate control), global power projection using space directed technologies, and creating the capability to control the pathway (called the gravity well) to and from Earth. NASA, with our tax dollars, continues to develop the necessary technologies to successfully 'mine the sky' for precious resources. We've already seen Obama privatise some aspects of the space programme as the technology matures. The plan is ultimately for full privatisation of space mining operations with the Space Command ensuring control of the gateway to outer space on behalf of particular corporate interests.

All of this will be very expensive to build. For years the Pentagon has been saying that Star Wars, this military space technology system, will be the largest industrial project in the history of our planet. Even after the US government, now under control of the corporations, cuts what little social programmes we have left, the Pentagon will still need more money.

The US and NATO are today discussing how to integrate their space technology programmes because the Pentagon needs the allies to help pay for this very expensive programme. But have no doubt – even though NATO partners will help pay for these military space programmes the US intends to stay in control of the system.

Russia and China have been trying for years to get the US to agree to negotiate a new treaty called Prevention of an Arms Race in Outer Space (PAROS) but all US administrations since Reagan have blocked the process at the United Nations.

While the US continues on this dangerous, expensive, and destabilising programme of world domination on behalf of corporate globalisation, more bases and ports of call are needed in the Asia-Pacific. Thus the US has imposed pressure on South Korea to build the Navy base on Jeju Island where US ships can port, just 350 miles from the Chinese coast.

The Pentagon is directing a very unpopular expansion of their current war bases in Guam, Okinawa and Hawaii. The US is also in negotiations with the Philippines and Vietnam to allow US warships to return to their ports after many years' absence.

As the Pentagon ramps up this imperial expansion it must find willing partners to give moral, financial, and strategic legitimacy to this global military empire. This is where Britain comes into play. Downing Street gives its blessings, sends troops to Afghanistan, and deploys its own nuclear weapons on submarines in a show of the flag intended to say to Russia and China: 'We are with the US on this programme. We've got their backs.'

It's an amazing display of hypocrisy to watch the US and Britain justify their own 'weapons of mass destruction' while they set out to lecture Iran, North Korea, Pakistan and others about the evils of such instruments of indiscriminate death. But justify these incinerators of hell they surely do.

I've been heartened over the years to follow the movement against Trident at Faslane. In September of 2007 Dave Webb (who convenes the Global Network and chairs CND) and I were arrested for protesting there during Faslane 365. We wanted to make a statement that our work to stop the militarisation and weaponisation of space is inextricably linked to Britain's Trident programme. These military systems serve the same master – the same corporate imperial ambitions.

It is inspiring that resistance to Trident replacement continues and is growing in the UK. It is clear that Britain can't afford to fund a new generation of these nuclear weapons nor should it! Aren't there scores of unmet social needs across the UK clamouring for those same funds? Shouldn't Britain, and all countries, be slashing military spending and using the taxpayer's funds to deal with the coming harsh reality of climate change? Think of what could be done with those monies building alternative energy sources and remaking society in a sustainable way.

Why are so many climate change organisations so reluctant to mention that the Pentagon has the largest carbon boot print on Earth?

If human kind is to survive on this planet then we must immediately change our direction. Successful opposition to Trident replacement is a key to open this door to survival. Trident is anti-future, anti-survival, anti-security and anti-Mother Earth.

The militarisation of everything around us is a spiritual sickness. Native American holy man Lame Deer often talked about how the white man was blinded by his love for the dollar. His spiritual connection to the Mother Earth is broken.

We must all continue to connect the dots between human needs, the environmental crisis, endless war for corporate control, and the expensive and deadly weapons systems that are used by the US, Britain, and an ever-expanding NATO to maintain their 'military boot' on the necks of most of the world's people.

We join you in this historic undertaking to turn the global war machine toward a life sustaining direction. We stand with you always and send our best wishes.

CHAPTER SEVENTEEN

'The Future of the United Kingdom's Nuclear Deterrent': An Ethical Critique

PROFESSOR JOHN M. HULL

John M. Hull is Honorary Professor of Practical Theology in The Queen's Foundation for Ecumenical Theological Education and Emeritus Professor of Religious Education at the University of Birmingham. His web site is www.johnmhull.biz.

FOLLOWING A DEBATE in the House of Commons on 14 March 2007, the UK government by 409 votes to 161 voted to support the renewal of the UK nuclear deterrent. Government policy was based upon a paper published by the Ministry of Defence in December 2006 entitled, 'The Future of the United Kingdom's Nuclear Deterrent', with an introduction by the then Prime Minister, Tony Blair.[1] This paper examines the ethical character of the document. It does not deal with the wider issues of the ethics of nuclear warfare in general.

Eight areas of ethical concern will now be described

1 The Policy of Enduring Deterrence

Attempts have been made in the past to show that a policy of nuclear deterrence may be ethically acceptable if its duration is strictly limited. It must be nothing but a step on the way towards the complete elimination of nuclear weapons.

This limited ethical approval for the policy of deterrence was specified by Pope John Paul II in his message to the Special Session of the United Nations on Disarmament, no. 8 in June of 1982.

In current conditions, deterrence based on balance certainly not as an end in itself, but as a step on the way towards a progressive disarmament, may still be judged morally acceptable. Nonetheless, in order to ensure peace, it is indispensable not to be satisfied with this minimum which is always susceptible to the real danger of explosion...

In their statement 'The Harvest of Justice is Sown in Peace',[2] the Catholic Bishops of America declared:

> Nuclear deterrence may be justified only as a step on the way toward progressive disarmament...The nuclear powers may justify, and then only temporarily their nuclear deterrence only if they use their power and resources to lead in the construction of a more just and stable international order... [Such a policy] is the only moral basis for temporally retaining our deterrent.

This reluctant concession, offering a minimal ethical consent, gained whatever plausibility it had from the situation in the 1980s when the conditions of mutually assured destruction prevailed as a constraint between the two major nuclear powers. Even then it was a flimsy argument and it has become less and less convincing with the passage of time, and the changes in world politics. However, even this minimal condition is disregarded by the White Paper, which describes its nuclear policy as enduring.

It is immediately clear from the opening statement by the Prime Minister himself that what the White Paper has in mind is a very long term, if not a permanent feature of British defence policy:

> We believe that an independent British nuclear deterrent is an essential part of our insurance against the uncertainties and risks of the future...
> I believe it is crucial that for the foreseeable future British prime ministers have the necessary assurance that no aggressor can escalate a crisis beyond UK control.[3]

Mr Blair goes on to announce a reduction of about 20 per cent in the number of warheads, and that this 'means Britain continues to set an example for others to follow'.[4] However, the Prime Minister does not declare that this reduction is to be part of a long term plan involving further reductions. He says that there will be consideration of the possibility of reducing the number of submarines from four to three, but this will only take place if the three prove to have the same or similar capability as the present four.

Turning to the body of the document, we find the following declaration:

> We can only deter such threats in future through the continued possession of nuclear weapons... We therefore see an enduring role for the UK's

nuclear forces as an essential part of our capability for deterring black-mail and acts of aggression against our vital interests by nuclear-armed opponents.[5]

It is claimed that this is 'consistent with our commitment to work toward a safer world in which there is no requirement for nuclear weapons',[6] but there is no comment upon the hiatus between this claim and the policy of 'enduring possession' of nuclear weapons. It is true, as the report points out, that the UK of all the nuclear powers has the smallest stockpile of weapons, and that the UK is the only country to reduce its nuclear capability to a single arm, but such comments look to the past and do not constitute a programme of steady continued reduction such as to suggest that the ethical requirement is met which insists that deterrence can only be justified if it is a temporary measure on the way to something else. No doubt, the UK is 'working multi-laterally for nuclear disarmament and to counter nuclear proliferation'[7] but the ethical character of British policy cannot be assured by such international objectives unless supported by a compatible policy on the part of the UK itself.

The White Paper continues by speaking of:

> ... the continuing risk from the proliferation of nuclear weapons, and the certainty that a number of other countries will retain substantial nuclear arsenals, mean that our minimal nuclear deterrent capability... is likely to remain a necessary element in our security.[8]

It is a pity that the document does not indicate any actual measures that might be taken to minimise the risk of nuclear proliferation or to discourage other nations in the maintenance of their nuclear arsenals, in spite of such noble sentiments as the assertion that 'We stand by our unequivocal undertaking to accomplish the total elimination of nuclear weapons'.[9] But how? By what means? And in our lifetime? 'The fundamental principles relevant to nuclear deterrence have not changed since the end of the Cold War, and are unlikely to change in the future'.[10] If that is the case, deterrence will be permanent, and talk of nuclear disarmament is mere dreaming: 'Enduring principles underpin the UK's approach to nuclear deterrence'.[11]

It is thus clear that deterrence is not, as demanded by the moral teaching of the Catholic Church, to be a temporary provision pending a planned reduction but a permanent feature of the lives of British citizens.

2   The Principle of Discrimination

A basic principle for minimising the barbaric character of warfare is that deliberate attacks should be directed only at the opposing armed forces and not to civilian populations. It must be emphasised that observing this principle of discrimination does not make war ethical. When it is ignored, however, the unethical character of the military action would be undeniable. Admittedly, it is not easy to draw a clear distinction today between military personnel and civilians. We would have to consider the position of the many thousands of civilians who directly or indirectly maintained the armed forces. We would also have to distinguish between the deliberate killing of innocent bystanders and what today is called 'collateral damage' i.e. the unintended and unavoidable civilian casualties that occur in spite of the fact that the intended target is the enemy military. In the light of this principle it might be argued that tactical or battlefield weapons are consistent with the principle of discrimination because the target is not the civilian population of the area.

If this is the case, then we may ask whether the nuclear deterrent of the UK is conceived of as strategic or tactical. The White Paper asserts that 'Conventional capability cannot have the same deterrent effect'.[12] It is not easy to see why the limited use of tactical weapons on the battlefield would have a deterrent effect beyond that of conventional weapons, apart from the threat of escalation, and it would therefore appear that what the government has in mind is strategic weapons. This is supported by the following comment: 'Ballistic missiles are more effective than cruise missiles because they have much greater range and payload.'[13] Any remaining doubt is removed in the following sentence:

> The UK's nuclear weapons are not designed for military use during conflict but instead to deter and prevent nuclear blackmail and acts of aggression against our vital interests that cannot be countered by other means.[14]

The nuclear deterrent deters precisely because it is a weapon of mass destruction. Not only do such weapons not distinguish between military and civilian targets, their scale and impact upon surrounding areas, the environment and future generations means that they cannot do so: indeed this is precisely what they are intended to do. They are political, not military, because they are intended to terrify entire populations. Not only do they fail to comply with the principle of discrimination, they openly and shamelessly defy it. There can be no doubt, then, that these weapons are barbaric.

3 The Ethical Character of the Threat and of the Use in First Strike and Second Strike

Up to this point, most people would probably agree. Nobody denies that strategic nuclear weapons are terrible almost beyond imagination. The Government admits that it is reluctant to possess them: 'We would not want to have available the terrifying power of these weapons unless we believed it to be necessary to deter a future aggressor.'[15]

The purpose of these weapons is not to use them but to prevent their use. They are intended to forestall the massive destruction of civilian populations. They express the hope of securing peace through fear. We must ask, however, whether this kind of threat can be ethically justified even if the fear which produces it is reasonable. Nuclear weapons of this kind are in a class of their own. Every day illustrations such as threatening to give a bully a black-eye are misleading and inapplicable. The analogy might be rather to threaten not only the bully, but the entire household of the bully, the city in which he lives, hundreds if not thousands of miles of surrounding territory and the bully's descendants for several generations.

The ethical dilemma is highlighted today by the fact that the most likely source of a nuclear threat to Britain comes not from other nations but from terrorist groups who cannot be deterred by the threat because they are ready for a martyr's death. Not only is it unethical to threaten to kill millions of people in order to deter them from killing millions of your own people, but the threat loses whatever political integrity it had when it is poised, with all its horror, against a secret foe who cannot be deterred.

The deterrent implies the willingness to carry out the deed. To justify committing the deed on the ground that it will never be necessary to commit the deed is a strange and dangerous logic. Moreover, the policy is incompatible with a readiness to strike first.

The White Paper declares, 'We will not rule in or out the first use of nuclear weapons'.[16] If first use were against another nuclear power, would not that nation consider that retaliation was justified, for its own deterrent policy would then have failed? And if first use was against a non-nuclear power, how could it be justified on the grounds that a strategic nuclear attack had to be averted?

Let us now consider the possible second use of a strategic nuclear weapon. If such weapons are to be justified at all, it can only be as a deterrent. However, if the deterrent should fail, the ethical situation is substantially altered. Any use of the weapons following the failure of deterrence would no longer be deterrent but vengeful, retaliatory and murderous. Would it be ethical to murder millions of people because millions have already been murdered? This would be nothing more than the crudest form of blood feud raised to the ultimate limit of horror. The men in charge of the weapons in the submarine are placed in a position of terrible ethical paradox. The finger must be poised above the red button if a credible threat is to be maintained, but is the finger to come down on the button when that policy has failed? The same ethical paradox would confront the Prime Minister of the day, who faced with the report of a nuclear attack on a UK target, would have to decide whether it would be useful, appropriate and ethical to take out a foreign city in return for one of our own. Would that perhaps deter a second attack? But deterrence that failed the first time would perhaps fail again. So then is it to be city for city until the world is destroyed?

Let us suppose that the commander of a submarine were to make a mental decision, foreseeing this terrible emergency, that he would not accept the retaliatory order. That mental decision would forever have to remain a secret, for if it became known, or even rumoured, the credibility of the deterrent would have been compromised.

If deterrence fails, the resulting use of strategic nuclear weapons would no longer be deterrence but vengeance. It is not ethically permitted to destroy life in revenge. Moreover, since there is thus an ethical distinction between the success and the failure of deterrence, those responsible for firing the missiles would have to be informed as to whether the firing they had been instructed to initiate was deterrent or vengeful. If not, the moral status of the operatives would be impaired and their human rights ignored. In fact, the submarine crew are only given a set of coordinates and the instruction to fire. They do not know what or at whom the missile is directed. There can be no doubt that both the order and the response both severally and together commit a crime against humanity, their own and that of others.

In short, the ethical status of nuclear deterrents cannot be maintained because willingness to commit the act itself is implied in the deterrence.

4 The Principle of Last Resort

Moral reasoning demands that in order to meet the requirements of justice in warfare, it must be a last resort. The White Paper does not make this clear, but uses such expressions as 'in our vital interests' or 'to avoid blackmail'. These concepts are not explained, and suggest that the moral implications of last resort have not been grappled with.

In spite of the fact that earlier statements affirm that the UK nuclear deterrent would only be used when all other means had failed and the very existence of the state was threatened, the present paper is ambiguous on the issue. The favourite expression used is 'our vital interests'. The Prime Minister says, 'We cannot be sure that a major nuclear threat to our vital interests will not emerge'.[17] In the past, our deterrent has been used 'only to deter acts of aggression against our vital interests'.[18] The other phrase which is used to describe the situations in which the nuclear weapons might be used is to prevent what the White Paper calls 'blackmail'. We must not 'be constrained by nuclear blackmail by others'.[19] The purpose of the nuclear force is for 'deterring blackmail and acts of aggression against our vital interests by nuclear-armed opponents'.[20]

There is no discussion of what is meant by these expressions. Moreover, when the UK presses its vital interests, supported by nuclear force, other countries are likely to experience this as nuclear blackmail, just as the UK perceives blackmail when its vital interests appear to be threatened. In correspondence, the MOD has indicated that nuclear weapons would only be used as a last resort, when the very existence of the state was in danger. It is disturbing that no such statements occur in the White Paper. I am not suggesting that the UK Government might be prepared to use the threat of nuclear weapons merely to secure a trade agreement, but I am pointing out the superficiality and vagueness of the thinking behind the White Paper, its failure to work out the implications of its policy, and the shallow morality that underlies it.

5   The Principle of Proportionality

Justice in warfare also demands that action inflicted upon the enemy should be proportionate to the offence. Although the word 'proportionate' does occur in the document, it is not discussed or explained. 'Any state that we can hold responsible for assisting a nuclear attack on our vital interests can expect that this would lead to a proportionate response'.[21] It is difficult to see how, in response to blackmail or in order to secure vital national interests, it would be proportionate to launch strategic missiles against civilian populations on such a massive scale.

It might be argued that if an enemy attack were to obliterate a British city, the counter destruction of a comparable enemy city would be proportionate. This, however, assumes second strike, and to destroy an enemy city in advance would not be proportionate and would encourage retaliation. Moreover, a feature of nuclear weapons is their damaging effect not only upon the immediate victims but upon subsequent generations yet unborn, and upon populations within reach of the fall out, a factor difficult if not impossible to predict with any accuracy. For this reason alone, any use of strategic nuclear weapons must be regarded as disproportionate.

6 The Principle of the Minimisation of Suffering

Far from strategic nuclear weapons minimising human suffering, it is their very purpose to maximise suffering and thus to cause terror. The government document makes no reference to death, wounding, casualties, or suffering, and one could read it without penetrating below its surface to its human misery of which it speaks in calm technical terms. For example, consider the implications of the concept of greater payload: 'Ballistic missiles are more effective than cruise missiles because they have much greater range and payload...'[22]

7 Justice and Peace between the Nations

The Government has from time to time promised to adopt an ethical stance in international relations. This is confirmed by the assurances in the current White Paper that the country will continue to work for peace and toward the total elimination of nuclear weapons. However, the rationale for the continuance and upgrading of Britain's nuclear force is couched in very different language. The idea that the UK might be able to depend upon the continued protection of its allies to defend it in any ultimate crisis is dismissed, because a potential nuclear aggressor 'could gamble that the US or France might not put themselves at risk of nuclear attack in order to deter a nuclear attack on the UK or our allies'.[23]

On this kind of thinking every ally of the UK should develop its own nuclear facility, because one of their potential adversaries might also gamble that the UK might not risk an attack upon itself in order to deter an attack upon the ally. It is just this kind of perverse logic that makes progress towards multilateral nuclear disarmament so difficult. 'It is a key responsibility of Government', the White Paper claims, 'to be sure that the UK is properly protected should the future turn out to be less secure than we hope'.[24] But any government of any nation might make such a claim. Does not the Norwegian Government, and the Canadian Government also have the same obligation? How can nuclear proliferation be prevented if every government adopts a similar policy to secure its citizens against a nuclear future?

The White Paper illustrates this problem of security by pointing out the deficiencies of its intelligence services:

> There are limits to the extent to which intelligence can inform us about medium to long term changes in the nuclear capabilities of others, or give prior warning of a possible change in intent by an existing nuclear weapons State. We must therefore be realistic about our ability precisely to predict the nature of any future threats...[25]

This policy appears to be based upon a thinly disguised fear of the USA, France, Russia, India, Pakistan or China. No doubt any nation in the present state of human development will prefer its own interests to those of another state, but why should this affect the UK any more than Brazil, Japan or Sweden? Would we fear the nuclear states more if the UK were not a nuclear state? Probably not! In that case, we must live in fear, whether we have the nuclear weapons or not, and since fear would drive an arms race, there is little hope of preventing further proliferation. The White Paper claims that 'We will continue to work actively with all our friends and partners to enhance mutual trust and security...'[26] However, the meaning of this must be set against the following comment, 'We believe that our nuclear deterrent should retain our existing capability to deter threats anywhere in the world'.[27] It cannot be morally right to formulate a policy based on fear and mistrust which as such inhibits the development of peaceful relations between the nations. Policies that spring from fear lead to an increase of fear when implemented, and this contributes to a general increase in fear, to which more and more nations will succumb, and thus peace will recede.

8   The Ethics of Government

The fundamental weakness underlying the paper as a whole is its inadequate philosophy of government. This is expressed as follows by Mr Blair: 'The primary responsibility of any government is to ensure the safety and security of its citizens'[28]. The Executive Summary begins with a contrasting conception of governmental duty – 'The UK is committed to helping to secure international peace and security'[29] followed by a return to the first thought: 'The Government's primary responsibility is for the security of current and future UK citizens'.[30] The White Paper reveals some awareness of the tension between these two responsibilities, and seeks to reach a balance between them:

> We believe this is the right balance between our commitment to a world in which there is no place for nuclear weapons and our responsibilities to protect the current and future citizens of the UK.[31]

If these statements are true, and the nature of the balance between them is correct, then the weakness of this philosophy of government is sharply illuminated. If every government in the world conceived of its primary duty in such a manner, and in a context of general suspicion was satisfied with this adjustment of the balance, the world would inevitably become a much more dangerous place, the threat now hanging not only over the UK but over all humanity being intensified.

It is the function of the state not only to maintain the security of its citizens, but also to restrain evil and to promote and secure justice. Since the intentions of the government, or at least of the MOD and the Prime Minister, are to continue with an enduring manufacture and deployment of weapons of mass destruction, since the character of the fairness they profess is not divulged, since they persist in the legitimacy of a world divided into nuclear and non-nuclear states, and since they do not announce a planned future reduction of nuclear arms in a series of steps, the philosophy of the state to which they adhere must be denounced as incompatible with the demands of justice.

There can be no doubt that the spiritual consequences of the policy of this Government, as announced in the White Paper, will lead to a further deterioration of the moral and spiritual quality of the people of the UK. This is because they will be encouraged to adopt an attitude of fear and suspicion towards the world, and in so doing, to be prepared to use weapons which constitute a crime against humanity.

Moreover, the people of this country would have to live day by day in the knowledge of the fact, if it becomes a fact, that every day for at least ten years and maybe 25 years, they were willing to spend many millions of UK pounds to make it possible for them to threaten to destroy, and to actually annihilate if necessary, millions of other people in the most horrible circumstances. Most people could not live with this daily knowledge, and would therefore seek protection in ignorance, self-deception and pleasure. This would lead to a deadening of the conscience and a repression of natural human kindness.

Conclusion

It has become obvious during the course of this discussion that the moral insensitivity of the Government White Paper is not a matter of careless drafting. The problem goes deeper than that. The truth is that the more attention one were to pay to ethical questions, the less acceptable the document, and hence the policy itself, would become. The nature of the policy makes it necessary that the ethical questions should be avoided. But to avoid such questions is to avoid one's own humanity.

Notes

1 Ministry of Defence, *The Future of the United Kingdom's Nuclear Deterrent*: [https://www.gov.uk/government/uploads/system/uploads/attachment_data/file/27378/DefenceWhitePaper2006_Cm6994.pdf].

2 Catholic Bishops of America, 'The Harvest of Justice is Sown in Peace', 17 November 1993: [http://www.usccb.org/beliefs-and-teachings/what-we-believe/catholic-social-teaching/the-harvest-of-justice-is-sown-in-peace.cfm].

3 Tony Blair, 'Foreword' in Ministry of Defence, *The Future of the United Kingdom's Nuclear Deterrent*, p.5: [https://www.gov.uk/government/uploads/system/uploads/attachment_data/file/27378/DefenceWhitePaper2006_Cm6994.pdf].

4 Ibid, p. 5.

5 Ministry of Defence, *The Future of the United Kingdom's Nuclear Deterrent*, p. 7: [https://www.gov.uk/government/uploads/system/uploads/attachment_data/file/27378/DefenceWhitePaper2006_Cm6994.pdf].

6 Ibid, p. 7.

7 Ibid, p. 8.

8 Ibid, p. 12.

9 Ibid, p. 13.

10 Ibid, p. 17.

11 Ibid, p. 17.

12 Ibid, p. 7.

13 Ibid, p. 7.

14 Ibid, p. 17.

15 Tony Blair, Ibid, p. 5.

16 Ministry of Defence, Ibid, p. 18.

17 Tony Blair, Ibid, p. 5.

18 Ministry of Defence, Ibid, p. 6.

19 Tony Blair, Ibid, p. 5.

20 Ministry of Defence, Ibid, p. 7.

21 Ministry of Defence, Ibid, p. 19.
22 Ibid, p. 7.
23 Ibid, p. 18.
24 Ibid, p. 18.
25 Ibid, p. 18.
26 Ibid, p. 19.
27 Ibid, p. 22.
28 Tony Blair, Ibid, p. 5.
29 Ministry of Defence, Ibid, p. 6.
30 Ibid, p. 6.
31 Ibid, p. 8.

CHAPTER EIGHTEEN

Banning Nuclear Weapons: necessary and achievable (in our lifetimes)

REBECCA JOHNSON

Dr Rebecca Johnson FRSA is Co-Chair of the International Campaign to Abolish Nuclear Weapons (ICAN), co-founder of the Aldermaston Women's Peace Camp, and CND Vice President, as well as a member of Action AWE's Core Group.

> *The effects of a nuclear weapon detonation, irrespective of cause, will not be constrained by national borders, and will affect states and people in significant ways, regionally as well as globally.*

Norwegian Foreign Minister, Espen Barth Eide, Chair's summary, Oslo Conference on the Humanitarian Impacts of Nuclear Weapons, 5 March 2013

> *Nuclear weapons should be stigmatised, banned and eliminated before they abolish us.*

Federal President of Austria, Heinz Fischer, High Level Meeting of the UN General Assembly on Nuclear Disarmament, New York, 26 September 2013

AS LONG AS nuclear weapons exist, they may be used. That's the conclusion drawn by the world's leaders, from UN Secretary-General Ban Ki-moon to numerous presidents, including recent British Prime Ministers. Dr Hassan Rouhani, speaking for the first time as President of Iran and Chair of the 120 member Non-Aligned Movement during a ground-breaking High Level Meeting on nuclear disarmament held by the UN General Assembly in September 2013, made the obvious connection with abolition, saying: 'As long as nuclear weapons exist, the risk of their use, threat of use and proliferation persist. The only absolute guarantee is their total elimination.'[1]

Most, if not all, the nuclear-armed states say they want security without nuclear weapons, but they are carrying on with programmes to modernise and deploy them for many years to come. After decades in which treaty obligations such as 1968 Non-Proliferation Treaty (NPT) have been evoked to justify nuclear programmes and modernisation, it's time for those that really want to achieve disarmament to change our strategies. Despite all evidence to the contrary, we've continued to behave as if the NPT provides an adequate legal basis for disarmament and that step by step reductions will somehow lead to zero. By creating a multilateral process for a new treaty designed to prohibit nuclear weapons for everyone on an equal basis, we change the rules of the game. By re-framing nuclear disarmament in humanitarian terms we put the onus for disarmament action on the nuclear free as well as nuclear-armed governments. Under international humanitarian law, a multilateral treaty could be brought into force far more quickly and directly than through the processes of traditional arms control, which have to bow to the political interests of the states that wield these weapons of mass suffering for their own purposes. While it is desirable to pressure the nuclear-armed states as much as possible, it is not necessary to wait for them all to see the light. The humanitarian law approach makes it just as much the responsibility of nuclear free states – the majority by far – to negotiate a new, globally applicable treaty that would ban the use, deployment, production, transfer, transporting and stockpiling of nuclear weapons and require their elimination.

History shows that legal prohibitions generally precede and facilitate the processes of stockpile elimination, not the other way around. And history and experience also show that weapons that have been outlawed become more quickly stigmatised and taken out of circulation. They come to lose their political status, and so do not keep having money and resources invested in their production, modernisation, proliferation and perpetuation. That – though the major political parties don't yet acknowledge it – would be good news for Britain, where the current Government is still stuck on an outdated plan to replace Trident, costing billions that would be better spent on real human security needs. Most British people don't want these nuclear weapons, and the Scottish government is determined not to store the warheads at Coulport or deploy Trident-armed submarines at Faslane.

This chapter focuses on recent international approaches aimed at achieving a new international treaty to ban nuclear weapons and cut through all the objections of the reluctant weapons states. Already much work has been done to build alliances between governments and the International Campaign to Abolish Nuclear Weapons (ICAN) – a relatively new and fast-growing network of local, national and international civil society NGOs who have been working on humanitarian, rights and environmental issues as well as disarmament. ICAN's strategy is to create pressure and incentives for a significant cross-regional group of governments to start negotiations on a nuclear weapons ban as the next step towards eliminating nuclear weapons. This chapter looks at why this approach could become the tipping point to achieve nuclear disarmament once and for all, much sooner that previously envisaged.

Why do we need a new treaty?

Protecting all people's security and our fragile planetary environment must be a vital national security interest for all governments as well as an international security priority. The experiences of over 100 years of arms control and disarmament for many kinds of weapons – from biological and chemical weapons to land-mines, cluster munitions and laser blinding weapons – show us the importance of getting international negotiations to prohibit the use, deployment, manufacture, stockpiling and transfer of weapons of mass suffering, and to create international laws that unequivocally and without exception require their total elimination. The existence of such treaties doesn't remove all risks, but they play a vital part in reducing dangers and incentives and providing legal and political tools to deal with perpetrators and prevent any terrorist (state or non-state) use from escalating even more catastrophically.

Efforts to eliminate nuclear weapons have been an uphill struggle, in large part because of the double standards and nuclear myths of the Cold War.[2] Instead of banning nuclear weapons after they brought the world to the brink of annihilation in the 1962 Cuban Missile Crisis, the major powers decided on an approach aimed at non-proliferation – to keep their own arsenals but stop the spread of such terrible weapons to more countries. Over 40 years after the NPT entered into force, there are nine nuclear-armed states and over 17,000 nuclear weapons still at large.[3] The overkill capacity of the largest arsenals has been reduced from its Cold War peak of over 50,000 in the 1980s, but the five nuclear-weapon states recognised by the NPT – China, France, Russia, the UK and United States – have been joined by four more: Israel, with an undeclared nuclear arsenal of unknown strength and capabilities, estimated at over 80 warheads; India and Pakistan, which are locked into a competitive nuclear arms race and estimated to have built more than 100 weapons each since conducting nuclear tests in 1998; and North Korea, which left the NPT in 2003 and appears determined to test and deploy nuclear weapons. Others – such as Iran, despite claiming its unnecessary nuclear fuel cycle programme is for 'peaceful purposes' – are suspected of wanting to join these nuclear-armed states.[4]

For decades, the majority of governments have abided by the NPT and tried to get the nuclear-armed states to fulfil their part of the disarmament non-proliferation bargain. I have attended every NPT meeting since 1994 and worked with governments to develop principles, objectives and action plans with unilateral, bilateral and multilateral commitments.[5] If pursued as agreed, these step by step programmes would have brought us close to a nuclear-free world by now. But they were treated as paper words rather than binding legal commitments by the nuclear-armed states, who have kept modernising their weapons and spending billions on refurbishing their nuclear laboratories and facilities so that they could continue to design, make and deploy these inhumane weapons systems for the next century.[6] Constructed to ensure that the Cold War nuclear-armed states would maintain their power and control, the NPT has had the counterproductive consequence of marginalising the concerns of the nuclear free countries, impeding genuine disarmament, and assisting proliferation.

Despite years of legal advice, arguments, judgements and even the 1996 advisory opinion of the International Court of Justice (ICJ) on the use and threat of use of nuclear weapons,[7] the nuclear-armed states continue to claim that their possession, deployments, weapons collaboration programmes, and nuclear use doctrines are either consistent with or else not covered by the NPT.[8] Though the NPT has a weakly worded obligation under its Article VI to pursue nuclear disarmament 'in good faith', it has not had any effective legal impact on the nuclear-modernisation and perpetuation policies of the nuclear-armed states. As long as some countries insist that the NPT legitimises their possession of these weapons of mass suffering, proliferation and the risks of nuclear weapons use and accidents will remain a major threat to peace and security.

We're being conned by nuclear-armed leaders saying they want a world free of nuclear weapons while undermining effective steps to get there. US-Russian agreements to reduce their arsenals should be internationally welcomed, but do not contribute to disarmament while they pour money into their nuclear labs to refine and modernise the thousands they still deploy. Claiming legitimacy under the NPT, in 2010 the British and French governments signed a new agreement on nuclear collaboration. The 'Teutates Treaty' committed these two nuclear-armed states to share technologies and use each other's nuclear weapons facilities to enhance and maintain their nuclear arsenals for the next 50 years.[9] China keeps its weapon numbers below 500 but continues to upgrade and modernise its warheads and delivery systems, while India and Pakistan would like to benefit from the NPT if they were allowed in as 'nuclear-weapon states'.

It is a glaring omission and anomaly in international law that nuclear weapons – the most destructive and inhumane of all weapons – are not yet subject to an explicit treaty prohibition. On entering into force, the treaties prohibiting biological and chemical weapons created the unequivocal recognition that any use of such weapons would be a crime against humanity and war crime under international law. By contrast, nuclear 'deterrence' doctrines – whether 'first use' or 'retaliatory' – indicate that nuclear-armed states do not recognise that they would be guilty of crimes against humanity and war crimes if they unleash their nuclear weapons. As the reaction to the use of chemical weapons in the Syrian war showed, the biological and chemical weapons treaties provide invaluable legal and political tools to hold perpetrators accountable and eliminate the weapons; the international legal consequences of violating the biological and chemical weapons treaties' prohibitions are applicable to non-signatories once the core prohibitions have become embedded in international law.

Catastrophic humanitarian consequences – an imperative to ban nuclear weapons

Learning from the strategies that brought about the treaties banning land mines (1997) and cluster munitions (2007), ICAN has taken the lead in coordinating civil society to reawaken understanding that nuclear use and accidental detonations would cause unbearable suffering and unacceptable humanitarian consequences, and focus those concerns into pressure on governments to negotiate a global nuclear ban treaty. The information and arguments go beyond moral repugnance by providing a route towards a practical nuclear ban treaty under international humanitarian law. Disarmament advocates are being joined by humanitarian organisations such as the Red Cross and Red Crescent Societies, which since 2010 have produced information and adopted resolutions to reawaken the understanding and argue for them to be outlawed.[10]

No-one who has seen photographs of the devastation and misery caused by the two atom bombs used on Hiroshima and Nagasaki can deny that a single detonation would create unimaginable horrors for the people directly affected. We've probably all heard about the intense heat, blast and fire storms that would kill hundreds of thousands immediately. Radiation sickness would kill many more in the first days, weeks and months to follow. Radioactivity would also be deposited in a wide area as fall-out from the nuclear mushroom clouds, and this would contaminate agricultural lands and homes across a far wider area, depending on wind and weather patterns. But fear of these dreadful consequences receded at the end of the Cold War. Most people thought the dangers were being reduced, while others believed that it was moral for some states to have nuclear weapons for the purposes of 'nuclear deterrence' and prevention of war.

That complacency is being shaken by historical analyses that cast doubt on the theories of nuclear deterrence and use of nuclear weapons for war prevention[11] and also by updated scientific studies showing that 'nuclear winter' and widespread famine would occur if only a small fraction of today's arsenals were used against cities in a regional war.[12] Soviet President Mikhail Gorbachev was persuaded to pull back from the brink and kick-start disarmament talks in the mid-'80s by reports from US and Soviet scientists that demonstrated that nuclear war would cause planet-wide 'nuclear winter'.[13] Such studies are becoming influential once more, after being updated with data and calculations from the past 30 years of climate change research.

Based on the use of only a small fraction of today's arsenals in a 'limited' or regional nuclear war, climate scientists have demonstrated that the explosions and fires would propel millions of tonnes of soot, smoke and debris into the upper atmosphere, darkening the skies, causing temperatures across the planet to plummet and disrupting rainfall and agriculture everywhere on earth.[14] These effects could persist for over a decade, with devastating consequences for food resources and the health and life cycles of many species. Building on this research, scientists and physicians have conducted analyses on the health and humanitarian consequences of various 'limited scenarios'. Bearing in mind increases in global population and urbanisation since the 1980s, Dr Ira Helfand and others have concluded that in addition to the millions that would die from the direct effects of a regional nuclear war, over one billion people around the world would be put at risk of starvation and death due to famine and the epidemics and other health and security disasters that breed on the backs of large-scale hunger and malnutrition.[15] To put this into perspective, that level of appalling global disruption would be caused if one or more nuclear-armed states detonated just 0.5 percent of current nuclear arsenals – equivalent to less than half the explosive power carried on board one Trident-armed British submarine.

Further British-based studies have analysed the humanitarian consequences of various scenarios involving attacks on UK cities and, since we are also responsible for the weapons fired in our name, if one UK submarine launched Trident missiles at Russian cities. The studies show a scale of destruction, death and suffering that is truly shocking, confirming that nuclear winter and global famine could be caused by a relatively small number of nuclear detonations. In addition, in this interconnected world we have to think about how the lives of survivors would be made extremely difficult as the effects of nuclear weapons destroyed electronic communications and the transporting of blood, medical supplies and food resources around the world. And radiation would continue to contaminate wide areas for many generations.[16]

Most people prefer not to think about nuclear weapons being used, but these studies show that we must. It is irresponsible of leaders to hide behind glib assertions that 'the point of having nuclear weapons is to deter people and not to use them' (David Cameron, 2010) or that they are an 'ultimate insurance' (Tony Blair, 2006). Deterrence is not a property of a weapon but a relationship between potential adversaries, and history shows how often deterrent communications and threats can go wrong. The 'use them or lose them' logic and quick, computerised, launch operations associated with nuclear deterrence policies makes it more rather than less likely that nuclear weapons will be used, especially in times of conflict, uncertainty and mistrust. As well as the catastrophic humanitarian harm that just one or a few nuclear weapons would create, an unforeseen or badly managed conflict involving nuclear-armed leaders could escalate into nuclear war. Millions of people in countries far from the weapons' intended targets would suffer from contamination, climate disruption and nuclear-induced famine. As long as nuclear weapons are deployed, the risks of nuclear use, accident and war remain unacceptably high.

Civil society and government partnership to ban and eliminate nuclear weapons

ICAN has been persuading governments that in view of the transnational effects and consequences of nuclear detonations, accidents and war, the non-nuclear countries have their own compelling security imperative as well as the responsibility to initiate and carry through negotiations to ban and eliminate nuclear weapons. While it goes without saying that the nuclear-armed states should be encouraged and pressured to join in this collective endeavour to make the world safe from nuclear weapons, they should not be allowed to control or block the process. The non-nuclear countries need to move forward now. Whether or not the nuclear-armed states feel ready to participate at the start, the proposed nuclear ban treaty would change the political and legal context and remove the special status accorded to the countries that wield nuclear weapons.

These strategies are already putting humanitarian disarmament onto the international agenda. Following a UN General Assembly resolution in 2012, an UN-mandated 'open-ended working group' has been meeting in Geneva to discuss how to move forward on nuclear disarmament. Shockingly, the 'P5' nuclear-weapon states boycotted these multilateral talks in 2013.[17] In March 2013, the Norwegian government hosted an international conference in Oslo to consider the humanitarian impacts of nuclear weapons. Though 127 governments participated, the P5, Israel and North Korea boycotted the conference. Nonetheless, Mexico has taken the next step of convening a further international conference in February 2014, to further and deepen governments' understanding of the humanitarian consequences of nuclear weapons and consider what to do to prevent future catastrophe. The humanitarian train, as noted by one high ranking diplomat, has left the station. Civil society has to make sure that it heads towards a nuclear ban treaty, which is increasingly being recognised as the next station towards nuclear disarmament.

Following the Oslo Conference, 80 NPT member states co-sponsored a strong statement at the NPT 'PrepCom' meeting in 2013 – up from 16 the year before. Aware that boycotting Oslo and the UN Open-ended Working Group backfired on them, Britain, France and the United States tried a different tack by attending the September 2013 High Level Meeting on Nuclear Disarmament held at the United Nations, using a joint statement to criticise other governments for directing energy towards humanitarian nuclear disarmament initiatives. They tried to guilt-trip them into working only through the NPT – which confers special privileges on five nuclear-armed states – and the Conference on Disarmament and UN Disarmament Commission, which have been deadlocked and passive for over 18 years.[18]

Intended to be effectively multilateral by being open to all and blockable by none, the humanitarian strategies are much harder for the nuclear-armed states to prevent or block than disarmament programmes that have been proposed through the NPT, Conference on Disarmament or via traditional arms control approaches.[19] Contrary to the criticisms of some nuclear-armed states, the humanitarian disarmament concerns build on the NPT, which at its 2010 Review Conference clearly stated NPT parties' 'deep concern at the catastrophic humanitarian consequences of any use of nuclear weapons and reaffirms the need for all States at all times to comply with applicable international law, including international humanitarian law.'[20] The 2010 Final Document also declared that 'all States need to make special efforts to establish the necessary framework to achieve and maintain a world without nuclear weapons' and noted, for example: the five-point proposal for nuclear disarmament of the Secretary-General of the United Nations, which proposes, inter alia, consideration of negotiations on a nuclear weapons convention or agreement on a framework of separate mutually reinforcing instruments, backed by a strong system of verification.[21]

A major reason why the humanitarian disarmament strategies in several different fora are making the nuclear-armed states nervous is that they are creating new opportunities and better mechanisms to bring about disarmament. Most importantly, they enable the states that have renounced nuclear weapons by joining the NPT and various nuclear-weapon-free zone treaties to play a larger role in stigmatising and eliminating the weapons globally – based on their own national and international security. The reinvigorated international movement for a nuclear ban remains supportive of the NPT's disarmament and non-proliferation objectives, but it is strategically aimed at getting a treaty that will reinforce the regime by fundamentally changing the legal and political context within which nuclear-armed states and proliferators operate. The aim is a universally applicable prohibition under international law that will apply equally to all. No more privileges for nuclear 'haves' that Britain and others can use to justify continuing to make and deploy nuclear weapons. No more 'let-outs' for states that don't sign on to the treaty, like India, Pakistan and

Israel. Since this would be first and foremost a treaty for international and collective security, it would not promote nuclear energy and would create obligations and regulatory frameworks to ensure that nuclear technologies could not be used to supply or support nuclear weapons programmes.

Once the treaty is concluded and enters into force it will become part of the body of international law, alongside the NPT, Geneva Protocols, Mine Ban Treaty, Cluster Munitions Convention, Chemical Weapons Convention, Biological and Toxin Weapons Convention and CTBT.[22] A nuclear ban treaty does not have to negotiate a schedule for the weapons to be eliminated.[23] It is recognised that dismantling and destroying all the existing weapons will take time, and requires careful dismantling, security and verification processes. The weapons labs are equipped to accomplish these sensitive technical tasks, and a treaty would shift the burden of proof and make it more clearly in the nuclear-armed states' interests to develop effective ways to monitor and verify each other. Instead of wasting our billions on designing and making new warheads, Aldermaston scientists and the British government should take the lead in developing technically safe and secure methods to accomplish the total and verified elimination of all nuclear armaments, as they did for verifying the CTBT. They've had over 40 years experience of dismantling weapons deemed surplus to requirements, but under the NPT they have simply carried on making new ones. Disarmament histories show that they are more likely to accelerate the practical tasks of eliminating all their weapons – individually or together – if a treaty is already in place that unequivocally makes this an obligation, and includes universal prohibitions on the use, deployment, production and stockpiling of the weapons.

A multilateral nuclear ban treaty – the next step off the nuclear treadmill

For the past 30 years, British people have paid billions to deploy the current Trident system from Faslane (against Scotland's wishes) and keep producing nuclear warheads at AWE Aldermaston and Burghfield. This was a decision taken in 1979 on the basis of 'expert' projections about future Soviet threats and developments that were proved spectacularly wrong. By the time the first Vanguard submarine headed out to see with its Trident missiles in 1994, the Cold War was over. Now British politicians are tying themselves in knots to justify spending another £100 billion on the next generation of Trident for another 30–50 years of nuclear prolif-eration, risks and fears. Once again, their analyses have got it wrong, badly misjudging future trends and developments in international security, and costing British people billions in wasted military resources.

British politicians have lined up to say they want a world free of nuclear weapons, but everything that they do is geared towards perpetu-ating nuclear arsenals, not only for themselves but for others. Rather like the sad old 'joke' about a smoker who keeps going to France to load up his car with duty free cigarettes while praying 'Lord, help me to stop – but not yet'. Like that smoker, the nuclear-armed states think that they can carry on making and deploying nuclear weapons until they decide – in their own, sweet, unhurried time – that they ought to stop. Decades ago, it was assumed that smoking was an individual right or choice, and that the smokers had to be cajoled with appeals about their own health and welfare. Those approaches had limited impact. The real change in behav-iour and incentives occurred when non-smokers led the way to prohibit smoking in public spaces and workplaces. Similarly, international prohi-bition treaties like the Chemical Weapons Convention and Mine Ban Treaty have significantly changed the behaviour of states that did their utmost to prevent negotiations in the first place. As the treaties entered into force under international law they also embedded norms, taboos and expectations.

Local, national and international security demands that we bring together campaigns like Action AWE with CND and ICAN, to integrate global efforts to ban nuclear weapons with British public and political efforts to scrap Trident. By contrast with the 'not in my lifetime' caveats of the nuclear-armed states, recent, game-changing strategies by nuclear free people and governments are bringing a global nuclear ban treaty within reach.

Action AWE is building on Trident Ploughshares and the Aldermaston Women's Peace Camp(aign) to mobilise activists – from environmental and poverty campaigning as well an established civil society organisations like CND. In turn, UK activism to prevent Trident replacement can inspire and boost international initiatives and ICAN's global campaigning for a nuclear ban treaty. At all levels, we have necessary and important roles to play in halting further nuclear weapons production and deployment and creating political pressure for our governments to negotiate and conclude a fully comprehensive nuclear ban treaty without further delay.

Even before this treaty enters into full legal force, it will give us more effective tools in international law to ensure that our governments are held accountable for halting nuclear production and proliferation and eliminating their arsenals as quickly, safely and securely as possible. Such a treaty will stigmatise nuclear weapons and make sure that state and non-state actors understand that using and preparing to use nuclear weapons constitute crimes against humanity and war crimes, and that perpetrators, suppliers and others who violate the legal norms established by a nuclear ban treaty will be prosecuted and brought to the International Criminal Court, even if they come from countries that have not yet signed.

The table below graphically shows the key differences between the status quo arms control approach and the humanitarian disarmament approach. Our challenge now is to choose the most effective actions, arguments and approaches to create a tipping point that will require and enable the world to ban nuclear weapons. This in turn will require and enable Britain, NATO and the other nuclear-armed states to undertake genuine and irreversible steps to eliminate their current arsenals and stop wasting further resources on replacements.

Arms control and non-proliferation premises and UK government assumptions	Humanitarian disarmament premises and new thinking about tackling nuclear weapons
Proliferation is bad but can be managed.	Proliferation is bad and isn't being safely managed.
Proliferation is best stemmed by tightening nuclear security procedures and controls on the non-nuclear-weapon states	Stemming proliferation also requires halting the acquisition, modernisation and spread of nuclear weapons and stigmatising nuclear as well as other WMD as unusable, inhumane and its use as pariah/ha'aram
Nuclear weapons are essential for deterrence but cause insecurity if in the 'wrong' hands.	Nuclear deterrence is a dangerously misguided belief system, and doctrines of use and deployment create greater humanitarian threats, risks and instabilities than other deterrence tools.

Arms control and non-proliferation premises and UK government assumptions	Humanitarian disarmament premises and new thinking about tackling nuclear weapons
'We' can't 'give up' nuclear weapons before others. We need them as long as anyone else has some.	Scrapping nuclear weapons first will help move the process forward without compromising anyone's security because these weapons have no real military or security utility.
Status quo possession is stabilising, and proliferation is not affected by the actions and policies of recognised nuclear-weapon states.	The high value accorded to possessing nuclear weapons is a salient proliferation driver.
Nuclear weapons are by definition deterrents.	Deterrence is not a property or attribute of a weapon, but a complex, multifaceted relationship and process among potential adversaries, requiring accurate and effective communications and interpretations of information, intentions and cultural implications.
Nuclear deterrence requires credible scenarios and operations to demonstrate a readiness to fire and an ability to deliver 'unacceptable loss'.	The role of nuclear weapons in deterrence is questionable, unproven and unprovable. Threatening 'unacceptable loss' is inhumane and won't deter non-state or many state adversaries. Other states' actions and intentions may be miscalculated or misinterpreted.
Nuclear deterrence ensures that responsible states can extend security to their allies and have freedom of action where necessary.	The illusions of deterrence lead nuclear-armed states to take more risks and think they can project regional or international power ('punch above their weight'), which is dangerous and destabilising.
Nuclear deterrence is necessary for 'us' and must be maintained (but may be possible to do with lower numbers).	Nuclear weapons are not necessary for deterrence, which is determined by factors other than the number or size of nuclear weapons a country possesses.

Arms control and non-proliferation premises and UK government assumptions	Humanitarian disarmament premises and new thinking about tackling nuclear weapons
Nuclear deterrence is not necessary for non-nuclear countries, unless they are in alliance with nuclear-armed states.	If nuclear deterrence worked as theorised, every state should have the right to nuclear weapons of their own. That would of course be a recipe for insecurity and humanitarian disaster.
It is not necessary to consider the consequences of nuclear detonations because nuclear deterrence will ensure that these nuclear weapons won't be used.	When nuclear deterrence fails, the humanitarian consequences will be catastrophic.
Regional nuclear-weapon-free zones (NWFZ) and incremental steps have to be taken first.	Regional and international nuclear problems are interconnected, and international initiatives to ban nuclear weapons will reinforce and accelerate strategies to conclude further NWFZ.
Nuclear weapons have to be greatly reduced and eliminated before there can be any question of prohibiting them with a treaty.	A nuclear ban treaty will change the legal and political context and push the nuclear-armed states to accelerate the total elimination of their arsenals.
Working towards a nuclear weapons convention or other comprehensive nuclear treaty will undermine and distract from the NPT.	Working towards and achieving a nuclear ban treaty will help to fulfil the aims and objectives enshrined in the NPT, just as the 1996 Comprehensive Test Ban Treaty (CTBT) reinforced and fulfilled the 1963 Partial Test Ban Treaty (PTBT).

Arms control and non-proliferation approach (status quo reinforcing)	Humanitarian disarmament approach (game-changing)
The NPT is the cornerstone of the non-proliferation regime and is okay as long as we keep talking about disarmament and universality.	As a cornerstone dating back to the 1960s, the NPT needs to be built on with new treaties and agreements in order to achieve nuclear disarmament and create a non-discriminatory and universally effective regime to prohibit and eliminate nuclear weapons.
The NPT is useful for enabling the 'recognised' nuclear-weapon states to take the lead in managing this high value, important and desirable weapon while stopping its spread to others, unless they have already successfully developed their weapons outside the NPT in which case we will protect their interests along with our own.	It is time to ban and abolish this inhumane, unusable weapon that is contrary to humanity's interests and threatens our future survival. The nuclear-free governments and civil society must take the lead to achieve a non-discriminatory, universal treaty that will ban the use, deployment, production, stockpiling and transporting of nuclear weapons and require their total elimination.
Objective: do enough to appease nuclear free states in the NPT and keep the non-proliferation regime going with the 'recognized nuclear-weapon states' in charge.	Objective: accelerate the elimination of all nuclear weapons through a universally applicable nuclear ban treaty that will change the legal and political context of nuclear decision-making.
Focus on stabilising status quo among nuclear 'haves' and counter-proliferation and 'nuclear security' to prevent nuclear weapons being acquired by new or 'bad' actors.	Focus on changing international law and delegitimising nuclear weapons use and doctrines of threatened use (including nuclear deterrence).
Talk about step by step reductions in the context of the NPT while maintaining infrastructure and options for the current nuclear-armed states to keep modernizing and rearming.	Use all available multilateral fora and opportunities to highlight the catastrophic humanitarian conse quences of nuclear weapons and make the case for a nuclear ban treaty that would transform the legal

Arms control and non-proliferation approach (status quo reinforcing)	Humanitarian disarmament approach (game-changing)
	and political context for everyone and give us new, stronger tools to stop proliferation, close down nuclear programmes and bases, and hold our governments accountable.
Emphasis on reducing numbers of largest arsenals and maintaining more modern less expensive nuclear arsenals (for the foreseeable future).	Emphasis on banning use, deployment, production, stockpiling and production on nuclear weapons for all nuclear-armed states and providing obligations to create a more irreversible context for reducing and eliminating arsenals now.
Maintain national security and strategic stability, especially among nuclear-armed states, and projecting security with nuclear weapons.	Promote human security, create more sustainable national, regional and international security without nuclear weapons for everyone, and prevent harm to potential victims, including preventing catastrophic humanitarian consequences if nuclear weapons are detonated
Maintain (and if necessary adapt) nuclear deterrence as a potent doctrine of security, insurance and power projection.	Challenge and discredit nuclear deterrence beliefs and postures, as these perpetuate proliferation and impede disarmament.
Nuclear weapons and disarmament questions are a primary national security interest for the states that have them.	Nuclear weapons are a major human and global security issue, and nuclear disarmament is everyone's responsibility and in everyone's interests.
The most important actors are the nuclear weapons states, military and technical experts.	The non-nuclear weapon states must take more responsibility to initiate, lead and drive a humanitarian disarmament process with humanitarian agencies and NGOs and all sectors of civil society.

Arms control and non-proliferation approach (status quo reinforcing)	Humanitarian disarmament approach (game-changing)
The nuclear-weapon states must determine the pace and steps for nuclear disarmament.	Because of vested interests, the nuclear-armed states will fail to disarm without leadership from key nuclear-free states to ban nuclear weapons.
The non-nuclear states should support whatever the nuclear-armed states feel able to agree.	The nuclear-armed states are encouraged to participate in multilateral nuclear treaty negotiations but not empowered to block.
Processes include bilateral nuclear reduction negotiations between US and Russia, voluntary unilateral cuts; confidence building talks among the P5 nuclear-weapon states might eventually lead to negotiations.	Bring together a cross regional group of significant states to initiate multilateral negotiations on a nuclear ban treaty that can enter into force and create the conditions for accelerating the elimination of all nuclear arsenals.
Nuclear disarmament is impossible unless and until all nuclear-armed states are fully on board.	Even if the nuclear-armed states reject a multilateral nuclear ban treaty to begin with, it will change their policies and behaviour, making it much harder to keep modernising and perpetuating nuclear arsenals.

Notes

1   Dr Hassan Rouhani, statement on behalf of the NAM to the High Level Meeting of the UN General Assembly on Nuclear Disarmament, New York, 26 September 2013: [http://www.reachingcriticalwill.org/images/documents/Disarmament-fora/HLM/26Sep_NAM.pdf].

2   Rebecca Johnson, 'Rethinking the NPT's role in security: 2010 and beyond', *International Affairs* 86:2 (2010), Royal Institute of International Affairs, Chatham House.

3   SIPRI Yearbook 2013, Stockholm International Peace Research Institute: [http://www.sipri.org/yearbook/2013/files/SIPRIYB13Summary.pdf].

4   The NPT was useful in signing up most of the world (185 of its states parties joined as non-nuclear-weapon states) and developing a variety of additional procedures and agreements for nuclear monitoring, safeguards and export

controls. Iran is the most recent to cause concern for manipulating the Article IV nuclear energy provision. Concerns about the unintended consequences of both Article IV and Article VI, are underpinned by science and history: almost all the nuclear-armed states developed their weapons capabilities through nuclear energy programmes.

5   The most comprehensive plan agreed by NPT states parties was negotiated primarily between the P5 nuclear-weapon states and the New Agenda Coalition of seven non-nuclear states in 2000. Dubbed the 'thirteen steps', the disarmament plan of action was adopted by the 2000 Review Conference of the Parties to the Treaty on the Non-Proliferation of Nuclear Weapons, Final Document, May 20, 2000, New York, NPT/CONF.2000/28 Part I. The commitments were largely ignored by the nuclear-weapon states for the next ten years and then renegotiated in a much weaker form in the 2010 Review Conference of the Parties to the Treaty on the Non-Proliferation of Nuclear Weapons, Final Document, Volume I, Part I.

6   We should not be surprised that traditional arms control has failed to deliver disarmament. Human history, reason, and lawmaking experiences show that those with vested interests in a weapon, activity or crime are going to drag their feet if they think they can hang on to their privileges and avoid penalties for ignoring the security and needs of the community.

7   See the various analyses in Rebecca Johnson and Angie Zelter, eds. *Trident and International Law: Scotland's Obigations,* (Luath Press, 2011).

8   See for example the 2006 White Paper on 'The future of the UK's nuclear deterrent': [https://www.gov.uk/government/uploads/system/uploads/attachment_data/file/27378/DefenceWhitePaper2006_Cm6994.pdf], which paved the way for Tony Blair to tell the House of Commons in 2007 that the NPT gives Britain 'the right to possess nuclear weapons': [http://www.acronym.org.uk/uk/index.htm]; and Mohammed ElBaradei, *The Age of Deception: Nuclear Diplomacy in Treacherous Times,* Bloomsbury 2011. See also the 2013 Trident Alternatives Review, published by HM Government on 16 July 2013: [https://www.gov.uk/government/uploads/system/uploads/attachment_data/file/212745/20130716_Trident_Alternatives_Study.pdf] For analysis see Rebecca Johnson: Trident Alternatives Review: the elephant in the room, openDemocracy, 5 August 2013: [http://www.opendemocracy.net/5050/rebecca-johnson/trident-alternatives-review-elephant-in-room].

9   See Nuclear Information Service briefings: [http://nuclearinfo.org/blog/nuclear-information-service/2013/04/nis-presentation-uk-%E2%80%93-france-nuclear-weapons-co-operation, http://www.nuclearinfo.org/sites/default/files/NIS%20Anglo-French%20co-operation%20briefing%20November%202010.pdf].

10 For the first time since 1982, the International Red Cross and Red Crescent

Movement adopted a resolution on nuclear weapons, which called for their use to be prohibited and the weapons to be totally eliminated: 'Working towards the elimination of nuclear weapons', Resolution adopted by the Council of Delegates of the International Red Cross and Red Crescent Movement, Geneva, 26 November 2011. EN CD/11/R1.

11 Ward Wilson, *Five Myths about Nuclear Weapons*, Houghton Mifflin Harcourt, 2012.

12 See for example, Owen B. Toon, Richard P. Turco, Alan Robock, Charles Badeen, Luke Oman and Georgiy L. Stenchikov, 'Atmospheric effects and societal consequences of regional scale nuclear conflicts and acts of individual nuclear terrorism'; also Alan Robock, Luke Oman, Georgiy L. Stenchikov, Owen B. Toon, Charles Badeen and Richard P. Turco, 'Climate consequences of regional nuclear conflicts', Atm. Chem. Phys. 7 (2007); and Ira Helfand, 'Nuclear Famine: A Billion People at Risk', IPPNW, 2012.

13 Mark Hertsgaard, 'Mikhail Gorbachev explains what's rotten in Russia', *Salon.com*, 7 September 2000.

14 Toon, Owen B., Richard P. Turco, Alan Robock, Charles Badeen, Luke Oman and Georgiy L. Stenchikov, 'Atmospheric effects and societal consequences of regional scale nuclear conflicts and acts of individual nuclear terrorism'; also Robock, Alan, Luke Oman, Georgiy L. Stenchikov, Owen B. Toon, Charles Badeen and Richard P. Turco, 'Climate consequences of regional nuclear conflicts', Atm. Chem. Phys. 7 (2007).

15 Helfand, Ira, 'Nuclear Famine: A Billion People at Risk', IPPNW, 2012.

16 For example, see Rebecca Johnson, 'Unacceptable Risks: UK-relevant reports on the humanitarian consequences of nuclear weapons'; Richard Moyes, Philip Webber and Greg Crowther, *Humanitarian consequences: Short case study of the direct humanitarian impacts from a single nuclear weapon detonation on Manchester, UK*. Article 36, February 2013; Frank Boulton, *Blood Transfusion Services in the wake of the humanitarian and health crisis following multiple detonations of nuclear weapons*, Medact, February 2013; John Large, *The Lay-person's Alternative Guide to REPPIR Relating to the Atomic Weapons Establishment (AWE) Aldermaston and Burghfield*, Nuclear Information Service, April 2012; John Ainslie, *If Britain Fired Trident: The humanitarian catastrophe that one Trident-armed UK nuclear submarine could cause if used against Moscow*, Scottish CND February 2013; Philip Webber, *The climatic impacts and humanitarian problems from the use of the UK's nuclear weapons*, Scientists for Global Responsibility, February 2013 (revised from SGR Winter 2008). These reports are all available from the ICAN and Acronym Institute websites.

17 'P5' is UN jargon for the five permanent members of the UN Security Council

– China, France, Russia, the United Kingdom and United States – which are also the defined 'nuclear-weapon states' recognised by the NPT.

18 Alistair Burt, statement on behalf of France, the United Kingdom and the United States, to the High Level Meeting of the UN General Assembly on Nuclear Disarmament, New York, 26 September 2013: [http://www.reachingcriticalwill.org/images/documents/Disarmament-fora/HLM/26Sep_UKUSFrance.pdf].

19 Documents obtained through freedom of information requests have revealed that they are worried that when other governments discuss and understand the humanitarian consequences of nuclear weapons, the next logical step will be a process to prohibit the weapons and put the onus much more strongly on the nuclear-armed states to get rid of them. See the ICAN and Article 36 websites for further detail on these documents.

20 A (Principles and Objectives) v, Conclusions and recommendations for follow-on actions, 2010 Review Conference of the Parties to the Treaty on the Non-Proliferation of Nuclear Weapons, Final Document, Part 1.

21 B (Disarmament of Nuclear Weapons) iii, Conclusions and recommendations for follow-on actions, 2010 Review Conference of the Parties to the Treaty on the Non-Proliferation of Nuclear Weapons, Final Document, Part 1.

22 See the Acronym Institute website [www.acronym.org.uk] for information on these treaties and links to other organisations with knowledge and expertise in these areas. The CTBT has not yet formally entered into force, but as it has been signed by over 180 states and ratified by more than 150 it is generally viewed as part of the body of international law relating to nuclear weapons.

23 The recognition that effective new obligations can be created without negotiating all aspects of verification and elimination is the key difference between earlier civil society efforts to demonstrate the feasibility of nuclear disarmament through a detailed model 'nuclear weapons convention' (NWC), circulated in 1997 and 2007, and the humanitarian strategy to fast track negotiations for a simpler nuclear ban treaty. Advocates of both approaches acknowledge that the technical and physical eliminations require the agreement and participation of the nuclear armed states. As someone who initiated and helped draft the NGO model nuclear weapons convention, I think it did a good job of showing what a fully comprehensive treaty would have to do. As a political strategist analysing how narrowly perceived national interests of a handful of nuclear-armed states blocked negotiations on a small, incremental objective such as a fissile materials treaty in the Conference on Disarmament, I grew increasingly concerned

that the 'all or nothing' multilateral negotiations implied in the NWC approach put too much power in the hands of the most reluctant nuclear-armed states who would keep finding ways to stop NWC negotiations from ever getting started. By focusing on the legal necessity of prohibition – which can be achieved with or without the nuclear armed states – a nuclear ban treaty would irrevocably change the political calculus, creating obligations and removing existing justifications and incentives for impeding additional agreements on fissile materials, weapons reductions and verified elimination.

CHAPTER NINETEEN

Drones, Cyberwarfare and Democracy

PAUL MOBBS

Paul Mobbs is an independent environmental consultant, researcher, writer and engineer, specialising in work with community groups and grassroots campaigns. His website is www.fraw.org.uk/mei.

ON 17 OCTOBER 2013, Ben Emmerson – the United Nation's Special Rapporteur on 'the promotion and protection of human rights and fundamental freedoms while countering terrorism' – submitted his interim report[1] on the use of drone strikes to the UN General Assembly. A few days later, Human Rights Watch issued their own report[2] on the use of counter-terrorist drone strikes in Yemen. While both these reports clinically outline the use of automated machines to launch military action at a distance, both fail to encompass the precise nature of how this system functions. Looking at the issue of drones and robotic military technology at the point where people are killed is like trying to understand an iceberg by looking at the part which sticks out of the water – it tells you very little about the nature of the whole system you are trying to study.

It may seem a jump from drones to the revelations about surveillance by US whistle-blowers Edward Snowden[3] and Chelsea Manning,[4] but what both they and the UN's Special Rapporteur are describing are *the same* system. When we look at the 'networked state', surveillance, cyber warfare, the use of military drones, and the machines which enable all those systems to function together, they are one and the same. And when we consider the use of drones for targeted strikes against 'insurgents', again, considering recent military doctrines, it is difficult to separate the both the intelligence hardware which directs those strikes, and the long-term technology, foreign and security policies which have created it.

The 1980s: The first silicon war machines

To understand the significance of what is taking place today we begin not with the endpoint – *armed military drones* – but with the device which makes this entire system possible – *the programmable microprocessor*. If we look back over the last 40 years of the evolution of the microprocessor we might believe that we've come a long way – from pocket calculators to today's internet and smart phones. In fact, the power of the microprocessor has a long way yet to run, and could – in the space of just a decade or so – make the capabilities of today's 'intelligent' devices seem like the clunky operation of those 1970s pocket calculators.

In 1965, one of the founders of the semiconductor revolution, Gordon Moore, wrote a paper which predicted that the number of transistors (the *transistor count*) which could be packed into these devices would double every 18 months or so as the technologies to manufacture them developed. In turn, the power of these devices would double over the same period. That trend, now called 'Moore's Law',[5] has described the growth of computer processing power, data storage, and the capacity of data communications ever since it was made in the 1960s.

Despite the ultimate limitations on packing transistors into microprocessors,[6] Moore's Law might continue to apply for at least another decade or two. That being the case – as shown in the graph of *The Moore's Law trend* – the power of computer systems will dramatically accelerate over the next decade. In turn, the capabilities of those new systems to collect, process, interpret and report data will double every two years or so.

The "Moore's Law" trend

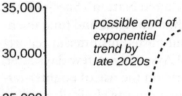

possible end of exponential trend by late 2020s

CPU power accelerating through late 2010s/early 2020s

Now turn that principle towards our recent knowledge about state surveillance or the use of autonomous drones... *and perhaps then you'll see where this phenomena is heading.*

The computer networks which laid the foundations of both the military and civil telecommunications and data network can be traced back[7] to the 1960s. However, the US military did not seriously engage with the power of computer networks until nearly 20 years later. In 1983, Ronald Reagan had initiated the *Strategic Defense Initiative,*[8] commonly called the 'Star Wars' project. It was a failure – primarily because it tried to achieve goals which were way beyond the capabilities of the technology which existed at the time.

From that failure the US military saw the potential of these technologies to assist their existing missions, and in the early 1990s the doctrine of 'full spectrum dominance' was created – a belief that computers, communications, and both ground- and space-based surveillance systems could achieve complete control over military operations. In 1996 this vision was outlined by the US Joint Chiefs of Staff as the *Joint Vision 2010*[9] – later updated as *Joint Vision 2020*[10] in May 2000.

From the 1980s, the military establishments of the developed nations funded new digital communications networks to create global systems for command, surveillance, and ultimately to direct offensive action. For the USA, the geographical location of their bases in the UK was a key part of

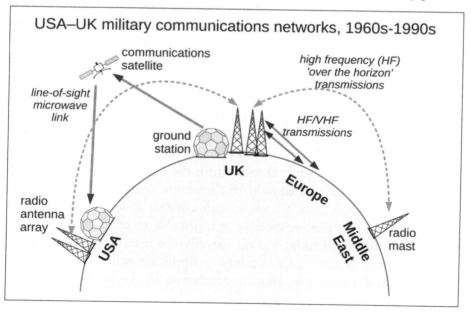

USA–UK military communications networks, 1960s-1990s

the operation of this global system. During the Cold War, military communications had relied on a network of radio stations using conventional high-frequency voice and radio-teletype (telex) links, with some low capacity satellite links. In Britain, us communications bases provided a staging post for communications routed from Europe, North Africa and the Middle East to the USA. British bases also provided a point to intercept radio communications from Eastern Europe and Russia. With the end of the Cold War it looked like these sites would become redundant, but the full-spectrum dominance doctrine gave them a new purpose in the global communications network.

The 1990s: Military theory meets evolving technology

Military academics have come to see warfare as evolving over different historical eras, each of which saw competing powers undergoing a race for tactical supremacy. During the late 1980s/early 1990s their vision was that we were moving into the fourth generation of warfare.[11] Fourth generation warfare is all about the *decentralisation* of conflict. The destructive potential of modern technology means that standing armies gain little from engaging directly, and so instead powers seek to engage each other indirectly by a variety of means. Rather than military foes meeting in high intensity conflict, this doctrine foresees conflict as a more drawn-out process involving political, economic and social subversion which seeks to degrade the ability of the state to function. More importantly, no longer are 'powers' limited to nation states. Any organised group, using the resources and technologies created by post-World War Two industrialisation, can now engage in this global battleground.

It was this changing view of military conflict which led the major military powers: to focus far more on intelligence and surveillance – because that is what's required to monitor the activities of decentralised or 'insurgent' forces; and to focus far more on small-scale offensive or policing actions – because the large-scale conflict of whole armies is no longer viable. From this perspective, it is possible to see the rationale for both the evolution of today's mass surveillance networks, and also the development of systems such as pilot-less drone aircraft.

The difficulty is that by viewing conflict as an essentially ideological struggle between small groups, rather than as an organised engagement between nation states, it is inevitable that these new technologies would be deployed against civilian populations – and even against the citizens of the states concerned. By polarising political or economic debates between the interests of 'the state' versus 'everyone else', democracy is no longer a dialogue between alternative ideas, but an ongoing militarised struggle between opposing ideologies.

Once again, within this new post-Cold War strategy, Britain is a key link in the chain of command and control – between the analytical capabilities of USA's foreign and domestic security agencies, and the peripheral information collection gathering capabilities of the global network. The US bases at Menwith Hill, Croughton and Alconbury provide not just a conduit for phone calls and emails, but also the command systems for drones, and the information generated by the various global monitoring and surveillance systems. The cooperation agreement between the UK and US intelligence agencies[12] also means the resources of British security agencies, such as GCHQ in Cheltenham, supply a valuable back-up to the USA's own systems.

Rather than the low capacity high-frequency radio links of the Cold War, these new systems utilise many more satellite-based systems (the USA launched over 200 military satellites between 1984 and 2013) – in effect militarising the control of space in accordance with the full-spectrum dominance doctrine. Microwave satellite communications only work by line of sight, and to span the globe satellite ground-stations have to be set up to supervise the flow of information from one region to another. Britain, strategically placed between the USA, Europe and the Middle East, acts as a way-station for US military/security networks. In addition, US agencies can access the European microwave and fibre-optic communications networks directly from the UK's telecommunications infrastructure to carry out surveillance of digital information traffic on the European continent.

The roll-out of new digital networks by military and civil agencies during the 1990s revolutionised communications and intelligence. When all communications – be it your telephone, email, credit card transactions or Internet browsing – are reduced to binary data, then all forms of economic and social activity in society are potentially available for surveillance. Also, because this is digital information, rather than having to engage many expensive human operators, banks of computers can quickly and cheaply sift these large quantities of information looking for patterns of activity which are deemed 'valuable'. Using digital technological rather than human-based systems, individuals can be tracked and their activity monitored to assess their potential threat to the state – enabling far larger scales of surveillance to be carried out than were possible before.

In the final instance, when individuals are considered a 'threat', they can be geographically located and then eliminated using the weapons systems linked into these networks. It is these 'targeted killings' which have recently caused some of the greatest civilian casualties[13], and created some of the greatest enmity to the use of remote-controlled war machines. One of the early examples of targeted killing was the assassination of the Chechen president Dzhokhar Dudayev in 1996; the Russian military tracked his satellite phone and then, when it was confirmed he personally was speaking on the phone, launched missiles onto that location. Today, with the increased sophistication of these technologies, and the deployment of pilot-less aircraft which can stay airborne for long periods, both the surveillance and offensive capacities of the most technologically advanced states have grown significantly; and will continue to do so whilst the key component which underpins those developments – the microprocessor – increases its operating capacity.

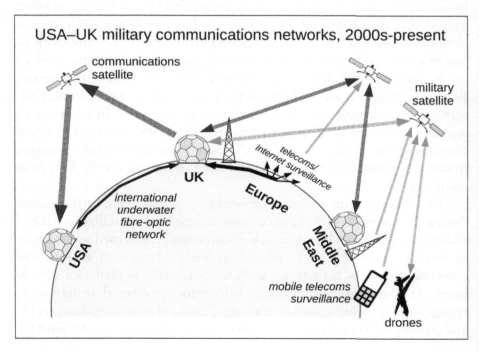

USA–UK military communications networks, 2000s-present

communications satellite

military satellite

telecoms/ Internet surveillance

UK

Europe

international underwater fibre-optic network

USA

Middle East

mobile telecoms surveillance

drones

The 2000s: The war against terror, mass surveillance and the rise of the drones

A significant milestone in the development of these systems was the attack on the World Trade Centre in September 2001. That not only legitimated the military's previous focus on non-state-based or 'insurgent' groups, it also created an environment where the states could justify the introduction of new surveillance laws (such as the Patriot Act in the USA; or the *Regulation* of Investigatory Powers Act 2000, Terrorism Act 2000 and Serious Organised Crime and Police Act 2005 in the UK) and spending ever greater amounts on security and surveillance.

As military and security agencies rolled out their new intelligence gathering capabilities in the wake of 9/11, and as the subsequent wars in Afghanistan and Iraq created new problems, this experience fed back into the development of a new understanding of how technology could be used by military and security agencies to 'project force' around the globe. In the USA, the military policies of the 1990s developed into new strategies for Information Age Warfare,[14] decentralising military operations,[15] and Network-Centric Warfare.[16] These updated the ideas of 'full spectrum dominance' to take advantage of the new computer networks and mobile telecommunications.

Central to the development of these ideas was a new agency set-up by US Defence Secretary Donald Rumsfeld – The Office for Force Transformation. Although it was disbanded five years later, this office was instrumental in getting technology companies and the military working together to develop new automated systems – even to the point where the technical staff of these companies were deployed with troops in action to develop and perfect their products. This reinforced the push towards the greater use of technology by the military, and led to a new emphasis on the use of automated systems in conflict zones – now generally called 'drones'.

Whilst we might use the term 'drone' to identify the infamous Predator or Reaper unmanned aerial vehicles (UAVs) there are in fact over 500 land, air and on/under-water 'drones' in production or development by the five leading manufacturing states (USA, UK, Israel, Russia and China) – and many countries are now buying these technologies as these states develop an export market for their products.[17] Contrary to the popular media depiction, drones come in all shapes and sizes. Some of the smallest aerial drones, designed for surveillance, will fit into your hand. Others, such as the PackBot, used by soldiers in Iraq and Afghanistan, are designed to scout ahead in dangerous situations (for example, a PackBot was sent in to the damaged reactor buildings following the Fukushima nuclear disaster to provide video surveys) and fit into a rucksack. Larger and heavily armed ground-based drones, such as the TALON, are being developed for offensive use as scouts or sentries – primarily in urban areas. The largest drones, like the Predator and Reaper, are self-guiding aircraft. However, one of the fast developing areas of technology is self-guided land vehicles. Originally a military concept, these are now being rapidly developed for civilian use – and will be licensed for use on the UK's roads by the end of 2013,[18] and Nissan expect to be manufacturing driver-less cars for sale by 2020.[19]

The important factor in the development of all these systems is that it is primarily private companies developing these systems for the military. Whilst these projects are initially Government-funded, the companies involved stand to make their greatest profits not from the military applications, but from their greater potential in the civil sector. If you look at the economics of driver-less vehicles, what will fund the roll out of this technology will be replacing the human driver with a fully automated 'delivery machine' – or, for example, self-driving taxis. Likewise the computer software developed by security agencies for mass surveillance has parallels within the 'big data' applications now being developed for use by commercial companies – and often it is the same companies involved in the production of systems for use by security agencies.

The Edward Snowden affair has been a very public example of the close relationship between the civil corporate IT sector and the use of 'big data' by the security services. Snowden worked for the civilian IT contractor Booz Allen Hamilton, working as a private analyst for the CIA and NSA. Following 9/11, the US Department for Homeland Security conceived a project called Total Information Awareness, intended to collect data from across the USA on the activities of every citizen. In 2003 the US Congress withdrew funding for that project, precisely because of concerns about the implications for civil liberties. Snowden saw that the objectives of that project were instead carried out by a covert NSA project codenamed PRISM. Another, XKeyscore, carried out similar operations on individuals globally. A similar project run by the British GCHQ, Tempora, sifted data intercepted from global telecommunications networks and then tracked large numbers of individuals. Whilst these projects had been cleared by the oversight committees within the agencies concerned, elected officials in government – even at Cabinet level[20] – were excluded from having knowledge of their existence or operation. Whether or not these projects broke either US, UK or European law is still a matter of official debate, and may take years of both public investigations and private litigation to resolve.

Of greater concern for society in general are the increasingly close links between the military and security services, defence and IT companies, and the wider body of corporate interests who those security companies service. As a result of these links the boundary between the military, the public and the private has becoming increasingly blurred. For example, in 2008, when climate change protesters were planning an action at a power station, officials at the UK's Department of Business gave police intelligence files to the plant's operators, EON.[21] Likewise, Canadian security officials routinely hold briefings for Canadian corporations to disclose information on rival foreign companies discovered during their surveillance operations.[22] In the USA – as recently outlined in the documentary *Gasland, Part 2* – companies involved in shale gas (or 'fracking') are advised by former US military personnel[23] on the use of military 'psychological operations' against both protesters, and the communities they're drilling around. More recently in the USA, freedom of information requests by the Partnership for Civil Justice Fund[24] revealed that the FBI and Department for Homeland Security were producing briefings on the Occupy movement for American corporations.

Returning to the change in military doctrines outlined earlier, that conflict is now viewed as existing between the state and small groups who might for various reasons 'disagree' with it, it's important to consider to what extent that this might become a self-fulfilling prophecy. As Nietzsche said, 'Beware that, when fighting monsters, you yourself do not become a monster.' Is the establishment seeing enemies because it wants to, or simply because these groups exercise their democratic rights to disagree?

Nafeez Ahmed, director of the Institute for Policy Research and Development, considers that such shifts in security strategy are the result of an uncertain political environment[25]. The fact that economic stagnation, resource depletion and climate change might create civil unrest is pushing the establishment towards a greater fear of the citizens of the developed world – just as much as it might fear the insurgent groups of the developing world. When the state mistrusts its citizens, does that create the very crisis it perceives to exist?

Tomorrow: What future for civil democracy in a cybernetic world?

Over the history of the modern state, war has required a general consensus within the population. This is because war is not only expensive, it also requires the active support of the public to provide the military personnel who engage in conflict. That same need for unanimity provides a check on the power of the state. That's not just because the state needs the people to fight for it; the debate over conflict allows for a broader range of views – let's call it 'common sense' – to be applied to the operations of both the military, police and security services.

Replacing people with machines breaks that check on administrative excess – *in many ways*. That's not just an issue with drones: the use of networked surveillance in the more affluent nations has parallels to the use of drone strikes in poorer nations. To begin to consider how, we need to examine what is happening today.

The United Nation's Special Rapporteur's interim report on the use of drone strikes lays out a complex picture of how automated systems are used to enact what is, put simply, extra-judicial killing – a sentence of death without the due process of an impartial trial. The Special Rapporteur does not say that the use of a drone strike is always unlawful. But when used outside a declared war zone, for example within Pakistan or Yemen, it is questionable as to whether such action is legal or is a war crime[26]. Human Rights Watch's report on drone strikes in Yemen states that some attacks were clear violations of international humanitarian law because they struck only civilians or used indiscriminate weapons; whilst others may have violated the laws of war because the individual attacked was not a lawful military target or the attack caused disproportionate civilian harm.

According to the UN Rapporteur's report, Yemeni government permission had been obtained for all strikes: while in Pakistan permission for strikes came from the military establishment, although whether that has the support of elected ministers is a matter of debate. In Pakistan, unconfirmed reports put the death toll at around 2,200, with over 600 serious injuries. However, because of the problems collecting data in these areas, the Government could only confirm 600 civilian deaths, with a further 200 regarded as 'non-combatants'. The report also covers the use of drones in Libya, Iraq, Gaza, Somalia and Afghanistan, and whilst in all areas it is accepted that civilian casualties have resulted from drone strikes, the problems of accurate data collection, or identifying targets, mean that producing confirmed figures is very difficult. The report identifies that the greatest problem in testing the legality of drone strikes is that it requires command accountability for their use, but that, 'the single greatest obstacle to an evaluation of the civilian impact of drone strikes is lack of transparency, which makes it extremely difficult to assess claims of precision targeting objectively'.

In terms of the impacts of recent Western military action, drones have thus far caused only a small fraction of the total casualties. However, as we move forward from today what might we expect to change? Already opposition groups in the Middle East are working on counter-measures to the use of drones – not just aerial drones, but also the ground-based systems used for scouting buildings in urban areas and defusing bombs. States such as Iran are using captured drones, or parts of them, to try and develop their own drone technologies. Some have already speculated that it is only a matter of time before we see conflicts involving the use of drones by both sides, or a significant terrorist incident using an 'insurgent drone'.[27]

As technology advances, it is arguably only a matter of time before an 'insurgent drone' arises. For example, in the US and Europe there is already amateur interest in, and readily available technology for the construction of 'DIY drones'.[28] The difficulty is, whilst it is possible to outline 'unconventional' drone attacks, there are a series of technical barriers which have to be crossed to get to that point. But as time passes, and the required technology improves and becomes more readily available, it is arguably not an implausible scenario.

Unfortunately, due to the speed and complexity of technology, the principal method of countering insurgent drones *is with more drones* – and then we enter a wholly different world. That's because to allow drones to counter the use of other drones we have to give our drones far greater autonomy. Technically we are still some distance from that point, but not far. Even so, the issue still arises as to how – in perhaps five or ten years time – a future UN Special Rapporteur might investigate the accountability and transparency of the targeting decisions of a machine intelligence. Where networks of machines are involved, for example where a machine responsible for detection and tracking sends instructions to a strike drone, it becomes an even more complex problem.

If we want an example of what full autonomy entails then we should examine the recent history of global stock and commodity exchanges. In automated financial (or 'algorithmic') trading reaction time is everything. In a mirror of the arms race, financial institutions have to use automated trading because 'everybody else' uses it, and they are all in a perpetual battle to 'win' the technological race surrounding automated trading. The problem, from the evidence of a decade or so of this practice,[29] is that while these systems work acceptably for much of the time, they are inherently unstable and prone to sudden, unexpected and aberrant behaviour. Basically, we let the machines loose and unsurprisingly, they don't behave like people!

Would drones behave any differently? If a trading machine malfunctions, a bank loses a few hundred million; when drones malfunction, many people might die. For example, consider the incident in 1983 when a Russian missile defence operator disregarded his instruments warning of a US missile strike because he didn't believe they were working correctly[30] – what would a machine have done?

In December 2013, the US Department of Defense published its 'Unmanned Systems Integrated Roadmap' – a detailed programme of how the greater use of remotely-controlled drone technologies, surveillance capabilities and high-power computing facilities would be rolled out to support all sections of America's armed forces and security establishments.[31] And of course, where America leads, other major military powers follow. Therefore irrespective of concerns about the viability or long-term efficacy of these technologies, defence establishments around the globe are now locking themselves into this pattern of supra-human-based technological development.

If we look at the evolving language which the military has used to describe the purposes of their technology since the 1990s – from Star Wars, across two decades to drones and cyberwarfare – it is about *command* and *dominance*. At the same time the notion of who these systems are meant to 'oppose' has shifted from whole nation states towards small groups of people. And whether those people are in poor societies being bombed by drones, or in affluent societies having their lives monitored, has little practical difference – it's the same underlying information and intelligence machinery which administers and co-ordinates that process. Likewise, whether or not the extra-judicial killing of suspects is legal under international law, or whether the mass surveillance of the populace by their government is lawful by their own national laws, is still being argued over today – and may be so for some time. That is because the alternate outcome to the military/security strategy of *command and dominance* would be *engagement and dialogue* – and whilst that seems antithetical to their expressed democratic principles, such a strategy is not open for debate within the leading Western states right now (perhaps not even with their own people).

Irrespective of how we resolve this problem – and right now there are many obstacles to any solution – set aside that objective and return to the beginning of this chapter. The implication of Moore's Law is that by the end of this decade the power of the machines involved in that system is likely to quadruple; and before we reach the limits of this trend we might see computing capacities 30 times greater than they are today. Quite literally, comparing today's drones to the drones of 2025 might be like comparing those 1970s pocket calculators to today's mobile phones.

The real issue here is not simply the use of machines by the state, or the controls over their lethality. The greatest flaw in the whole machine is the governing human element; and certainly – as shown by the debate over the use of drones or the disclosures over surveillance by Edward Snowden and Chelsea Manning – our fundamental problem is not one of control, it is of oversight, transparency and accountability. Solving that has little to do with machines and silicon diodes, but has much to do with how we value ourselves, our society, and how our human system chooses to govern itself.

Recommended reading

P.W. Singer, Wired for War: The Robotics Revolution and Conflict in the 21st Century (London: Penguin Books, 2011).

Benjamin Medea & Barbara Ehrenreich, Drone Warfare: Killing by Remote Control (London: Verso Books, 2013).

Daniel J. Solove, Nothing to Hide: The False Trade-off Between Privacy and Security (Connecticut: Yale University Press, 2013).

Recommended video

P.W. Singer: Military robots and the future of war, TED, February 2009 – [http://www.ted.com/talks/pw_singer_on_robots_of_war.html].

The Secret Drone War, BBC Panorama, 10 December 2012 – [http://www.youtube.com/watch?feature=player_embedded&v=ov5mmVIGrJc].

'Protest Policy of Full Spectrum Dominance', workshop with Bruce Gagnon, April 2013 – [http://www.youtube.com/embed/84EY-mOYjyM].

The Trigger Effect (series 1, episode 1), James Burke's Connections, BBC, 1978 – [http://www.youtube.com/watch?v=WgOp-nz3lHg].

Michio Kaku: Tweaking Moore's Law and the Computers of the Post-Silicon Era, YouTube, 13 April 2013 – [http://www.youtube.com/watch?v=bm-6ScvNygUU].

Websites

Dronewars – [http://dronewars.net/]

Drone Campaign Network – [http://dronecampaignnetwork.wordpress.com/]

Campaign for the Accountability of American Bases – [http://www.caab.org.uk/].

CND UK: Ground the Drones Petition – [http://www.cnduk.org/campaigns/anti-war/ground-the-drones-petition].

Global Network Against Weapons and Nuclear Power in Space – [http://www.space4peace.org/].

DIY Drones – [http://diydrones.com/].

Notes

1 Ben Emmerson, *Report of the Special Rapporteur on the promotion and protection of human rights and fundamental freedoms while countering terrorism*, United Nations, 18 September 2013: [http://www.fraw.org.uk/files/peace/un_sphr_2013.pdf].

2 *Between a Drone and Al-Qaeda: The Civilian Cost of US Targeted Killings in Yemen*, Human Rights Watch, 22 October 2013: [http://www.hrw.org/sites/default/files/reports/yemen1013_ForUpload.pdf].

3 Edward Snowden, Guardian On-line news archive: [http://www.theguardian.com/world/edward-snowden].

4 Chelsea Manning, Guardian On-line news archive: [http://www.theguardian.com/world/chelsea-manning].

5 'Moore's Law', Croughtonwatch, January 2014: [http://www.fraw.org.uk/croughtonwatch/files/wikipedia-moores_law.html].

6 *Michio Kaku: Tweaking Moore's Law and the Computers of the Post-Silicon Era*, YouTube, 13 April 2013: [http://www.youtube.com/watch?v=bm-6ScvNygUU].

7 'History of the Internet', Croughtonwatch, January 2014:[http://www.fraw.org.uk/croughtonwatch/files/wikipedia-history_of_the_internet.html].

8 'Strategic Defense Initiative', Croughtonwatch, January 2014: [http://www.

fraw.org.uk/croughtonwatch/files/wikipedia-strategic_defense_initiative. html].

9   *Joint Vision 2010*, US Joint Chiefs of Staff, July 1996: [http://www.fraw. org.uk/files/peace/us_dod_1996.pdf].

10 *Joint Vision 2020*, US Joint Chiefs of Staff, May 2000: [http://www.fraw. org.uk/files/peace/us_dod_2000.pdf].

11 'Fourth-generation warfare', Croughtonwatch, January 2014: [http://www. fraw.org.uk/croughtonwatch/files/wikipedia-fourth_generation_warfare. html].

12 'UKUSA Agreement', Croughtonwatch, January 2014:[http://www.fraw.org. uk/croughtonwatch/files/wikipedia-uk_usa_agreement.html].

13 'Targeted killing', Croughtonwatch, January 2014: [http://www.fraw.org. uk/croughtonwatch/files/wikipedia-targeted_killing.html].

14 David S. Alberts, *Understanding Information Age Warfare*, Command and Control Research Programme, US Department of Defense, 2001: [http:// www.fraw.org.uk/files/peace/alberts_2001.pdf].

15 David S. Alberts, Richard E. Hayes, *Power to the Edge: Command and Control in the Information Age, Command and Control Research Programme*, US DOD, 2003: [http://www.fraw.org.uk/files/peace/alberts_ hayes_2003.pdf].

16 *The Implementation of Network-Centric Warfare*, Office of Force Transformation, US Department of Defense, 2005: [http://www.fraw.org.uk/files/ peace/dod_ncw_2005.pdf].

17 P.W. Singer, *Wired for War: The Robotics Revolution and Conflict in the 21st Century*, (Penguin Books, 2011).

18 *Driverless cars to be tested on UK roads by end of 2013*, BBC News On-line, 16 July 2013: [http://www.bbc.co.uk/news/technology-23330681].

19 *Nissan: We'll have a self-driving car on roads in 2020*, CNN, 28 August 2013: [http://edition.cnn.com/2013/08/27/tech/innovation/nissan-driver-less-car/index.html].

20 Chris Huhne, 'Prism and Tempora: the cabinet was told nothing of the surveillance state's excesses', *The Guardian*, Sunday 6 October 2013: [http://www.theguardian.com/commentisfree/2013/oct/06/prism-tempo-ra-cabinet-surveillance-state].

21 Matthew Taylor and Paul Lewis, 'Secret police intelligence was given to EON before planned demo', *The Guardian*, Monday 20 April 2009: [http:// www.theguardian.com/uk/2009/apr/20/police-intelligence-e-on-berr].

22 Steven Chase, 'CSEC defends practices in wake of Brazilian spy reports', *The Globe and Mail*, Wednesday 9 October 2013: [http://www.theglobeand-mail.com/news/politics/nothing-illegal-about-spying-on-brazil-agency-chief-says/article14774444/].

23 Steve Horn, 'Fracking and Psychological Operations: Empire Comes Home', Truthout, Thursday 8 March 2012: [http://www.truth-out.org/news/item/7153:fracking-and-psychological-operations-empire-comes-home].

24 Partnership for Civil Justice Fund, FBI Documents Reveal Secret Nationwide Occupy Monitoring, 22 December 2012: [www.justiceonline.org/commentary/fbi-files-ows.html].

25 Nafeez Ahmed, 'Pentagon bracing for public dissent over climate and energy shocks', The Guardian, 14 June 2013: [http://www.theguardian.com/environment/earth-insight/2013/jun/14/climate-change-energy-shocks-nsa-prism].

26 Owen Bowcott, 'Drone strikes by US may violate international law, says UN', The Guardian, Friday 18 October 2013: [http://www.theguardian.com/world/2013/oct/18/drone-strikes-us-violate-law-un].

27 Eugene Miasnikov, Threat of Terrorism Using Unmanned Aerial Vehicles: Technical Aspects, Center for Arms Control, Energy and Environmental Studies, June 2004 (translated into English, March 2005): [http://www.armscontrol.ru/uav/report.htm].

28 Chris Anderson, 'How I Accidentally Kick-started the Domestic Drone Boom', Wired Magazine, 22 June 2012: [http://www.wired.com/dangerroom/2012/06/ff_drones/all/].

29 'Black box traders are on the march', The Telegraph, 27 August 2006: [http://www.telegraph.co.uk/finance/2946240/Black-box-traders-are-on-the-march.html]. 'Knight Capital Says Trading Glitch Cost It $440 Million', Dealbook – New York Times, 2 August 2012: [http://dealbook.nytimes.com/2012/08/02/knight-capital-says-trading-mishap-cost-it-440-million/]. 'Stock plunge raises alarm on algo trading', Reuters, 6 May 2010: [http://www.reuters.com/article/2010/05/06/us-market-selloff-idUSTRE6455ZG20100506]. 'Hoax Shows Growth in Algorithmic Trading', Wall Street Journal, 6 May 2013: [http://blogs.wsj.com/moneybeat/2013/05/06/the-twitter-hoax-shows-growth-in-algorithmic-trading/]; 'Too Fast to Fail: Is High-Speed Trading the Next Wall Street Disaster?', Mother Jones, January/February 2013: [http://www.motherjones.com/politics/2013/02/high-frequency-trading-danger-risk-wall-street].

30 'Stanislav Petrov: The man who may have saved the world', BBC News, 26 September 2013: [http://www.bbc.co.uk/news/world-europe-24280831].

31 'Unmanned Systems Integrated Roadmap', US Department of Defense, December 2013: [http://www.fraw.org.uk/files/peace/us_dod_2013.pdf].

Some other books published by **LUATH** PRESS

Faslane 365: A year of anti-nuclear blockades

Edited by Angie Zelter
ISBN: 978-1-906307-61-5 PBK £12.99

The Faslane campaign has been fantastic, it has encouraged people to act as the opposition to a government of false consensus and arrogance. Trident is an expensive stupid nuclear toy that creates an arms race, threatens to destabilise arms reduction treaties and lurches us into an uncertain future. It is a redundant dinosaur of the cold war era that has no place and serves no purpose, other than to aggrandise the military prowess of Britain's rulers. So when a state is uncivil, civil disobedience to the state becomes merely good manners. To everyone who locked themselves to the gates of Faslane, who blocked the roads, who dressed as pixies or swam across the loch to reach the submarines, I salute your lessons in civic etiquette.
MARK THOMAS, comedian and political activist

Faslane 365 is the story of the people and ideas that embodied the 365 day blockade of Fasland Naval Base, home of Britain's nuclear submarines. Combining poems, anecdotes, articles and observations, it details the preparation and demonstration of the blockades, documents Scotland's history of anti-nuclear resistance, analyses Britain's nuclear policy, examines the campaign's impact on Faslane's local community, and considers the international ramifications of disarmament.

With contributions from A. L. Kennedy, Adrian Mitchell, Eurig Scandrett and many others, this book documents an extraordinary year of history and is testament to the strength of 'people-power' and the value of dissent.

Trident on Trial: The case for the people's disarmament

Angie Zelter
ISBN: 978-1-842820-04-9 PBK £9.99

This is the story of global citizenship in action, a story of people's power and the right of individuals to prevent their state from committing very great wrongs. This book is about the women and men who are taking responsibility to prevent mass murder. It is about people's disarmament. I hope it will inspire you to join us.
ANGIE ZELTER

When three women – Ellen Moxley, Ulla Roder and Angie Zelter – boarded a research laboratory barge responsible for the concealment of Trident when in operation, they emptied all the computer equipment into Loch Goil. Their subsequent trial ended with acquittal for the 'The Trident Three' on the basis that they were acting as global citizens preventing nuclear crime. This led to what is thought to be the world's first High Court examination of the legality of an individual state's deployment of nuclear weapons. However the High Court failed to answer a number of significant questions...

Trident on Trial is Angie Zelter's personal account of Trident Ploughshares, the civil-resistance campaign of People's Disarmament. The book also includes profiles of and contributions by people and groups who have pledged to prevent nuclear crime in peaceful and practical ways, using public pressure to ensure that governments adhere to their international agreements on nuclear weapons.

This fine book should be read by everyone, especially those who have the slightest doubt that the world will one day be rid of nuclear weapons.
JOHN PILGER

Details of these and other books published by Luath Press can be found at:
www.luath.co.uk

Luath Press Limited

committed to publishing well written books worth reading

LUATH PRESS takes its name from Robert Burns, whose little collie Luath (*Gael.*, swift or nimble) tripped up Jean Armour at a wedding and gave him the chance to speak to the woman who was to be his wife and the abiding love of his life. Burns called one of 'The Twa Dogs' Luath after Cuchullin's hunting dog in Ossian's *Fingal*. Luath Press was established in 1981 in the heart of Burns country, and now resides a few steps up the road from Burns' first lodgings on Edinburgh's Royal Mile.

Luath offers you distinctive writing with a hint of unexpected pleasures.

Most bookshops in the UK, the US, Canada, Australia, New Zealand and parts of Europe either carry our books in stock or can order them for you. To order direct from us, please send a £sterling cheque, postal order, international money order or your credit card details (number, address of cardholder and expiry date) to us at the address below. Please add post and packing as follows: UK – £1.00 per delivery address; overseas surface mail – £2.50 per delivery address; overseas airmail – £3.50 for the first book to each delivery address, plus £1.00 for each additional book by airmail to the same address. If your order is a gift, we will happily enclose your card or message at no extra charge.

Luath Press Limited
543/2 Castlehill
The Royal Mile
Edinburgh EH1 2ND
Scotland
Telephone: 0131 225 4326 (24 hours)
Fax: 0131 225 4324
email: sales@luath.co.uk
Website: www.luath.co.uk